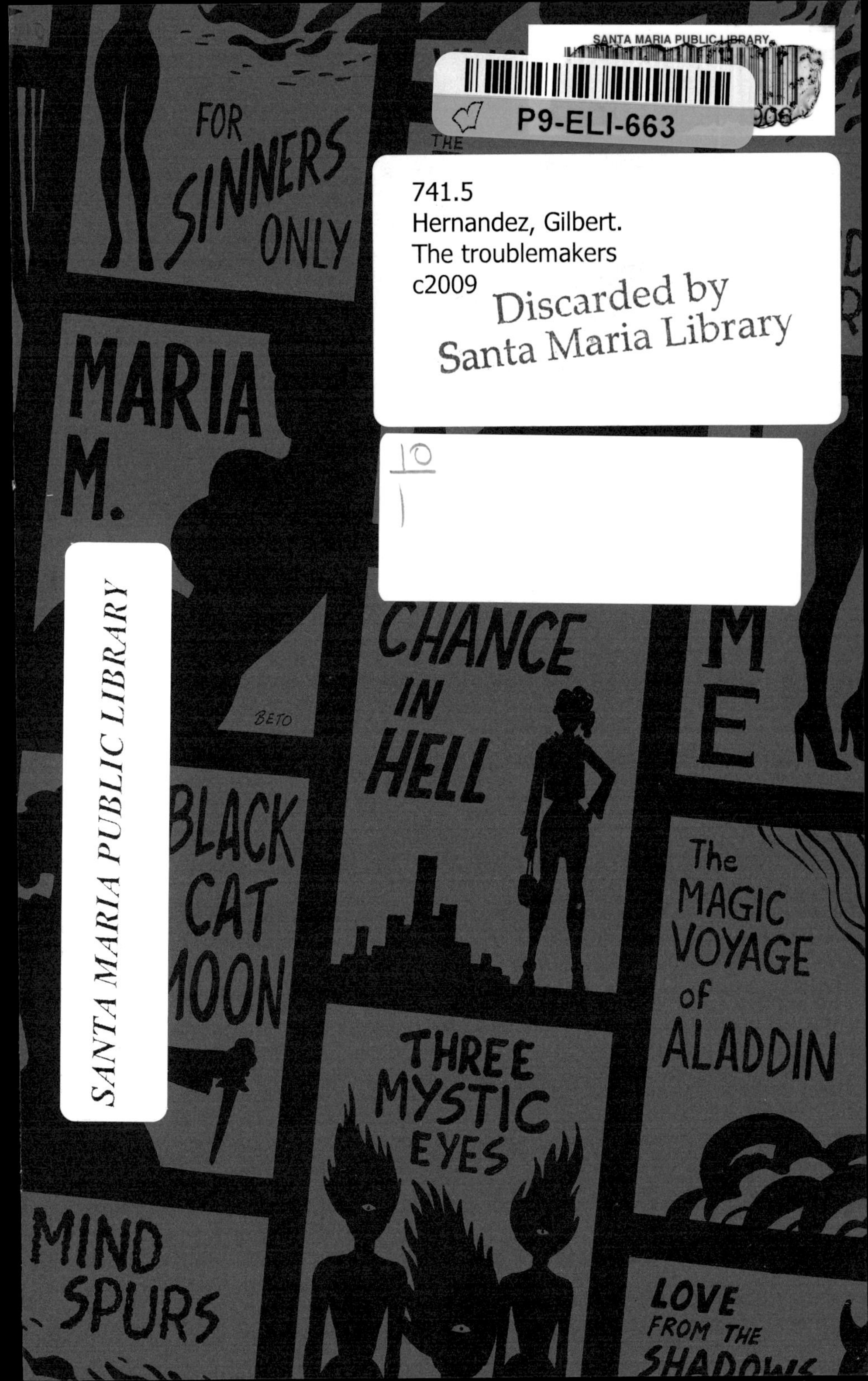
FOR SINNERS ONLY
MARIA M.
BETO
BLACK CAT MOON
MIND SPURS
CHANCE IN HELL
THREE MYSTIC EYES
ME
The MAGIC VOYAGE of ALADDIN
LOVE FROM THE

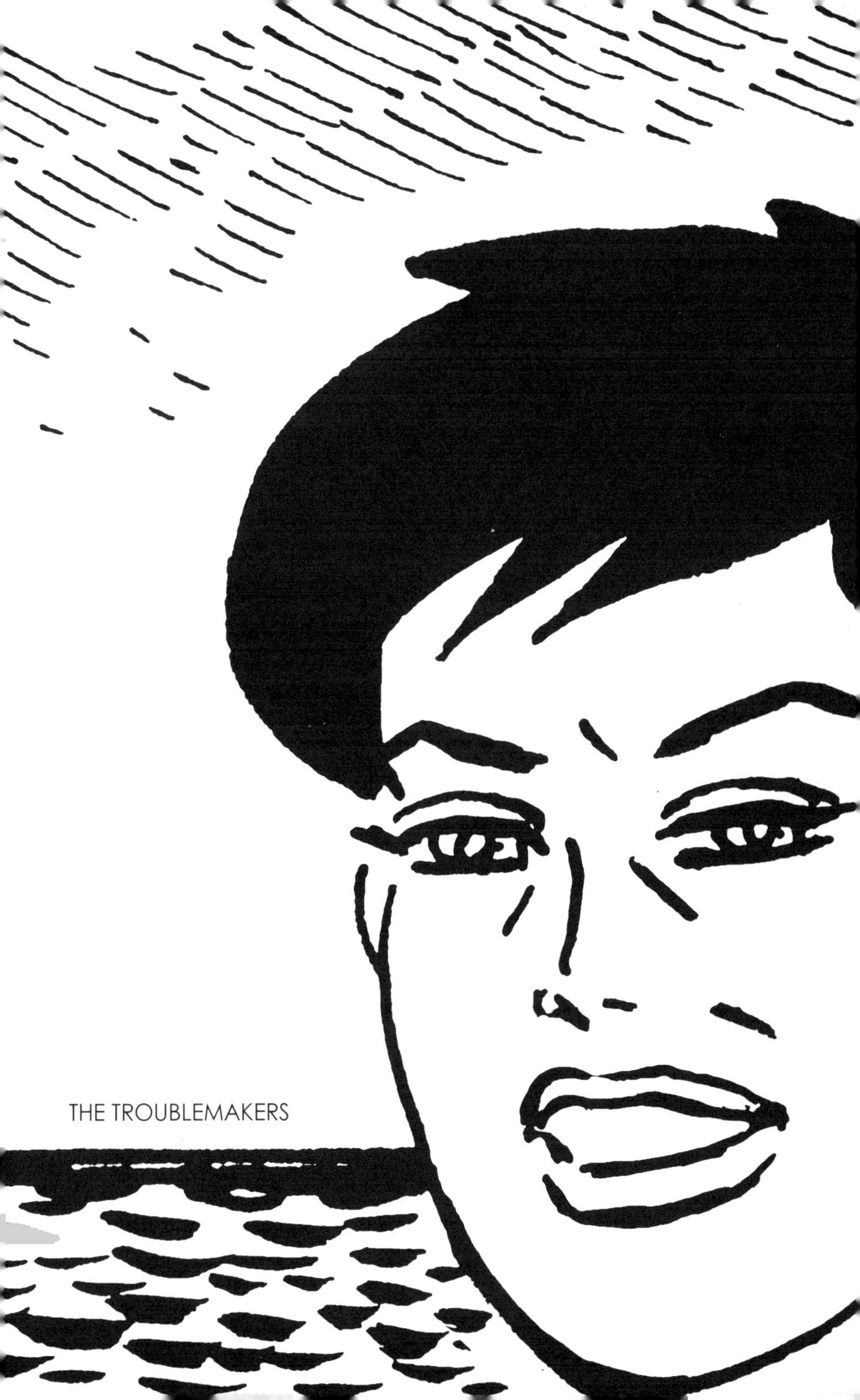

# THE TROUBLEMAKERS

# the
# TROUBLEMAKERS

A LOVE AND ROCKETS BOOK

BY GILBERT HERNANDEZ

FB FANTAGRAPHICS BOOKS

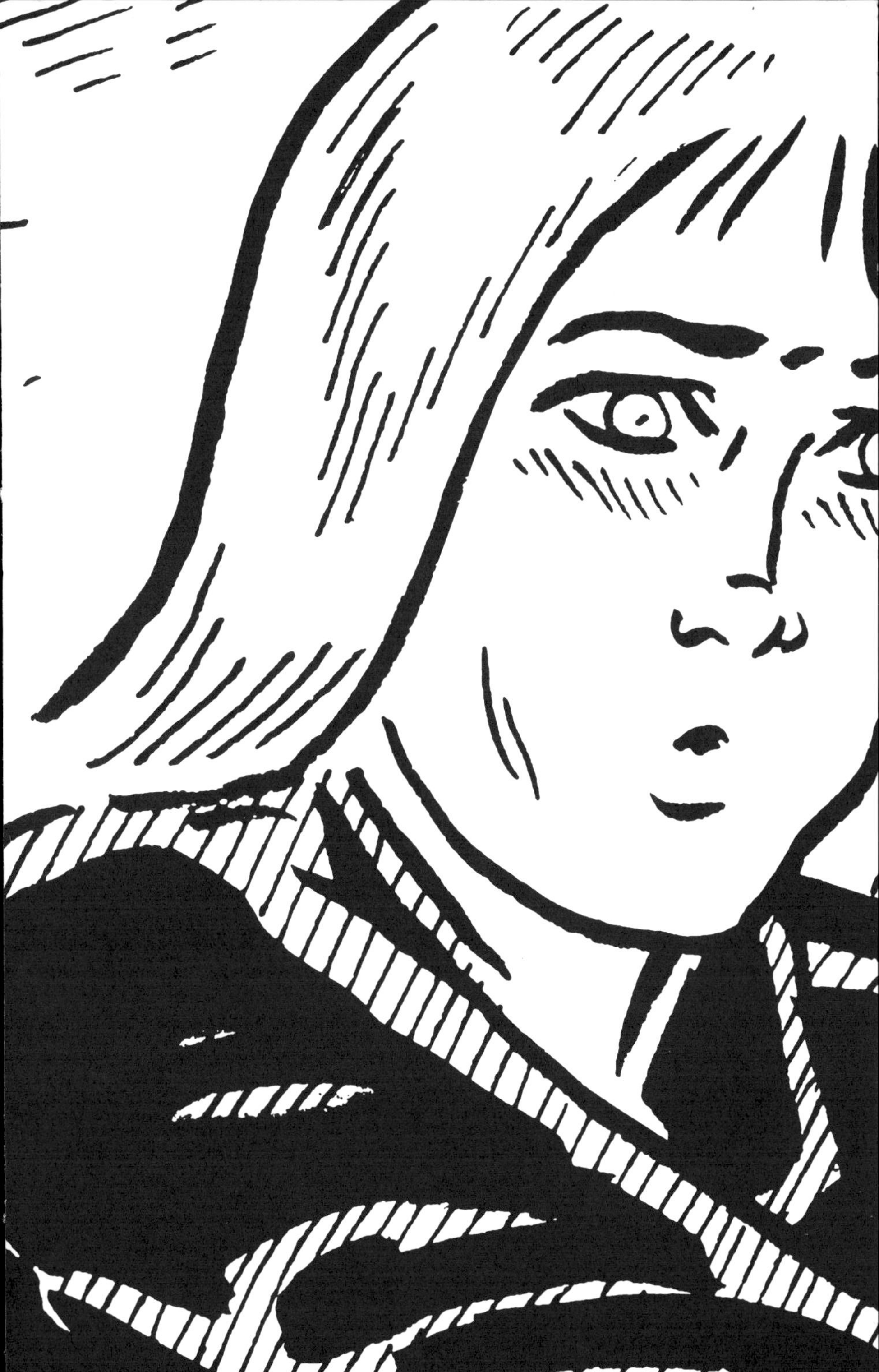

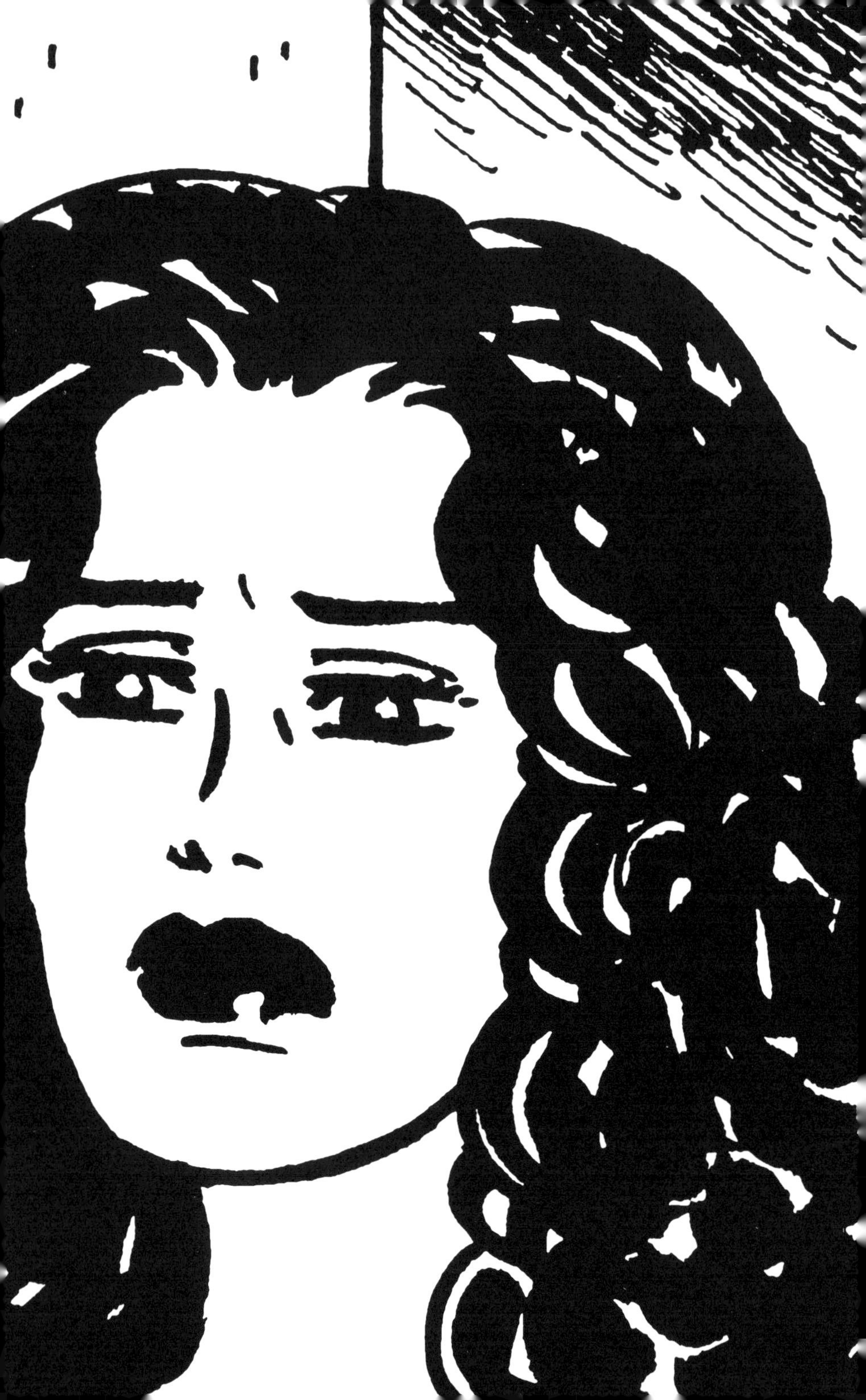

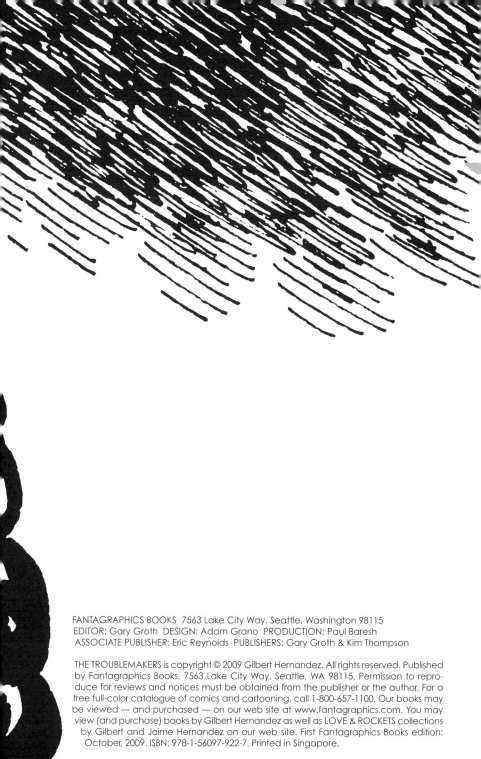

FANTAGRAPHICS BOOKS 7563 Lake City Way, Seattle, Washington 98115
EDITOR: Gary Groth DESIGN: Adam Grano PRODUCTION: Paul Baresh
ASSOCIATE PUBLISHER: Eric Reynolds PUBLISHERS: Gary Groth & Kim Thompson

 First Fantagraphics Books edition: October, 2009. ISBN: 978-1-56097-922-7. Printed in Singapore.

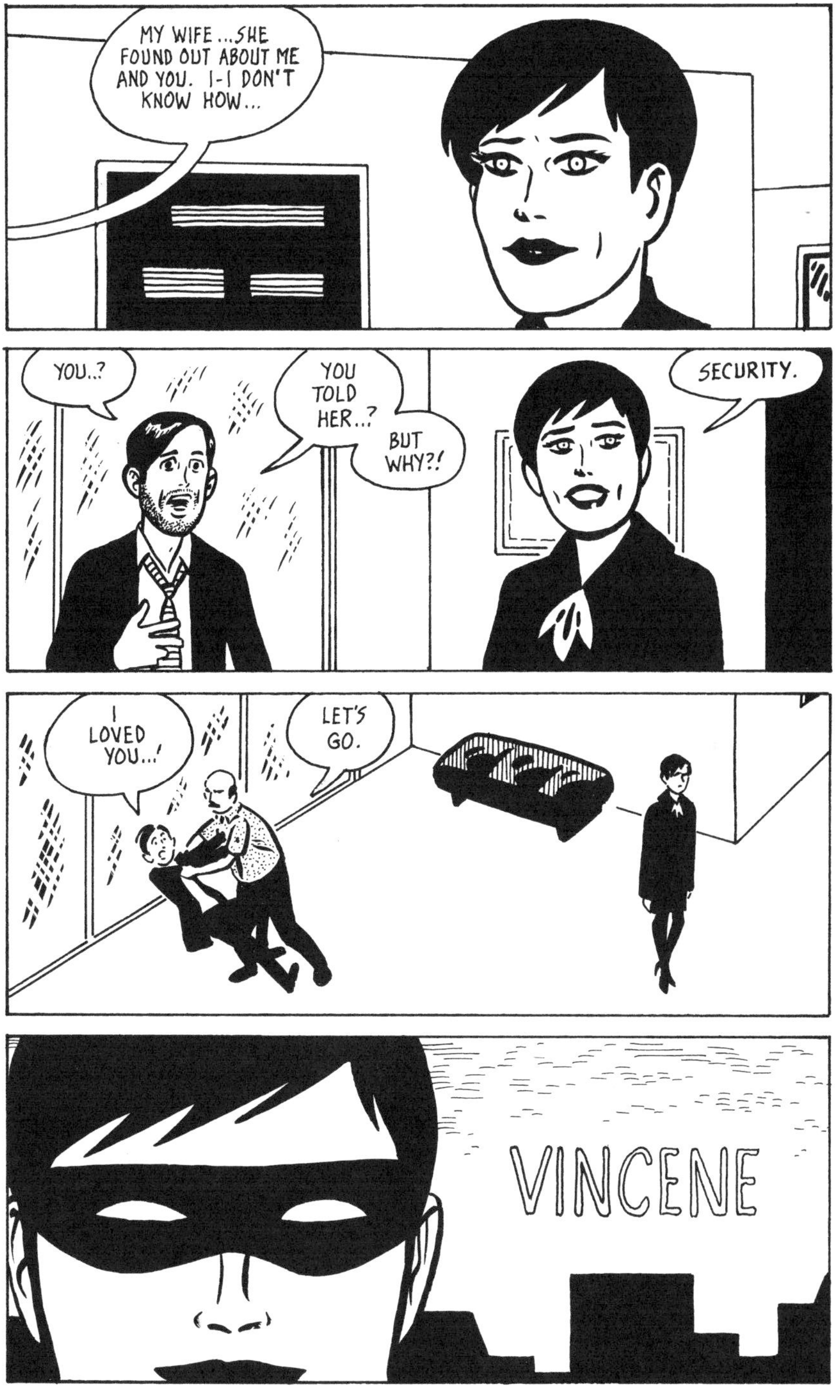
MY WIFE...SHE FOUND OUT ABOUT ME AND YOU. I-I DON'T KNOW HOW...
YOU..?
YOU TOLD HER..?
BUT WHY?!
SECURITY.
I LOVED YOU..!
LET'S GO.
VINCENE

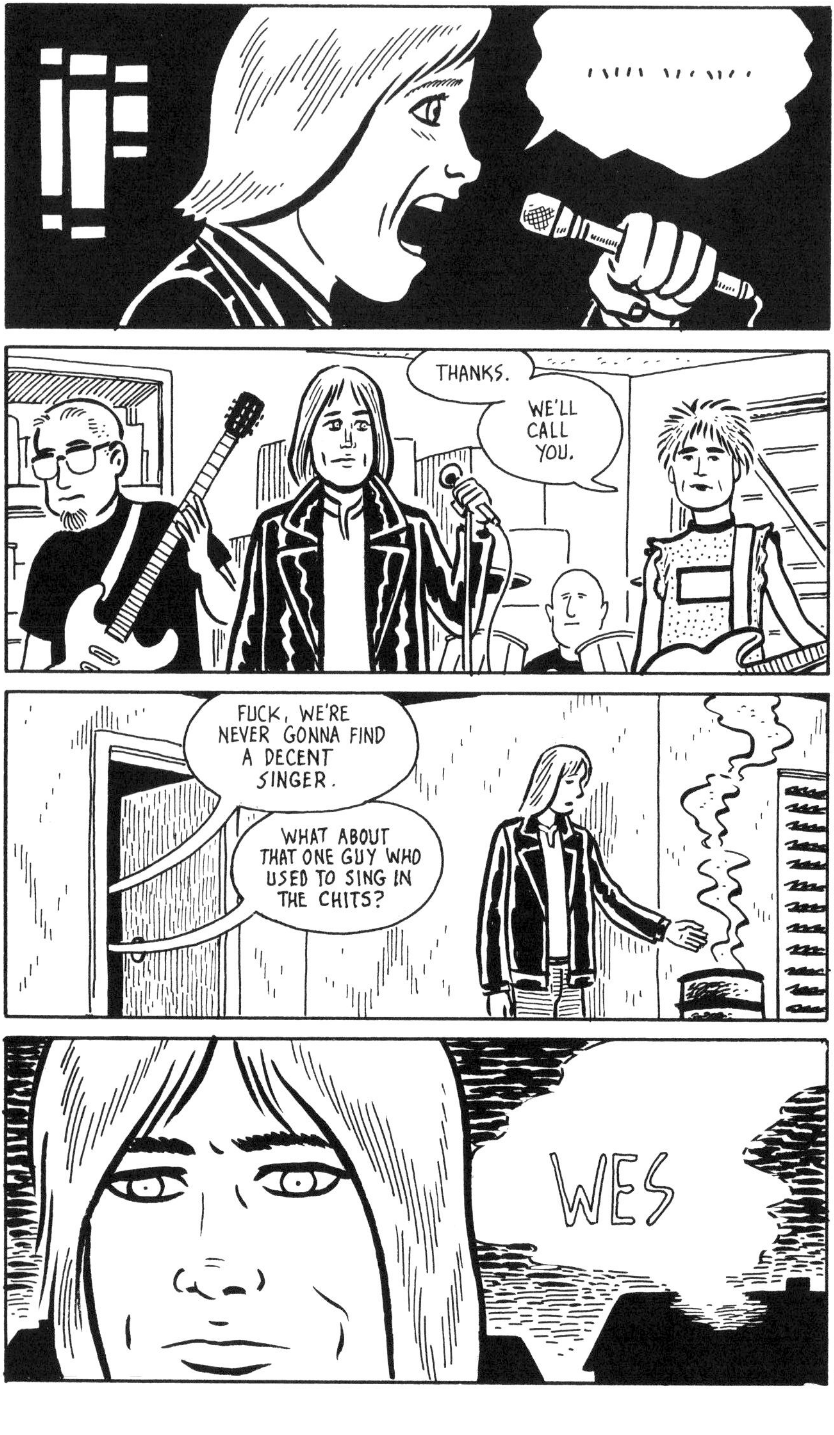
THANKS.
WE'LL CALL YOU.
FUCK, WE'RE NEVER GONNA FIND A DECENT SINGER.
WHAT ABOUT THAT ONE GUY WHO USED TO SING IN THE CHITS?
WES

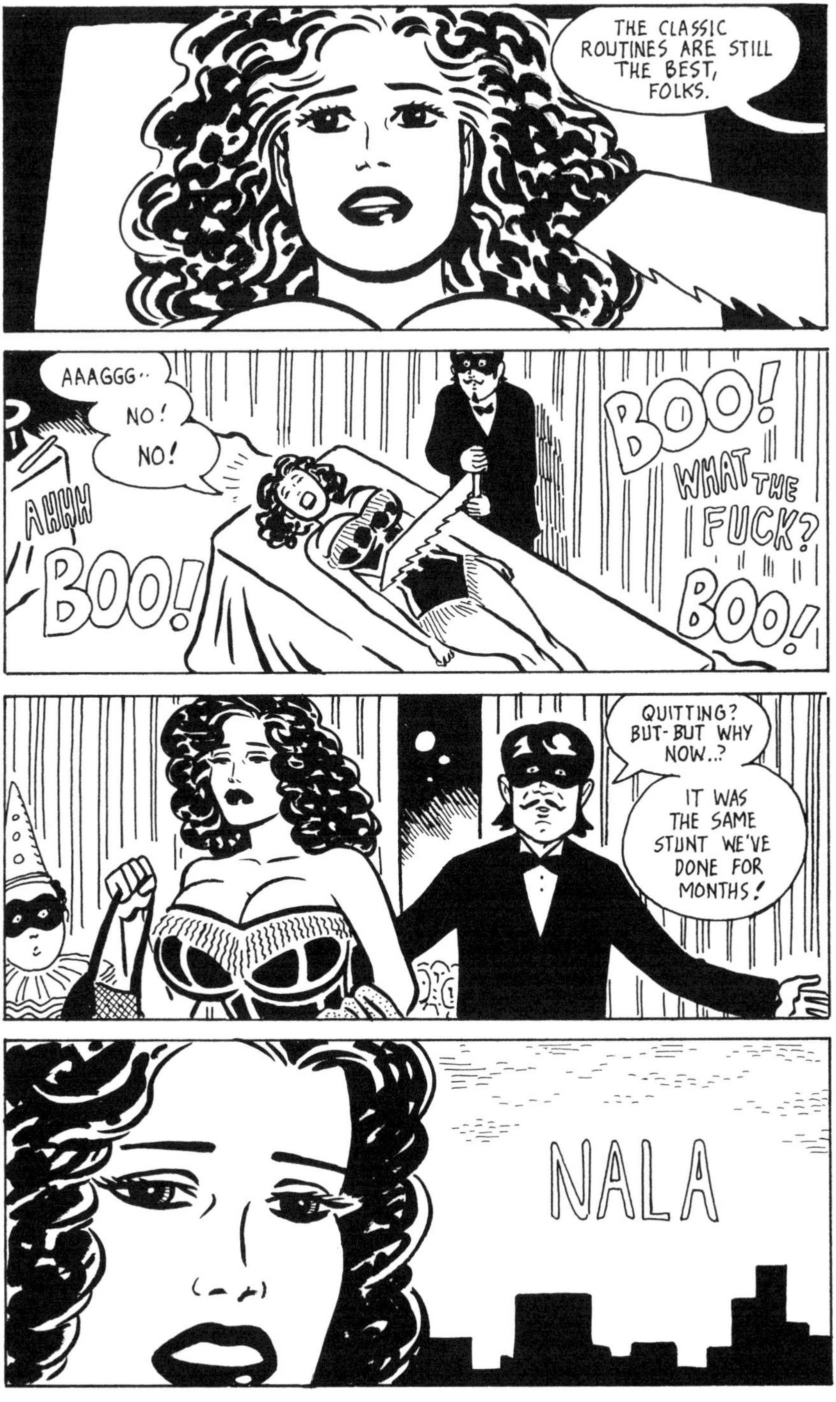
THE CLASSIC ROUTINES ARE STILL THE BEST, FOLKS.
AAAGGG.. NO! NO!
AHHH
BOO!
BOO!
WHAT THE FUCK?
BOO!
QUITTING? BUT-BUT WHY NOW..?
IT WAS THE SAME STUNT WE'VE DONE FOR MONTHS!
NALA

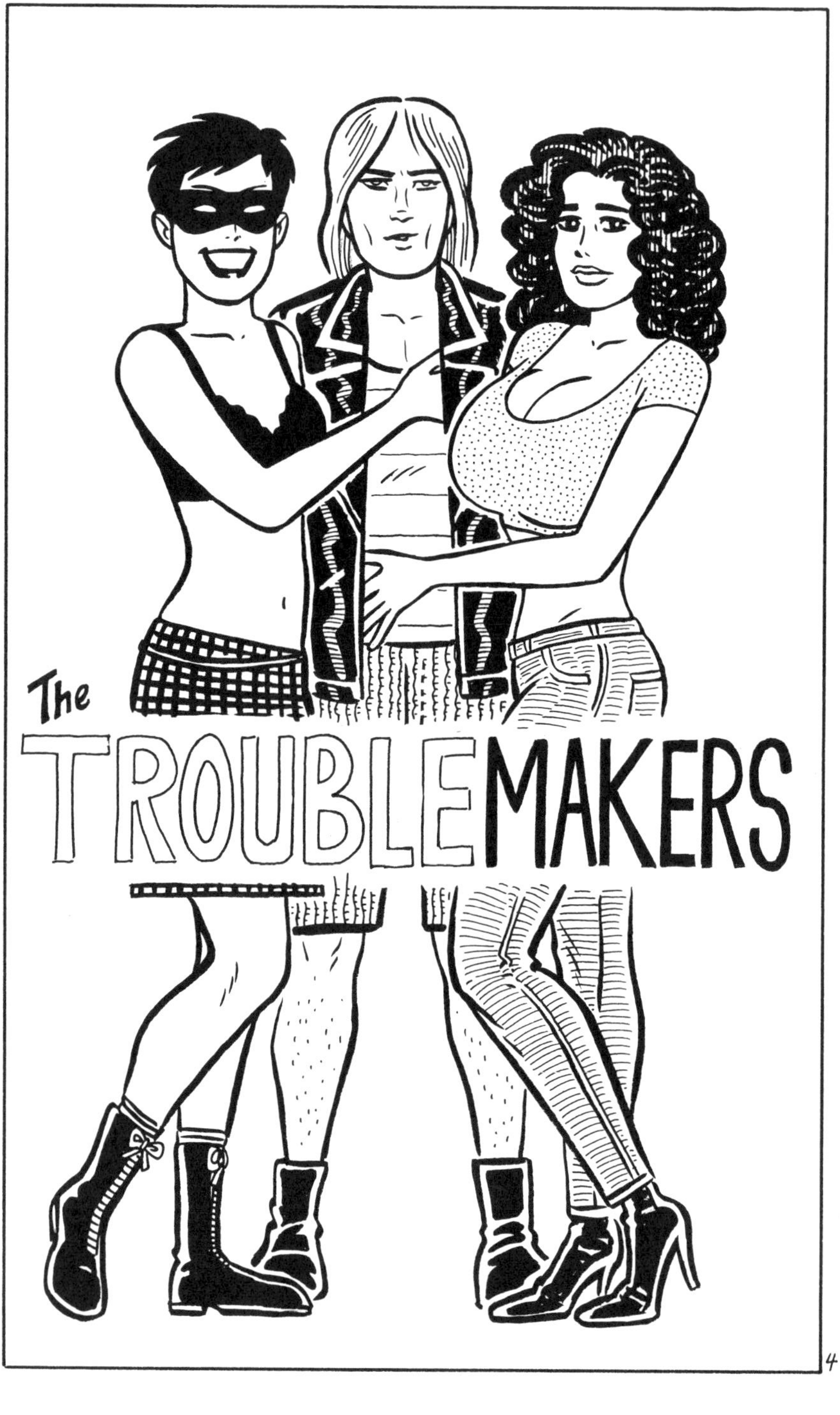
The
TROUBLEMAKERS

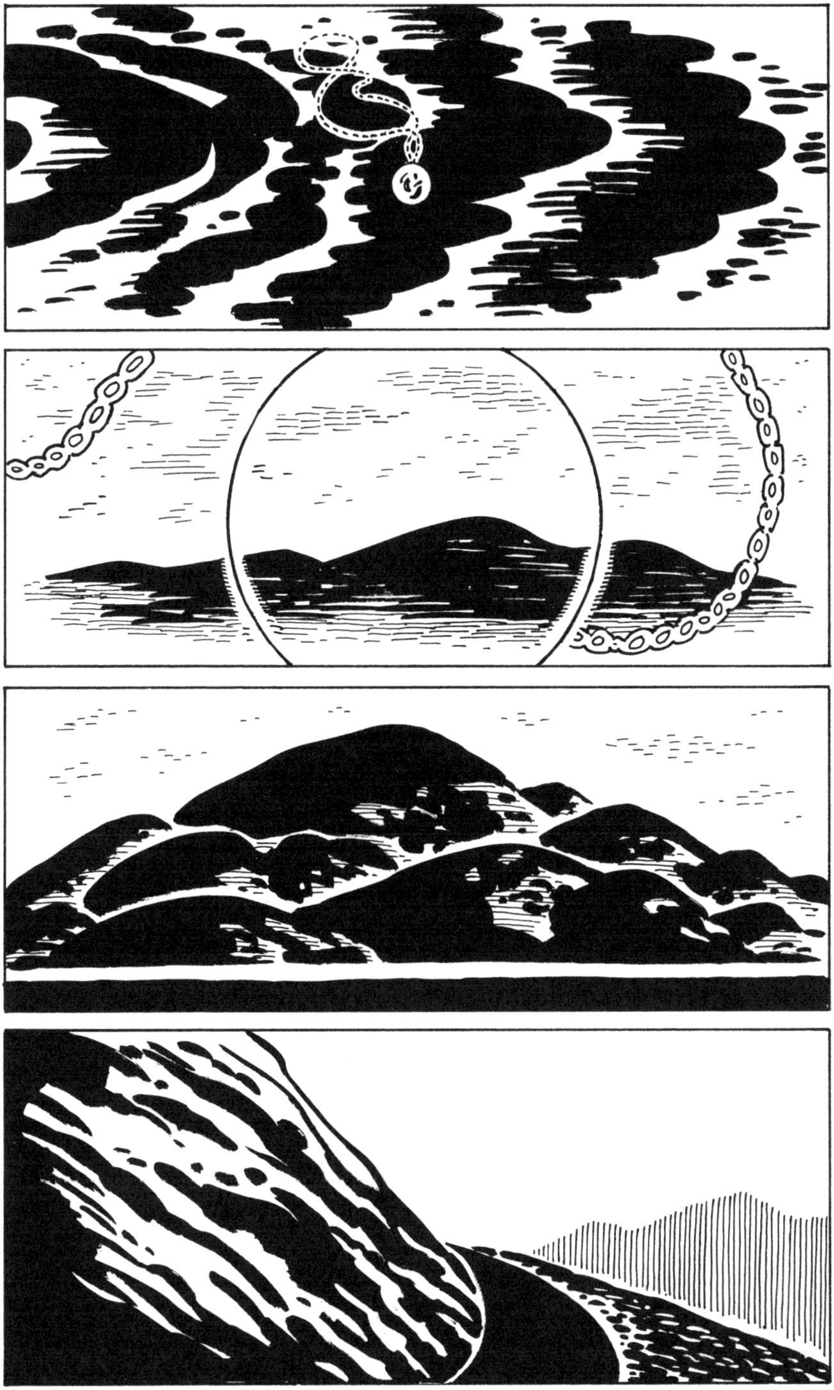

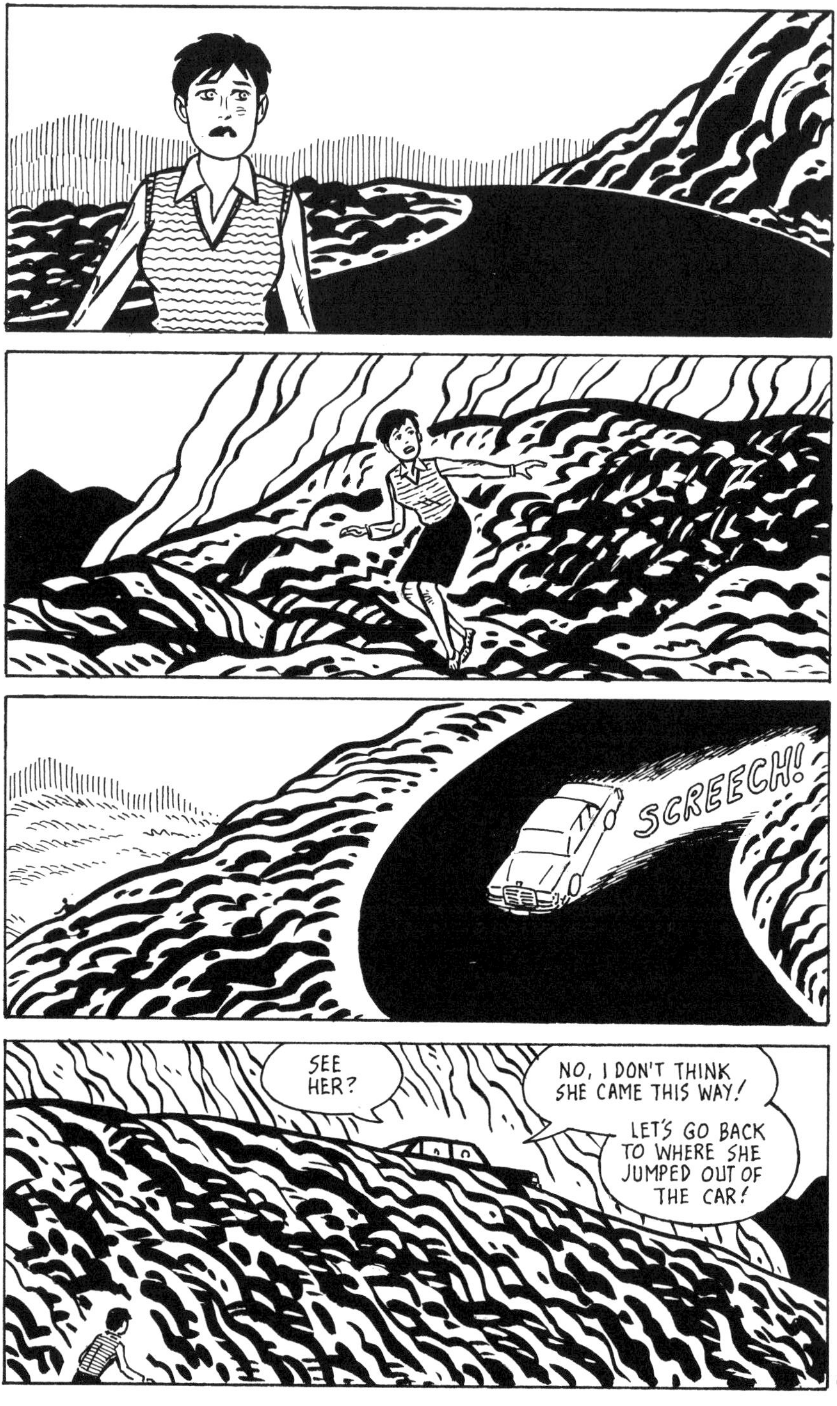
SCREECH!
SEE HER?
NO, I DON'T THINK SHE CAME THIS WAY!
LET'S GO BACK TO WHERE SHE JUMPED OUT OF THE CAR!

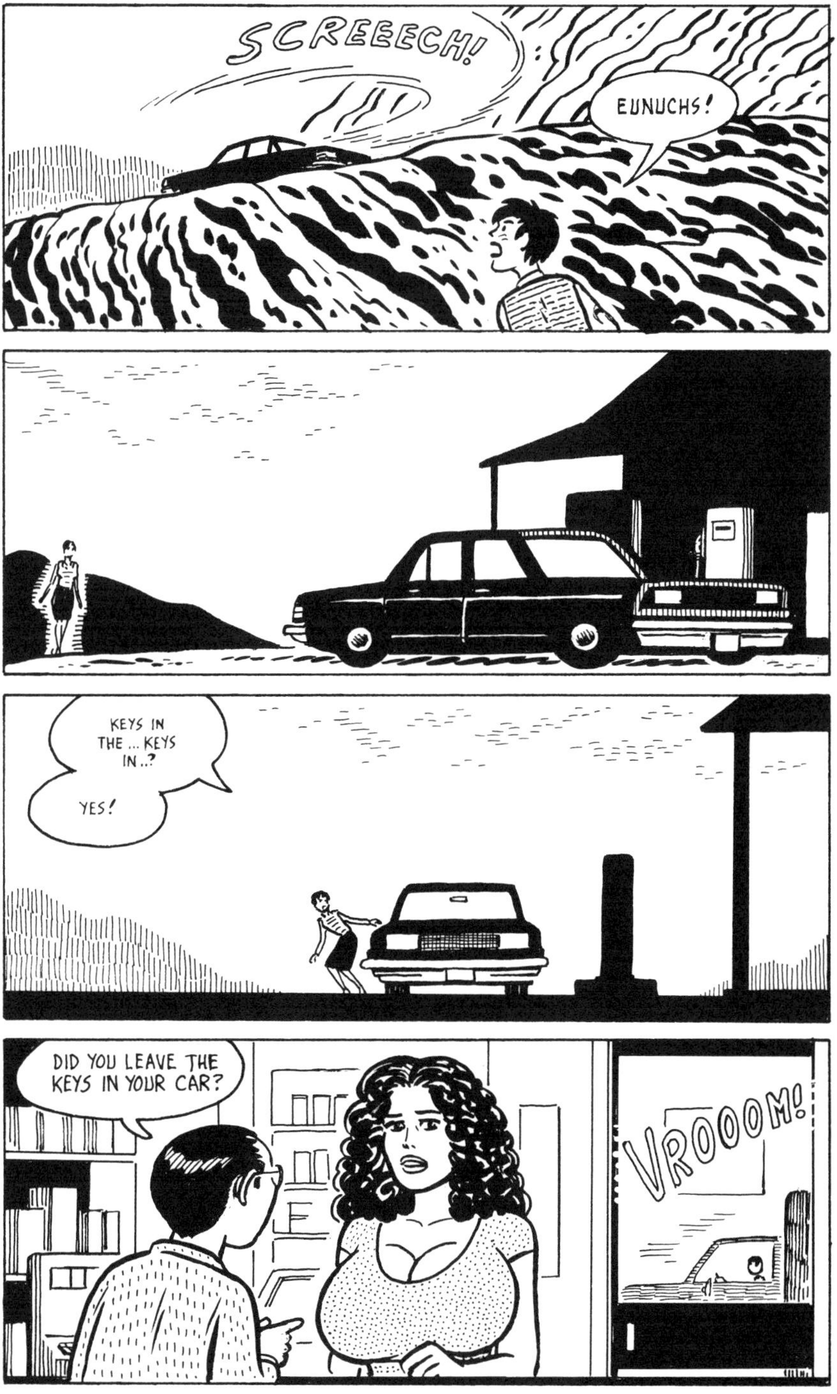
SCREEECH!
EUNUCHS!
KEYS IN THE ... KEYS IN..?
YES!
DID YOU LEAVE THE KEYS IN YOUR CAR?
VROOOM!

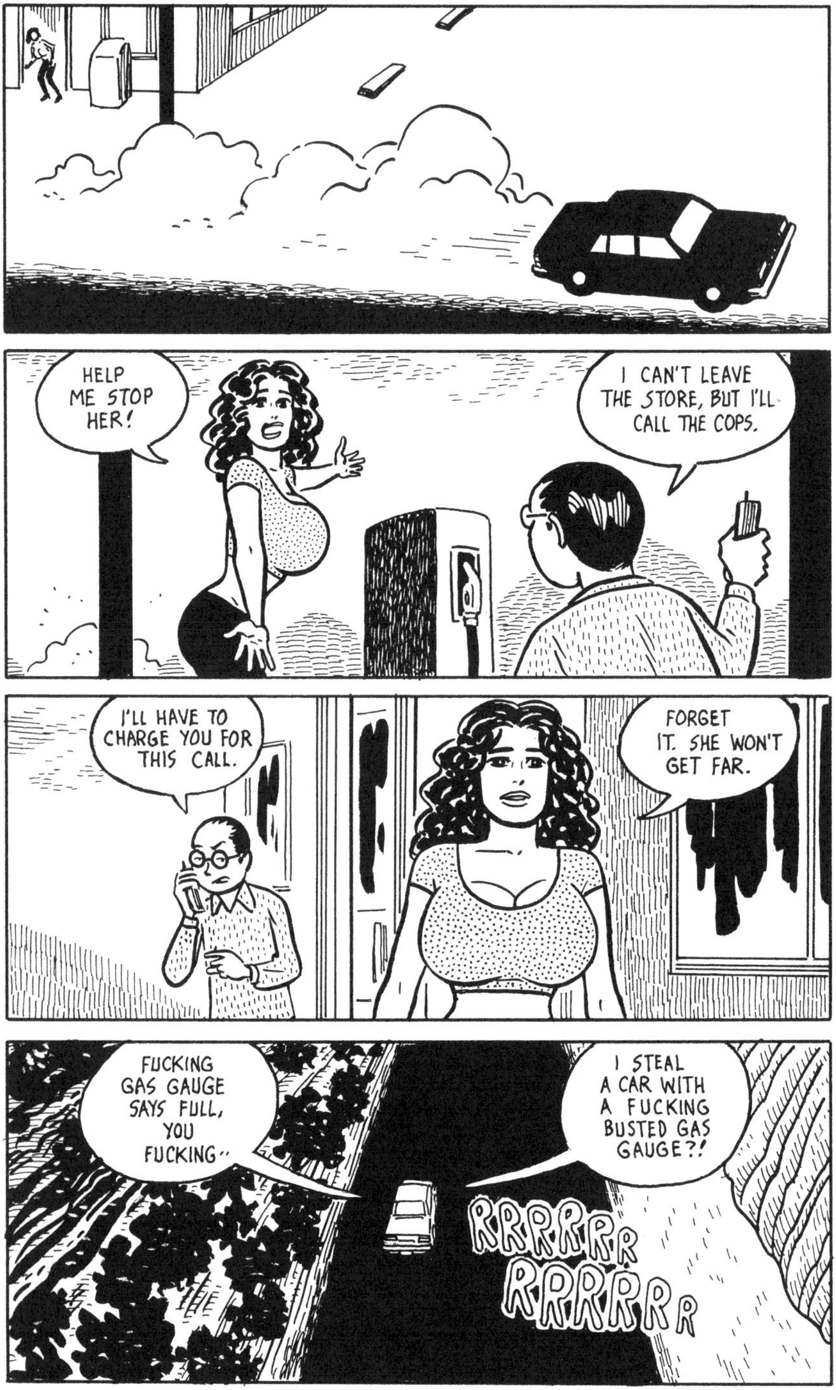

HELP ME STOP HER!
I CAN'T LEAVE THE STORE, BUT I'LL CALL THE COPS.
I'LL HAVE TO CHARGE YOU FOR THIS CALL.
FORGET IT. SHE WON'T GET FAR.
FUCKING GAS GAUGE SAYS FULL, YOU FUCKING..
I STEAL A CAR WITH A FUCKING BUSTED GAS GAUGE?!
RRRRRRR
RRRRRRR

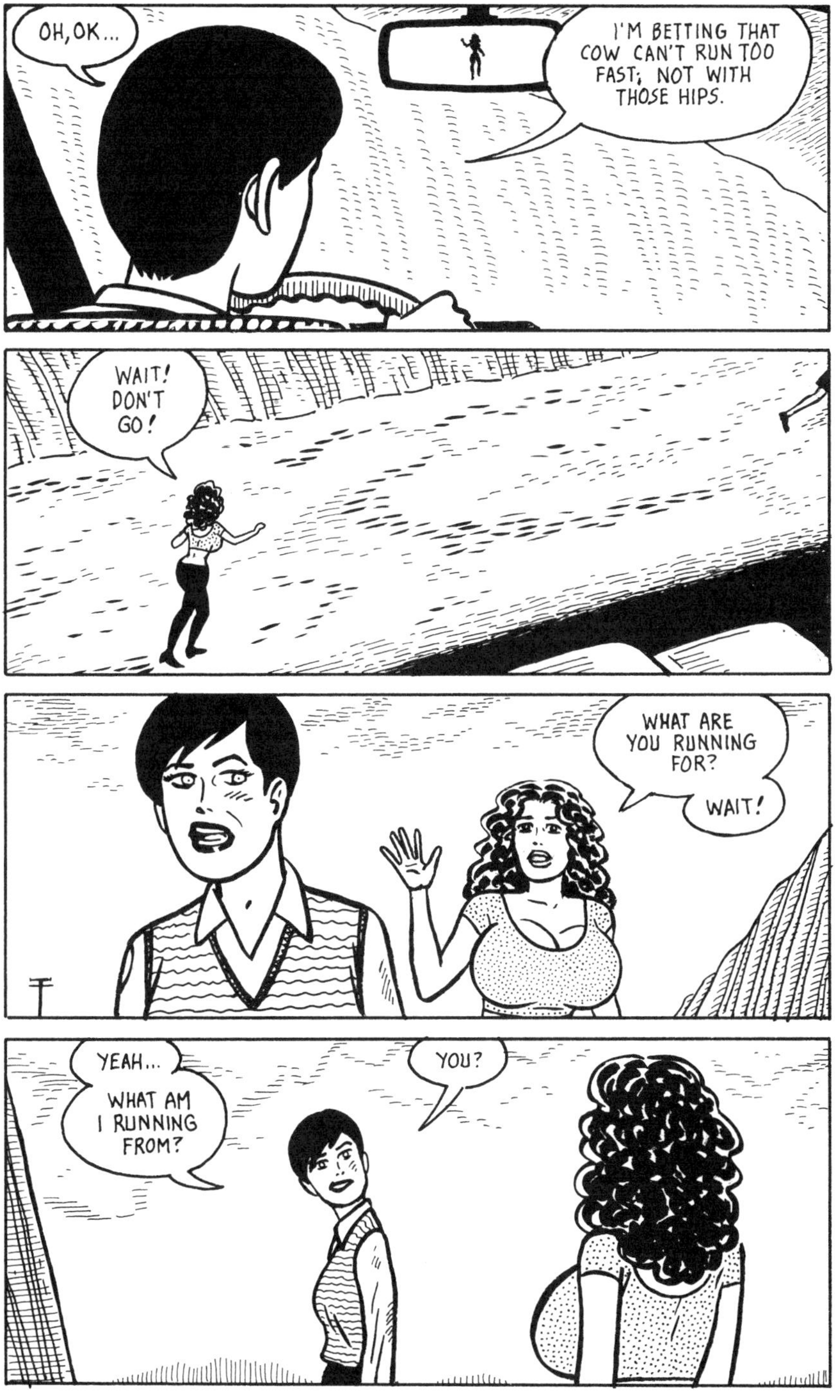
OH, OK...
I'M BETTING THAT COW CAN'T RUN TOO FAST; NOT WITH THOSE HIPS.
WAIT! DON'T GO!
WHAT ARE YOU RUNNING FOR?
WAIT!
YEAH... WHAT AM I RUNNING FROM?
YOU?

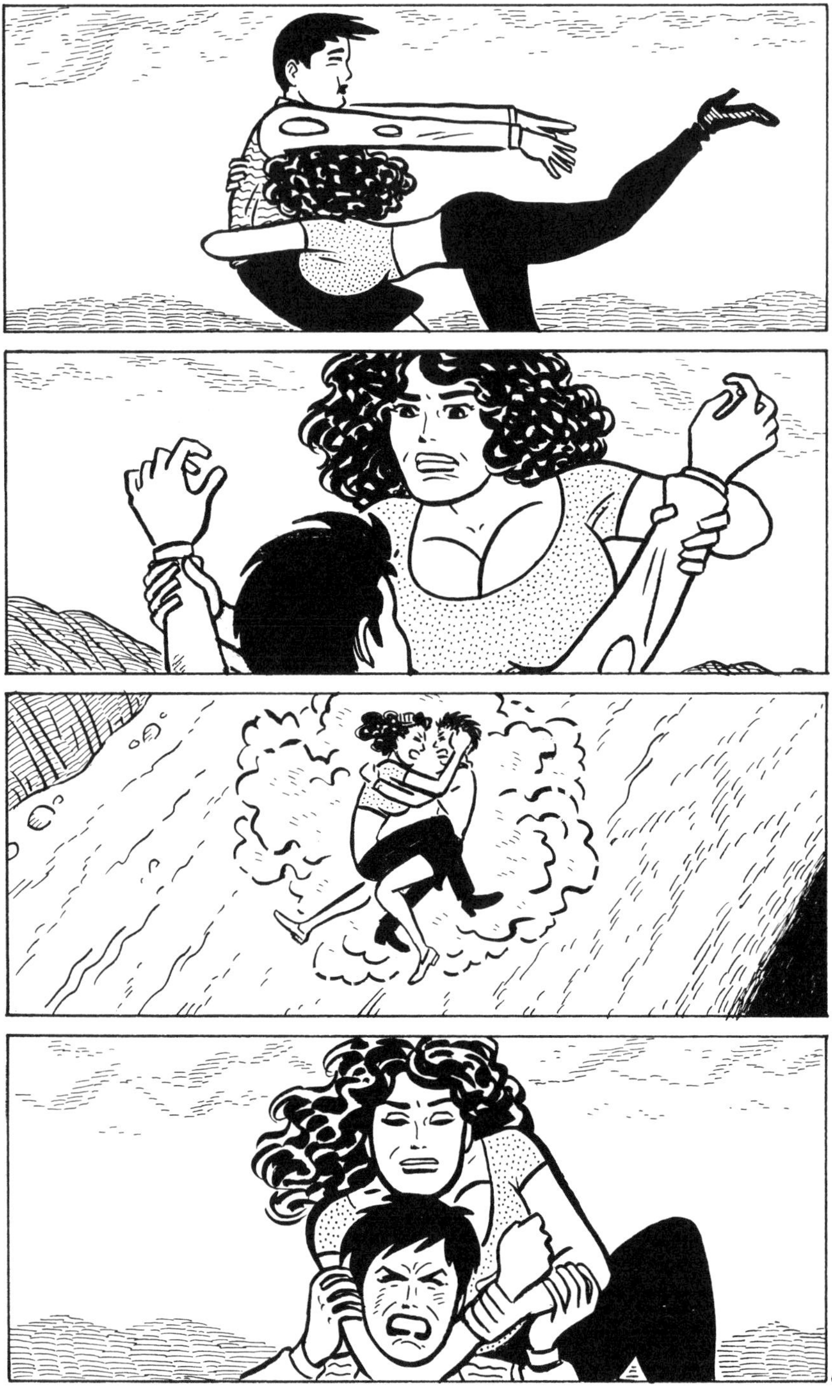

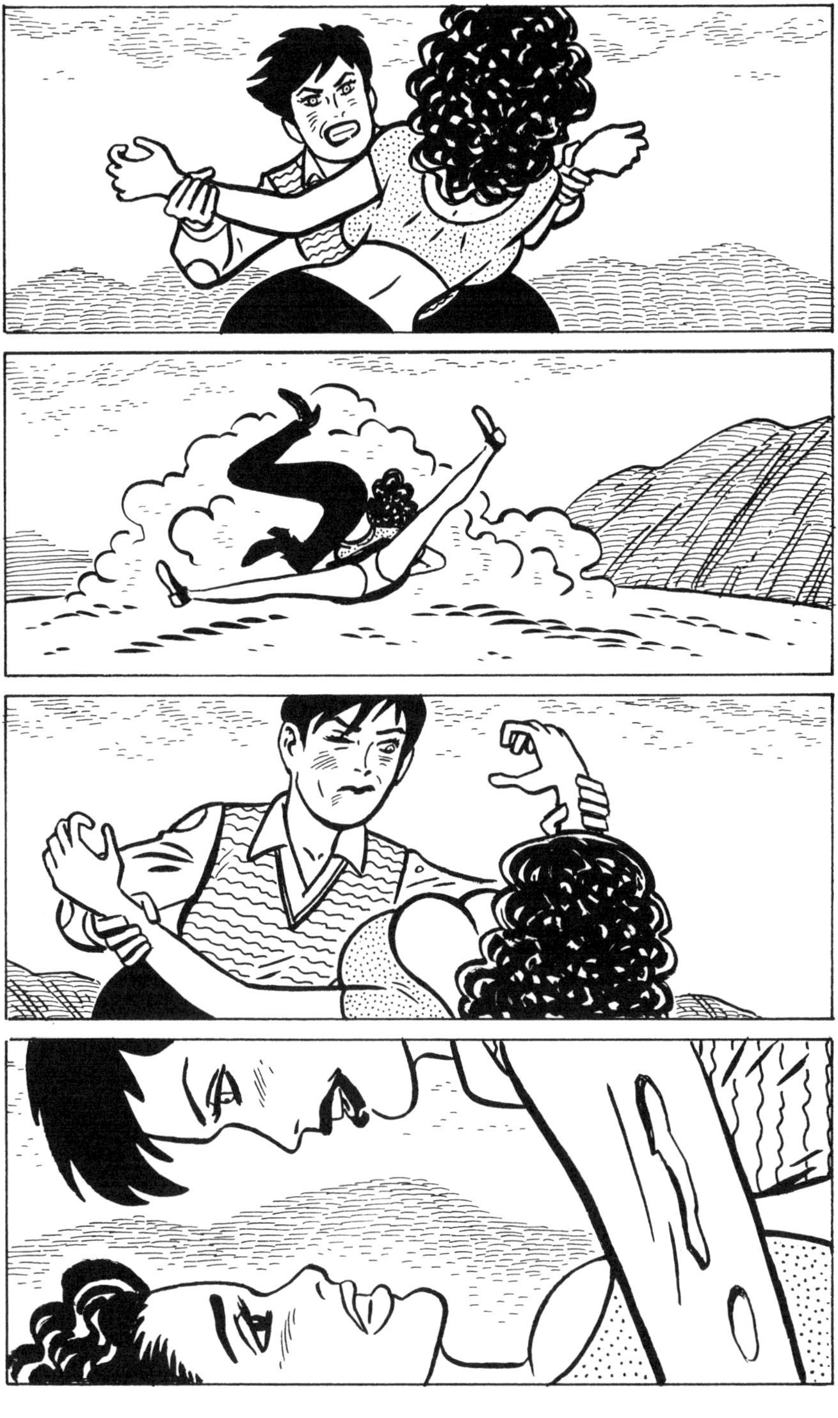

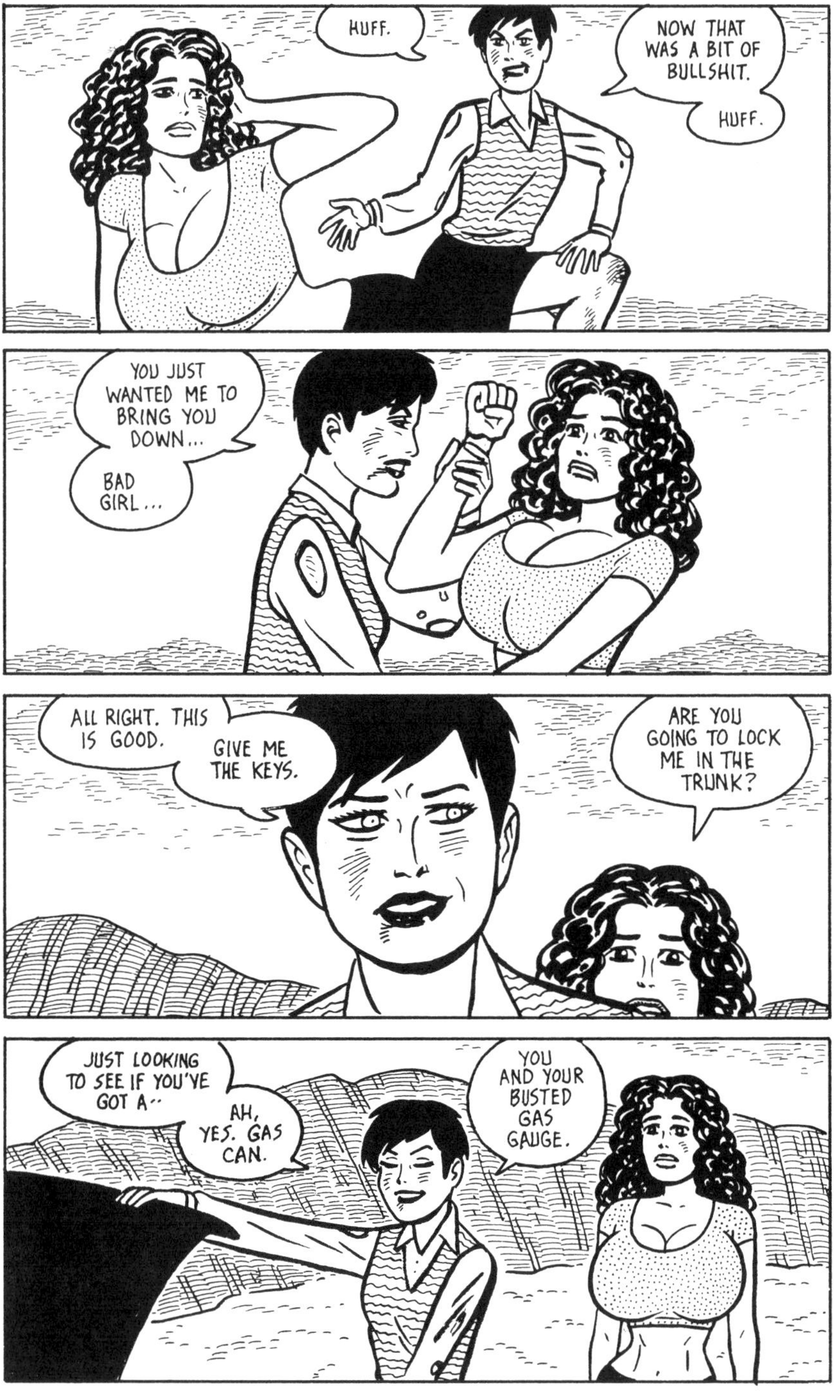
HUFF.
NOW THAT WAS A BIT OF BULLSHIT.
HUFF.
YOU JUST WANTED ME TO BRING YOU DOWN...
BAD GIRL...
ALL RIGHT. THIS IS GOOD.
GIVE ME THE KEYS.
ARE YOU GOING TO LOCK ME IN THE TRUNK?
JUST LOOKING TO SEE IF YOU'VE GOT A--
AH, YES. GAS CAN.
YOU AND YOUR BUSTED GAS GAUGE.

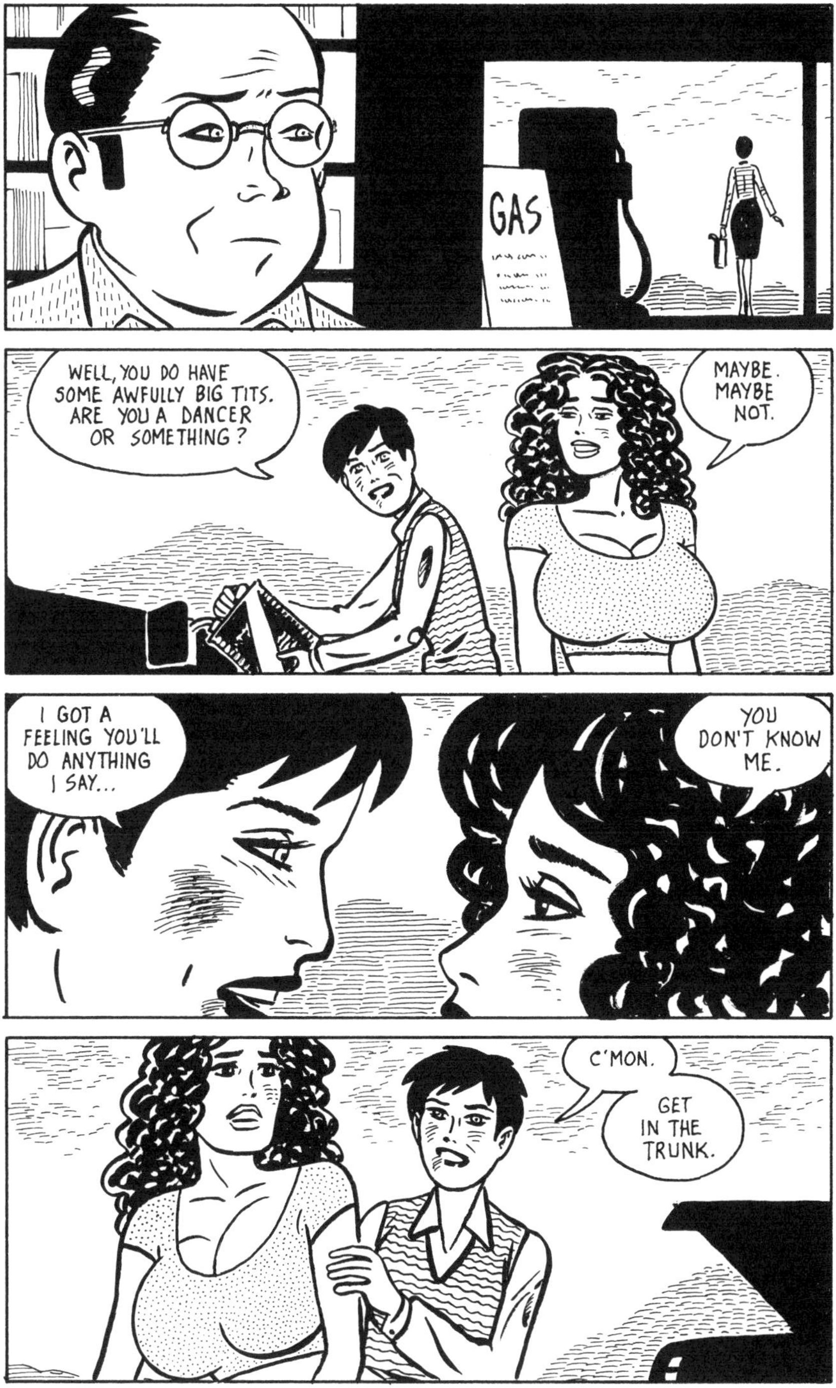
GAS
WELL, YOU DO HAVE SOME AWFULLY BIG TITS. ARE YOU A DANCER OR SOMETHING?
MAYBE. MAYBE NOT.
I GOT A FEELING YOU'LL DO ANYTHING I SAY...
YOU DON'T KNOW ME.
C'MON.
GET IN THE TRUNK.

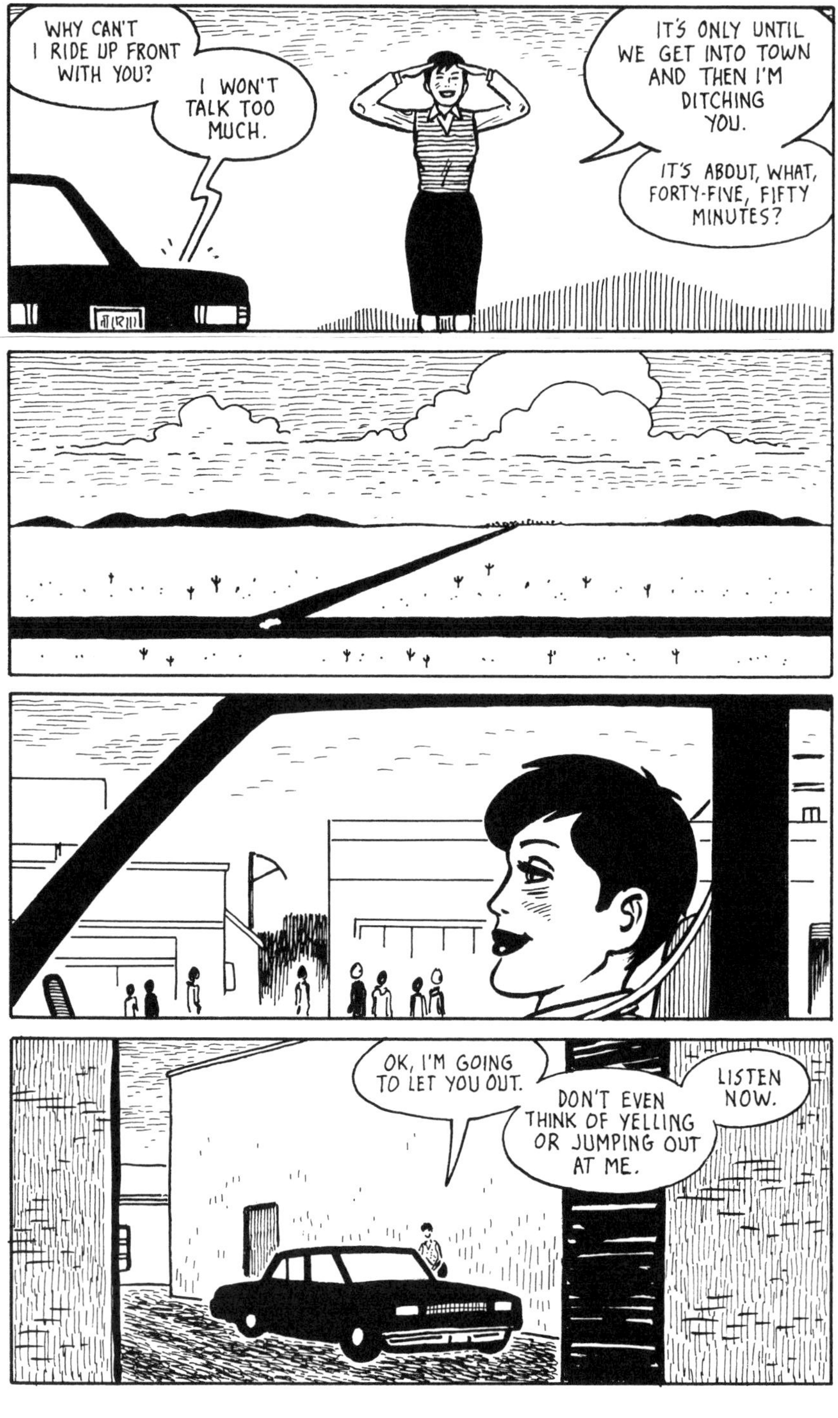
WHY CAN'T I RIDE UP FRONT WITH YOU?
I WON'T TALK TOO MUCH.
IT'S ONLY UNTIL WE GET INTO TOWN AND THEN I'M DITCHING YOU.
IT'S ABOUT, WHAT, FORTY-FIVE, FIFTY MINUTES?
OK, I'M GOING TO LET YOU OUT.
LISTEN NOW.
DON'T EVEN THINK OF YELLING OR JUMPING OUT AT ME.

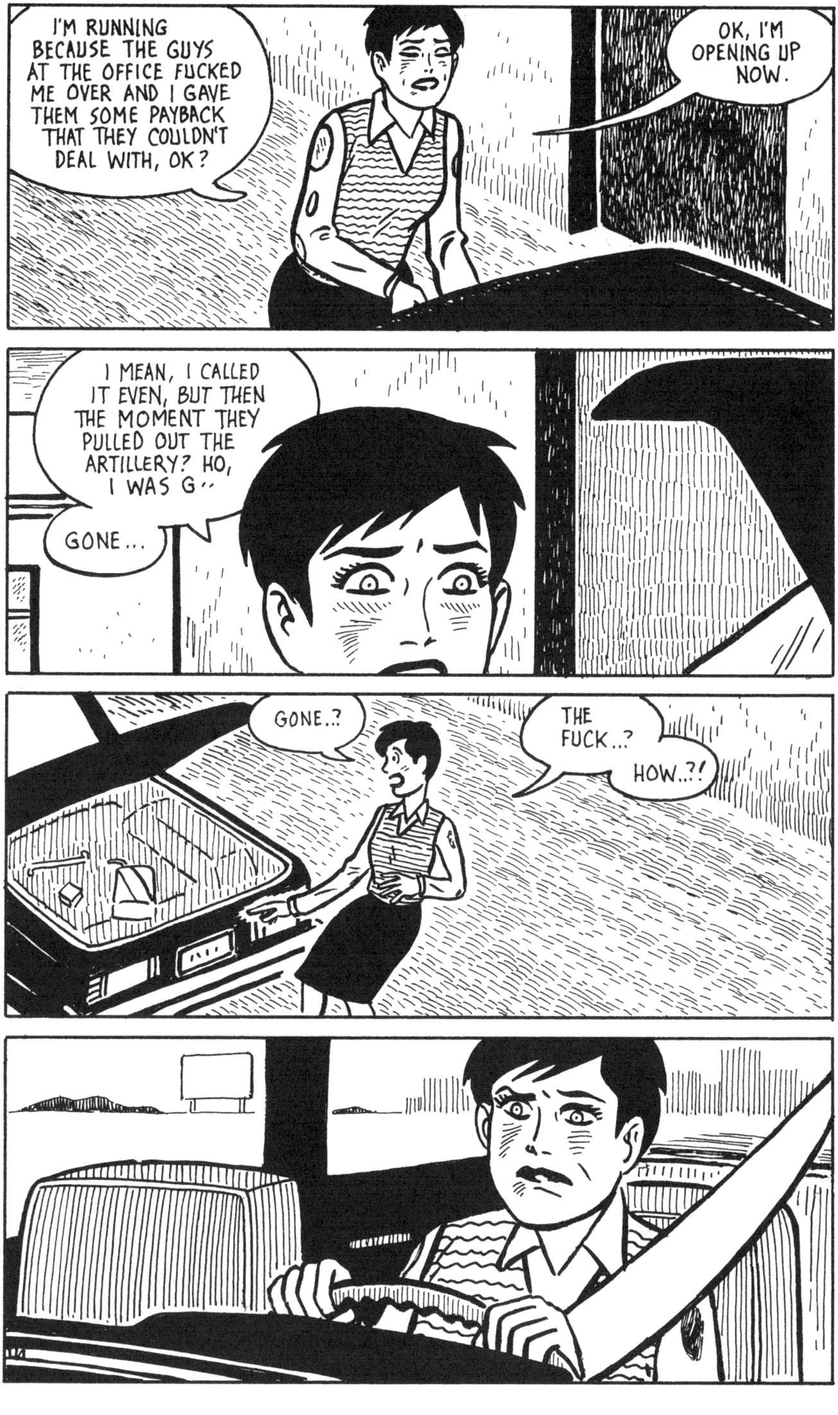
I'M RUNNING BECAUSE THE GUYS AT THE OFFICE FUCKED ME OVER AND I GAVE THEM SOME PAYBACK THAT THEY COULDN'T DEAL WITH, OK?
OK, I'M OPENING UP NOW.
I MEAN, I CALLED IT EVEN, BUT THEN THE MOMENT THEY PULLED OUT THE ARTILLERY? HO, I WAS G..
GONE...
GONE..?
THE FUCK..?
HOW..?!

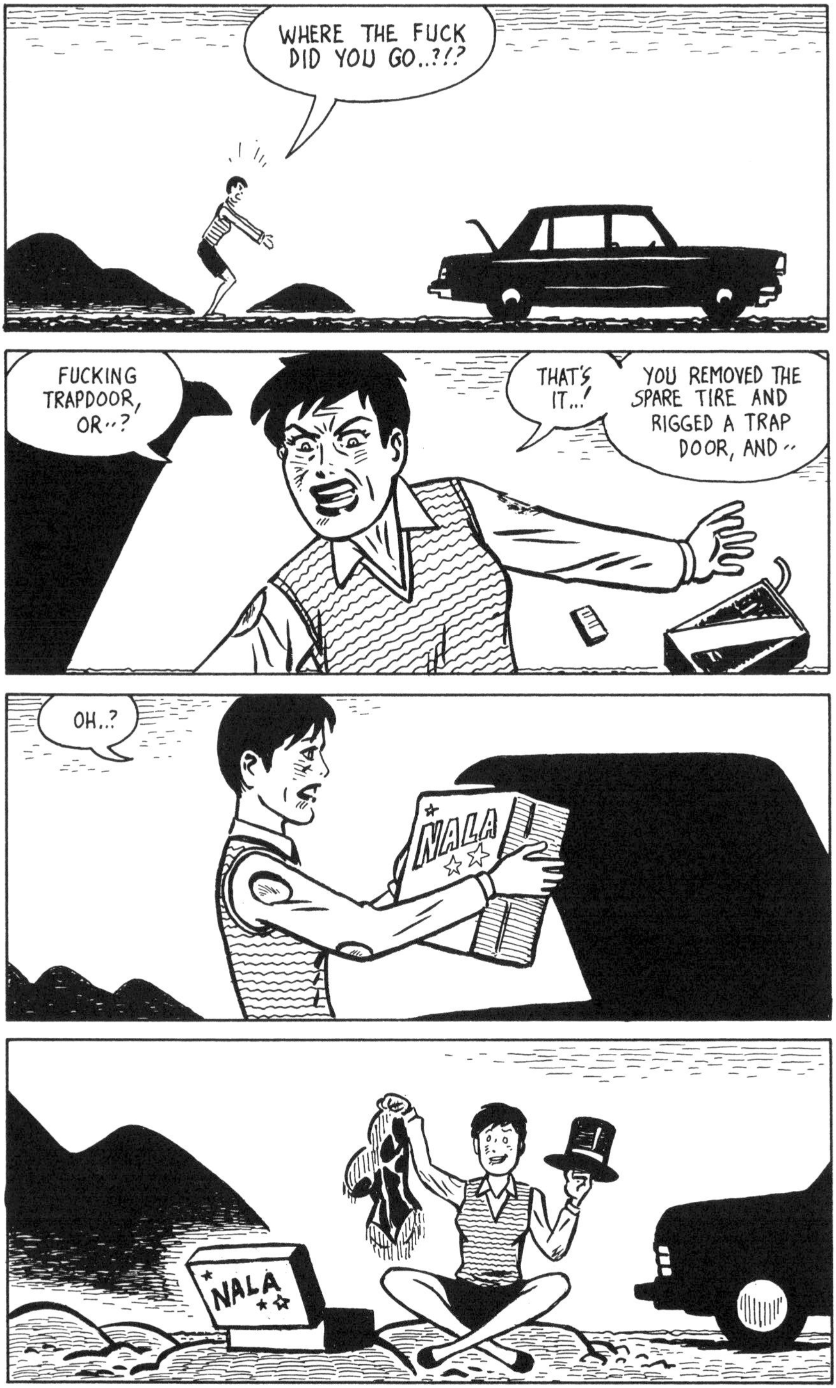
WHERE THE FUCK DID YOU GO..?!?
FUCKING TRAPDOOR, OR..?
THAT'S IT...!
YOU REMOVED THE SPARE TIRE AND RIGGED A TRAP DOOR, AND..
OH..?
NALA
NALA

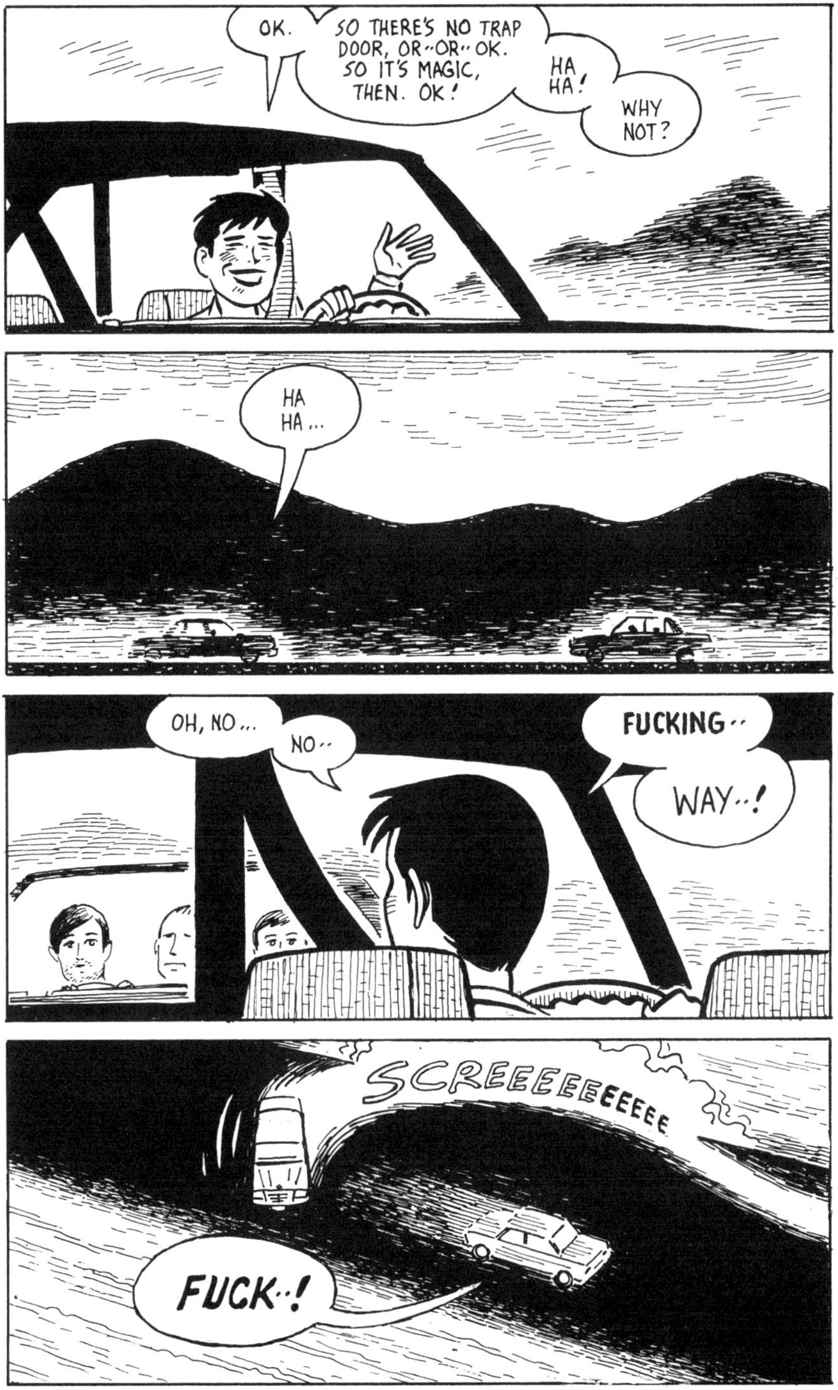
OK.
SO THERE'S NO TRAP DOOR, OR··OR·· OK. SO IT'S MAGIC, THEN. OK!
HA HA!
WHY NOT?
HA HA...
OH, NO...
NO··
FUCKING··
WAY··!
SCREEEEEEEEEEE
FUCK··!

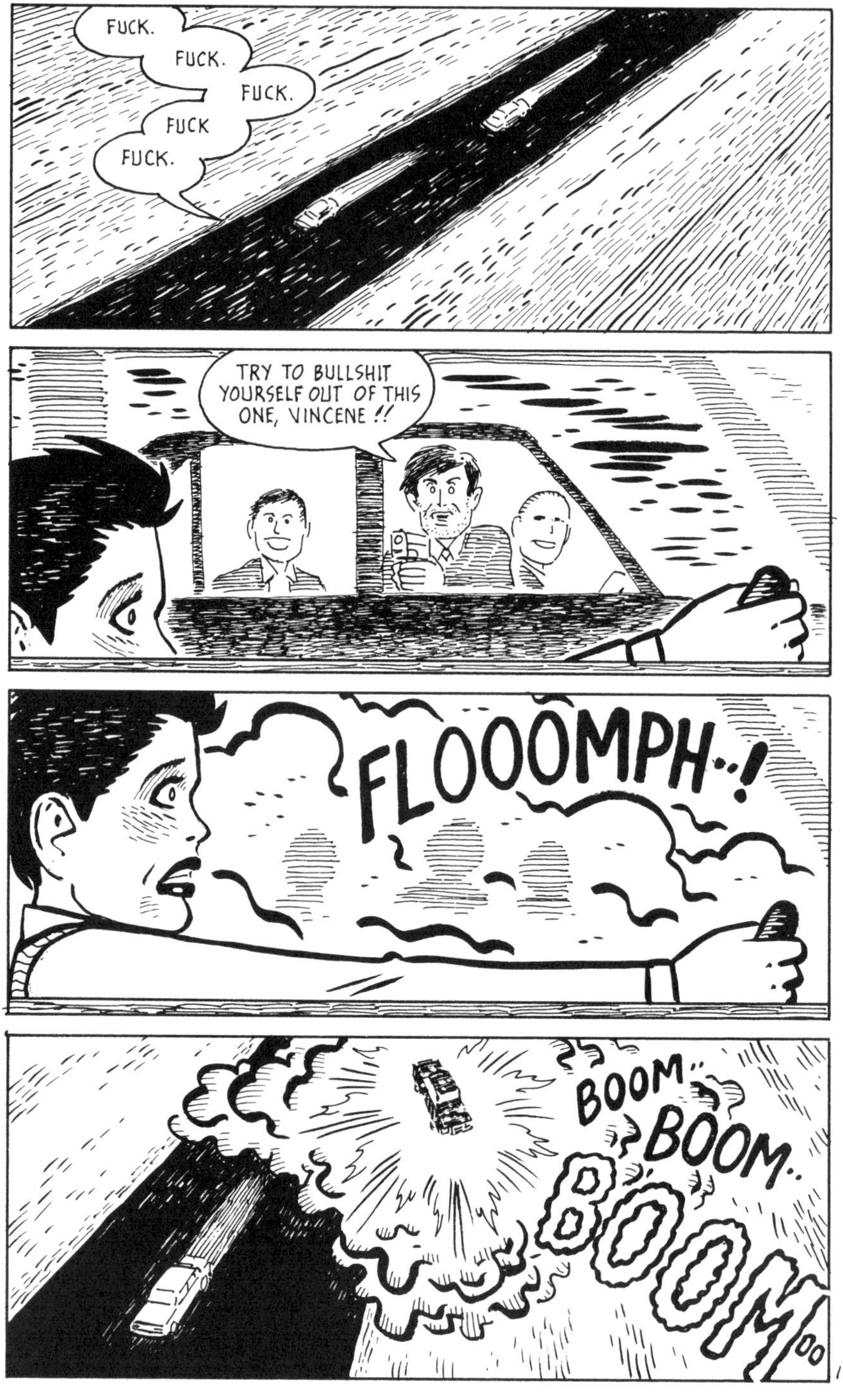
FUCK.
FUCK.
FUCK.
FUCK
FUCK.
TRY TO BULLSHIT YOURSELF OUT OF THIS ONE, VINCENE !!
FLOOOMPH..!
BOOM..
BOOM..
BOOOM

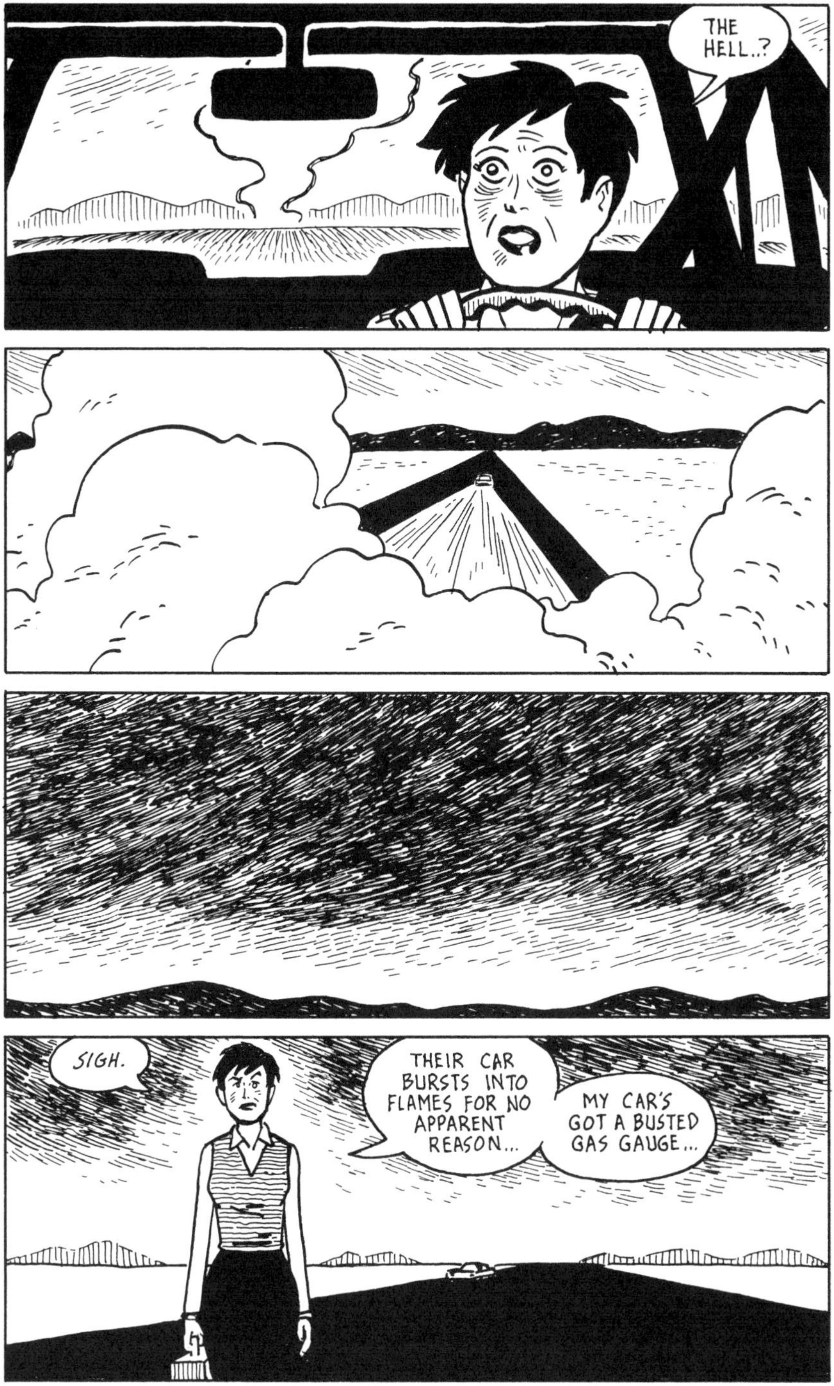
THE HELL..?
SIGH.
THEIR CAR BURSTS INTO FLAMES FOR NO APPARENT REASON...
MY CAR'S GOT A BUSTED GAS GAUGE...

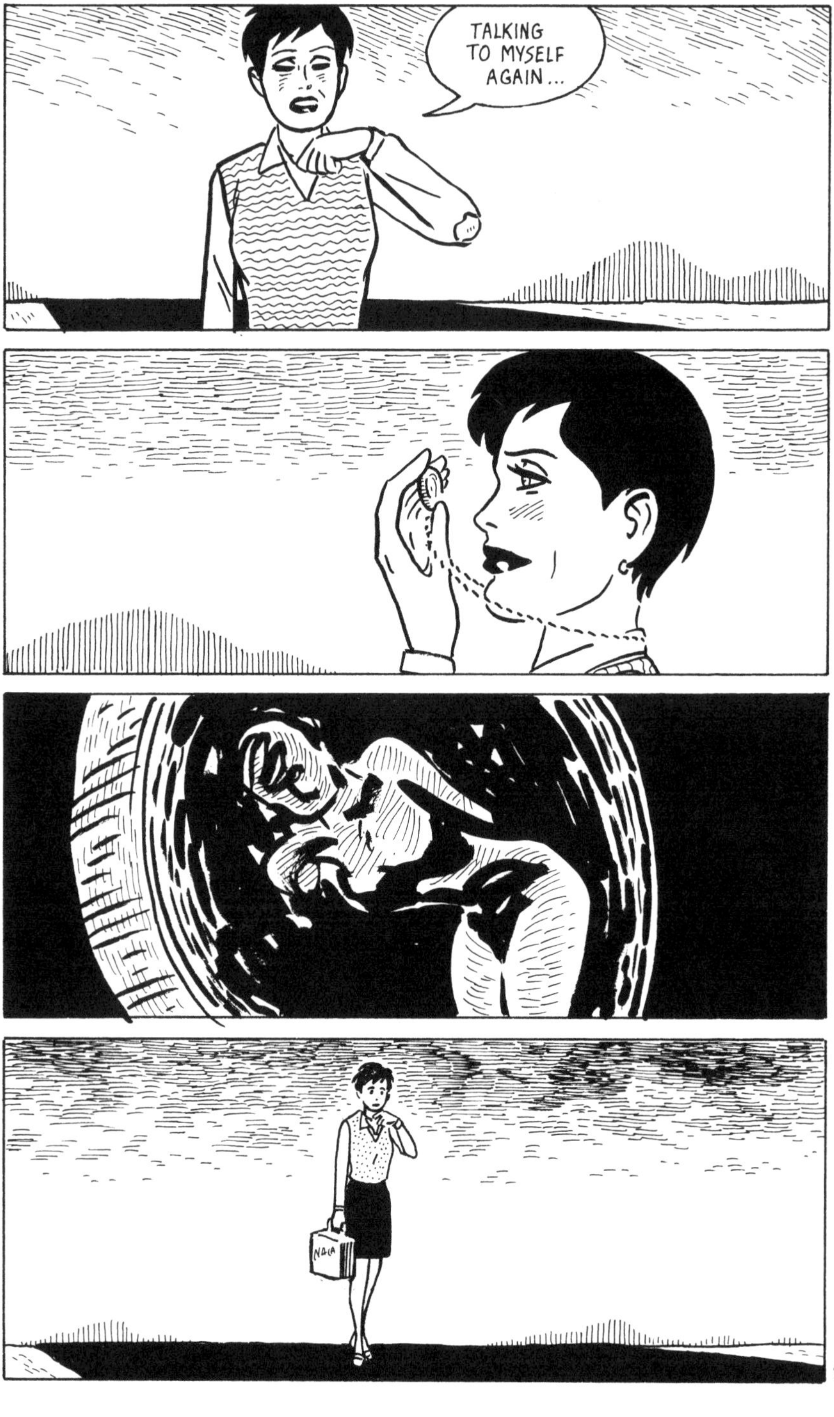
TALKING TO MYSELF AGAIN...
NALA

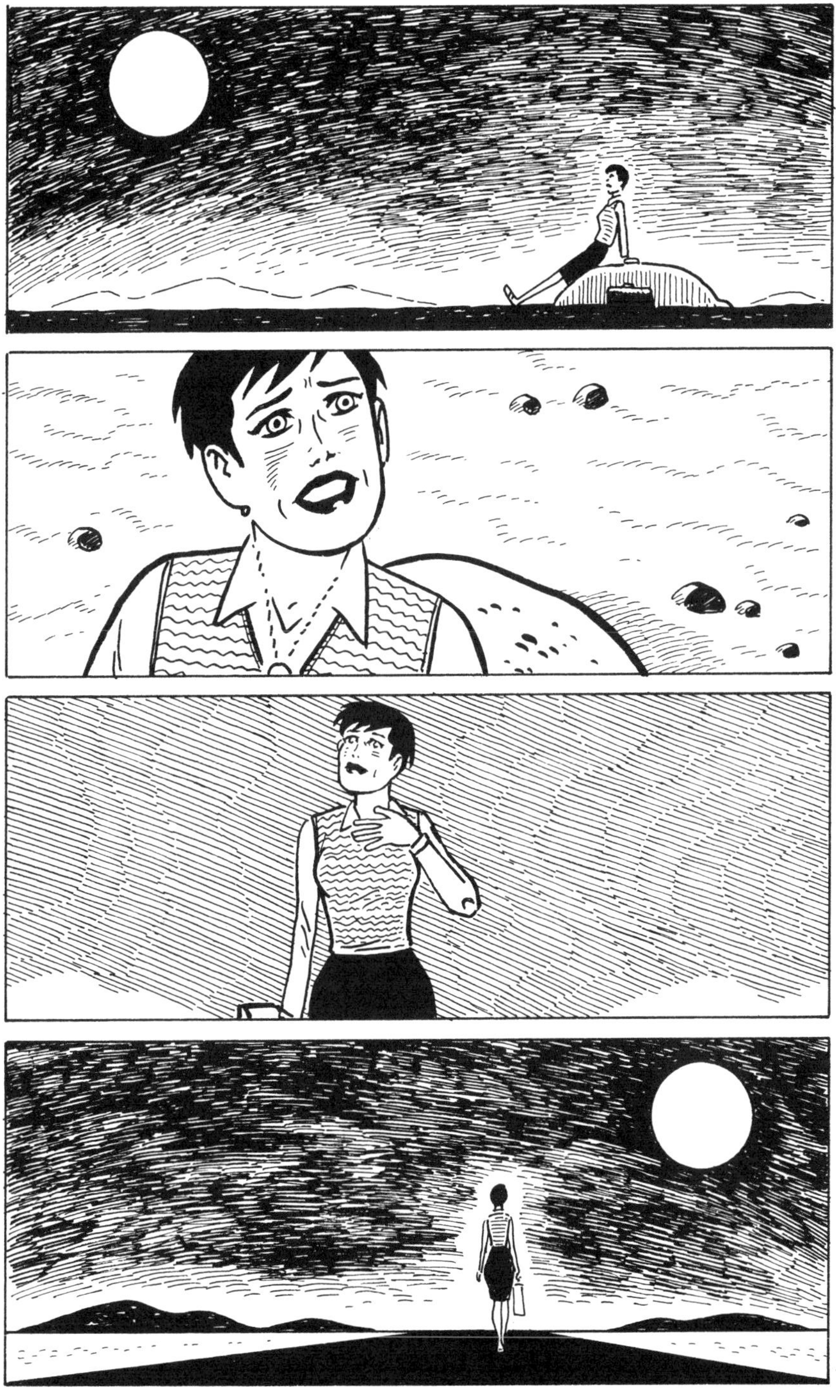

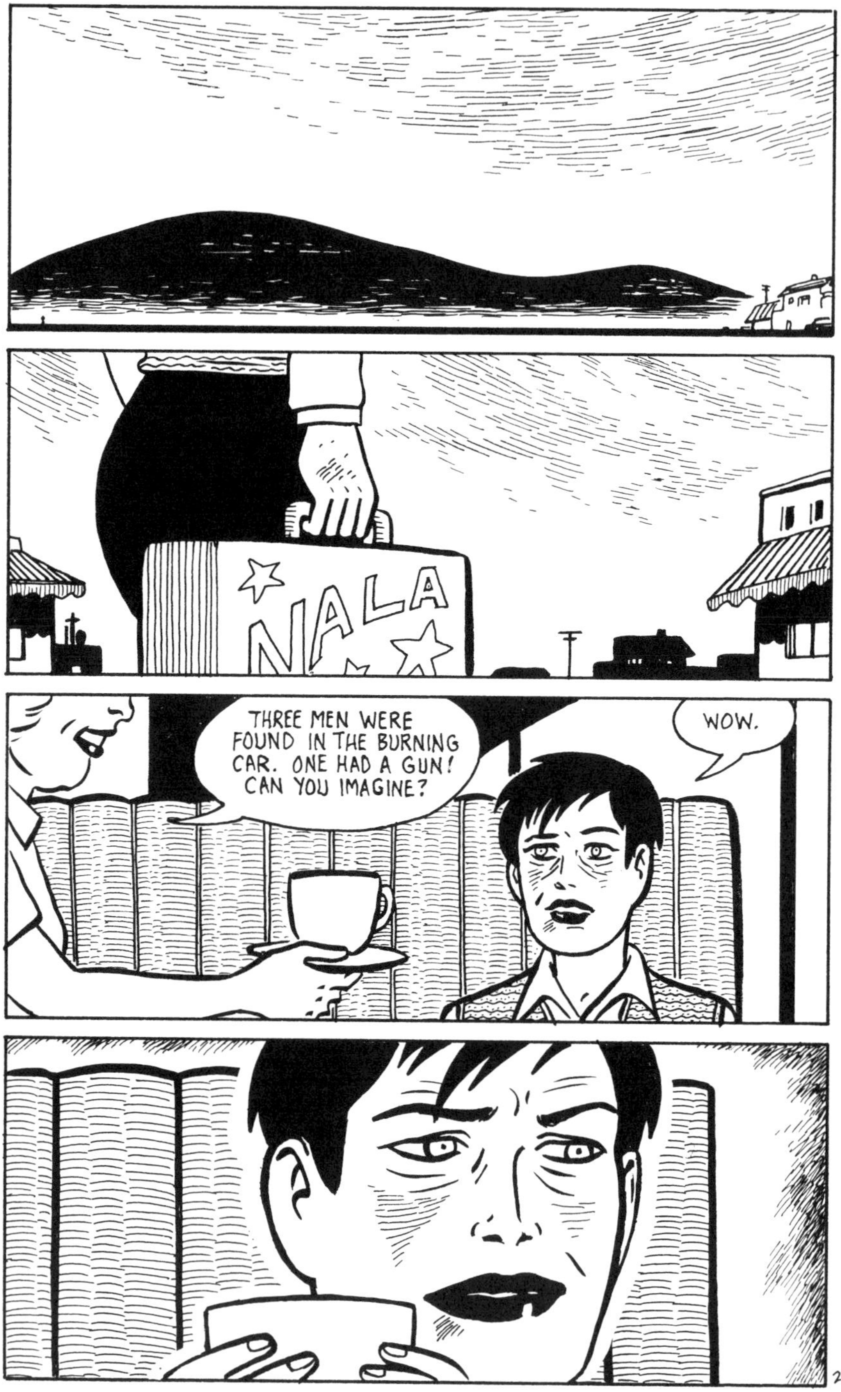
NALA
THREE MEN WERE FOUND IN THE BURNING CAR. ONE HAD A GUN! CAN YOU IMAGINE?
WOW.

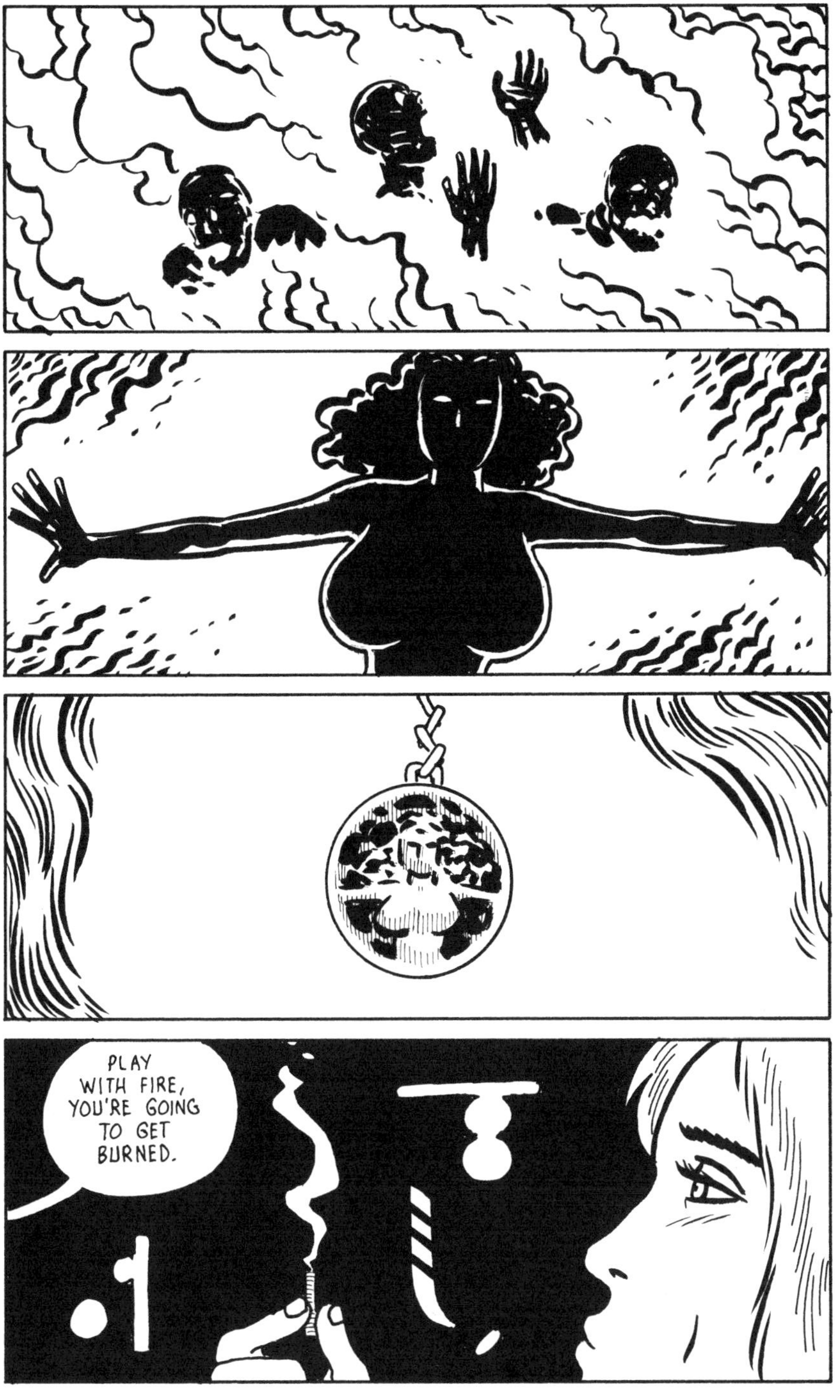
PLAY WITH FIRE, YOU'RE GOING TO GET BURNED.

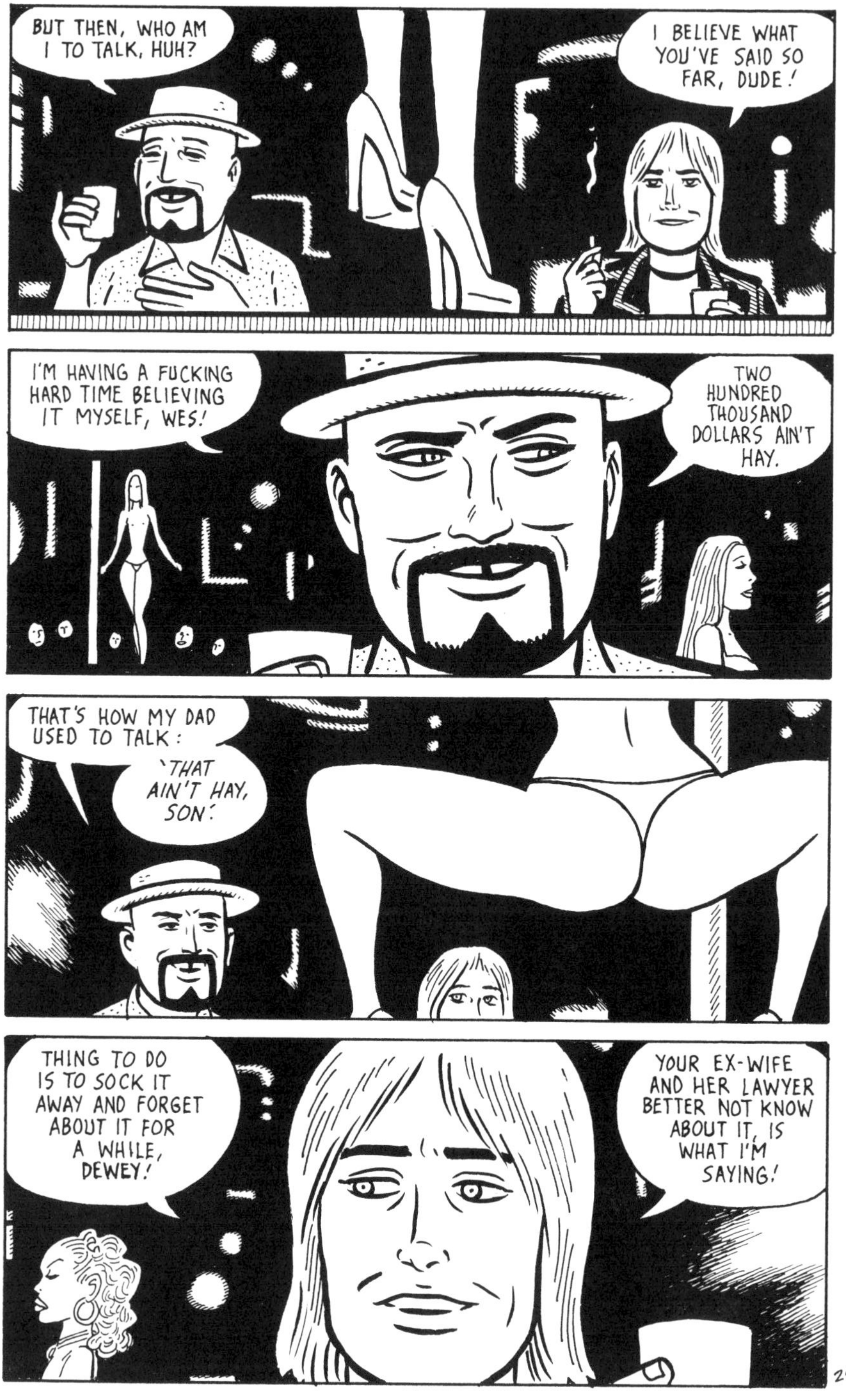
BUT THEN, WHO AM I TO TALK, HUH?
I BELIEVE WHAT YOU'VE SAID SO FAR, DUDE!
I'M HAVING A FUCKING HARD TIME BELIEVING IT MYSELF, WES!
TWO HUNDRED THOUSAND DOLLARS AIN'T HAY.
THAT'S HOW MY DAD USED TO TALK:
'THAT AIN'T HAY, SON.'
THING TO DO IS TO SOCK IT AWAY AND FORGET ABOUT IT FOR A WHILE, DEWEY!
YOUR EX-WIFE AND HER LAWYER BETTER NOT KNOW ABOUT IT, IS WHAT I'M SAYING!

OH YEAH, FUCK THEM! I RISKED IT ALL, THE FUCKING MONEY'S MINE!
TCH, THAT FUCKING GUN BARREL WAS STUCK BETWEEN MY EYES, NOT THEIRS!
DEWEY, I WOULD HAVE SHIT, I SWEAR. I DON'T KNOW HOW YOU GOT OUT OF THERE WITHOUT GETTING YOUR DICK BLOWN OFF.
IT WAS LIKE THE WILD FUCKIN' WEST, DUDE; FUCK, BULLETS WERE FLYING, BLOOD SPURTING..
FOX
I GRABBED THE CASH AND WAS OUT OF THERE WITHOUT A SCRATCH!
YEAH... DAD WOULD'VE BEEN PROUD.
GOD SURE SMILED UPON YOUR ASS THAT DAY, DEWEY.
AND MY LORD GOD AND SAVIOR IS SMILING UPON ME NOW, WES.

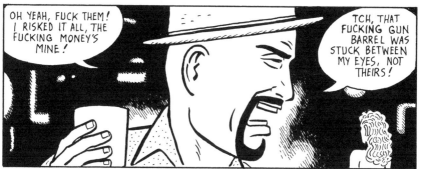

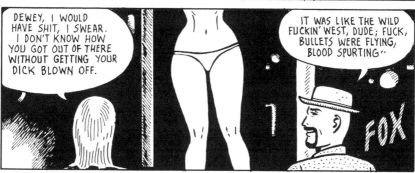

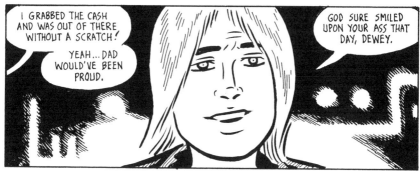

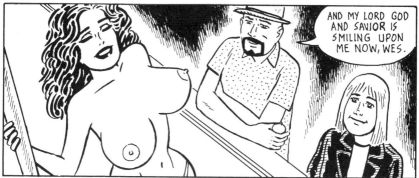

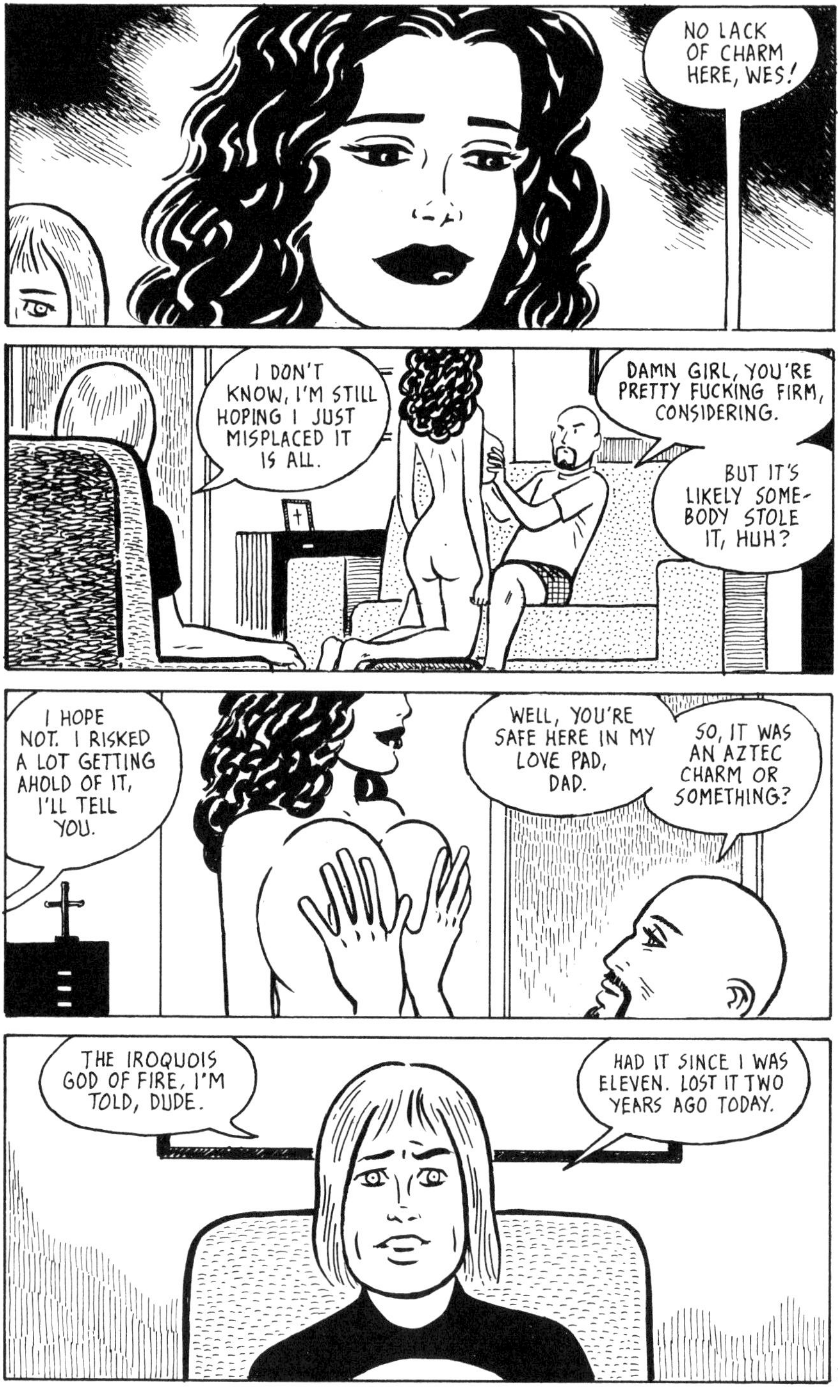
NO LACK OF CHARM HERE, WES!
I DON'T KNOW, I'M STILL HOPING I JUST MISPLACED IT IS ALL.
DAMN GIRL, YOU'RE PRETTY FUCKING FIRM, CONSIDERING.
BUT IT'S LIKELY SOMEBODY STOLE IT, HUH?
I HOPE NOT. I RISKED A LOT GETTING AHOLD OF IT, I'LL TELL YOU.
WELL, YOU'RE SAFE HERE IN MY LOVE PAD, DAD.
SO, IT WAS AN AZTEC CHARM OR SOMETHING?
THE IROQUOIS GOD OF FIRE, I'M TOLD, DUDE.
HAD IT SINCE I WAS ELEVEN. LOST IT TWO YEARS AGO TODAY.

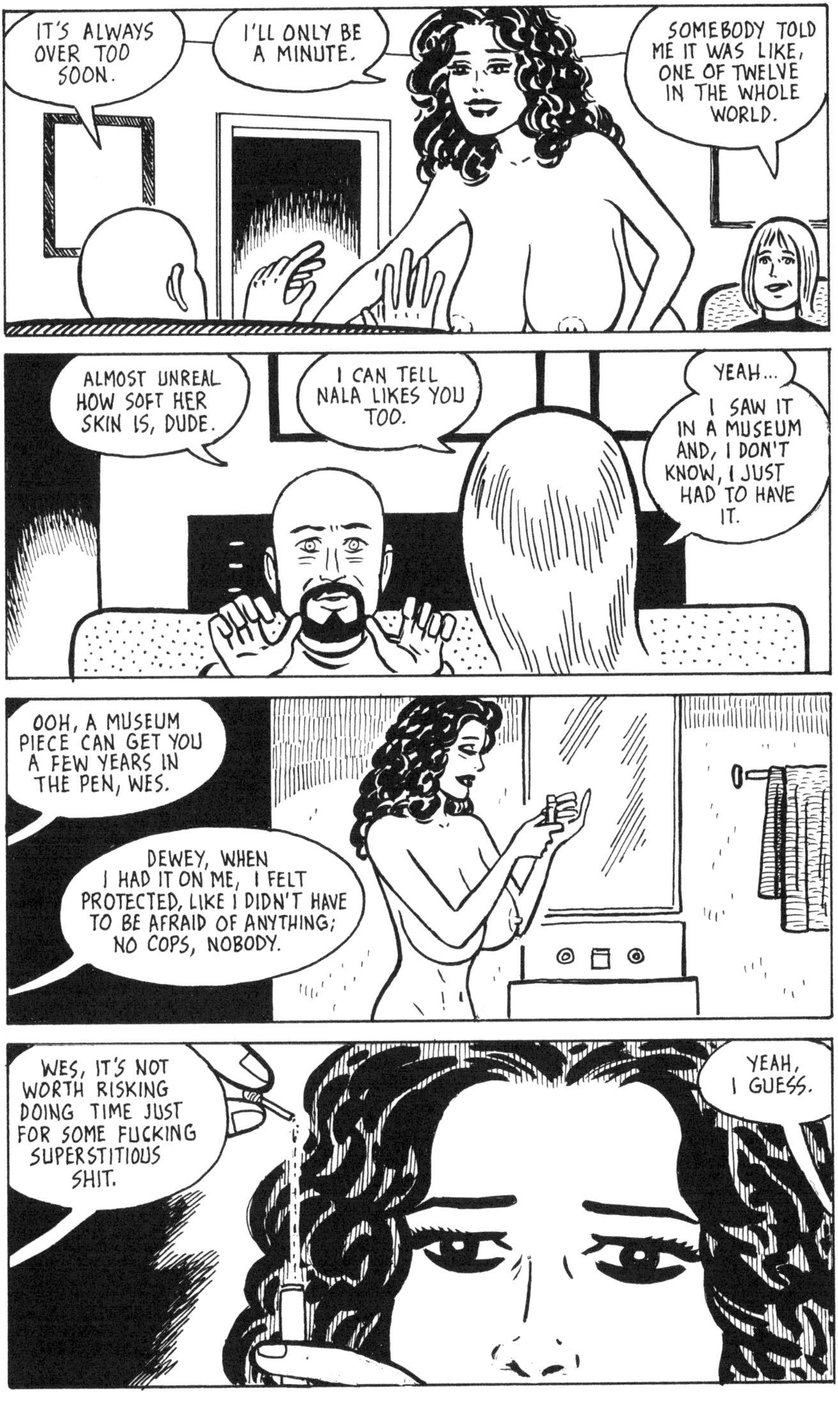
IT'S ALWAYS OVER TOO SOON.
I'LL ONLY BE A MINUTE.
SOMEBODY TOLD ME IT WAS LIKE, ONE OF TWELVE IN THE WHOLE WORLD.
ALMOST UNREAL HOW SOFT HER SKIN IS, DUDE.
I CAN TELL NALA LIKES YOU TOO.
YEAH...
I SAW IT IN A MUSEUM AND, I DON'T KNOW, I JUST HAD TO HAVE IT.
OOH, A MUSEUM PIECE CAN GET YOU A FEW YEARS IN THE PEN, WES.
DEWEY, WHEN I HAD IT ON ME, I FELT PROTECTED, LIKE I DIDN'T HAVE TO BE AFRAID OF ANYTHING; NO COPS, NOBODY.
WES, IT'S NOT WORTH RISKING DOING TIME JUST FOR SOME FUCKING SUPERSTITIOUS SHIT.
YEAH, I GUESS.

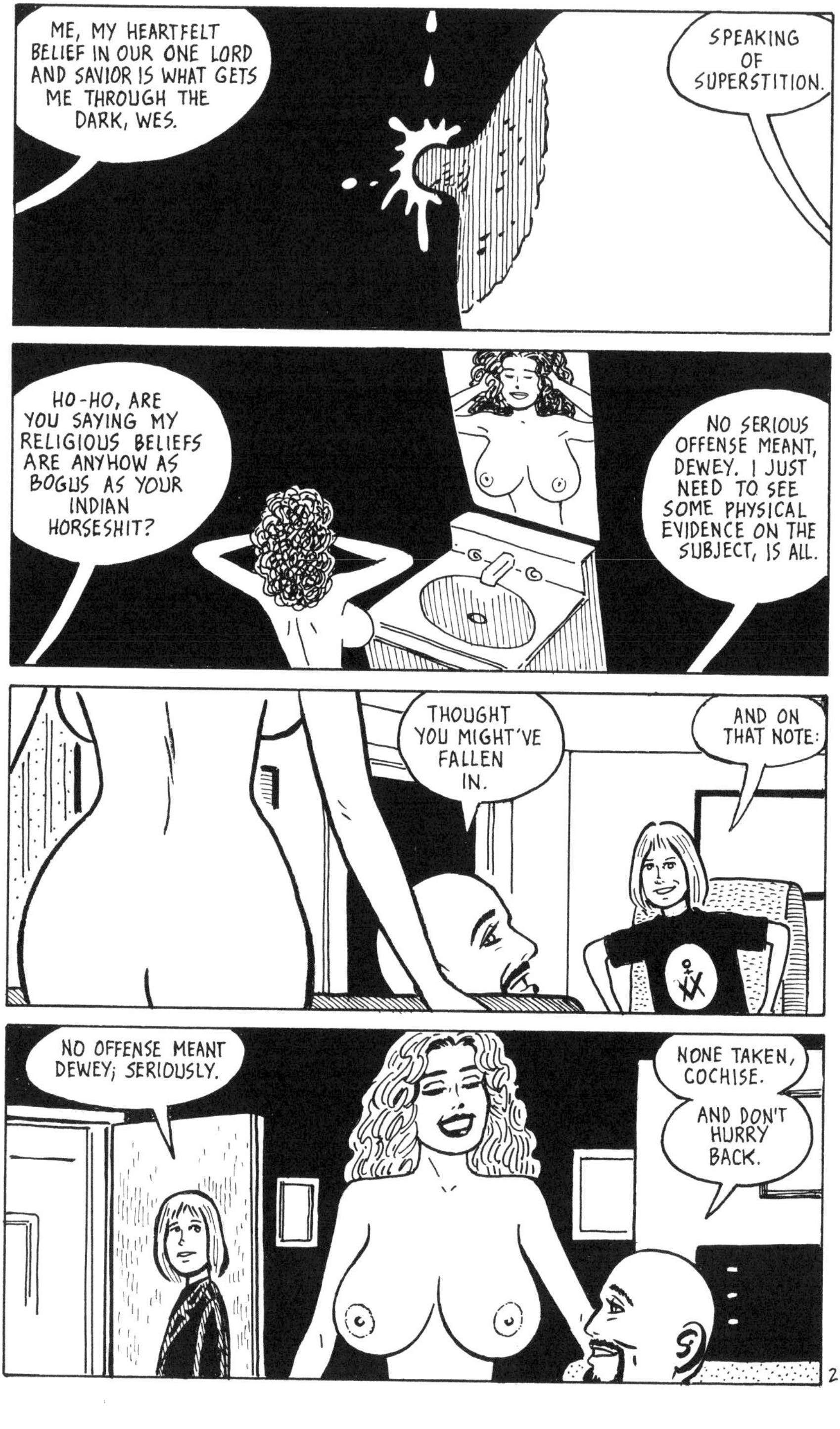
ME, MY HEARTFELT BELIEF IN OUR ONE LORD AND SAVIOR IS WHAT GETS ME THROUGH THE DARK, WES.
SPEAKING OF SUPERSTITION.
HO-HO, ARE YOU SAYING MY RELIGIOUS BELIEFS ARE ANYHOW AS BOGUS AS YOUR INDIAN HORSESHIT?
NO SERIOUS OFFENSE MEANT, DEWEY. I JUST NEED TO SEE SOME PHYSICAL EVIDENCE ON THE SUBJECT, IS ALL.
THOUGHT YOU MIGHT'VE FALLEN IN.
AND ON THAT NOTE:
NO OFFENSE MEANT DEWEY; SERIOUSLY.
NONE TAKEN, COCHISE.
AND DON'T HURRY BACK.

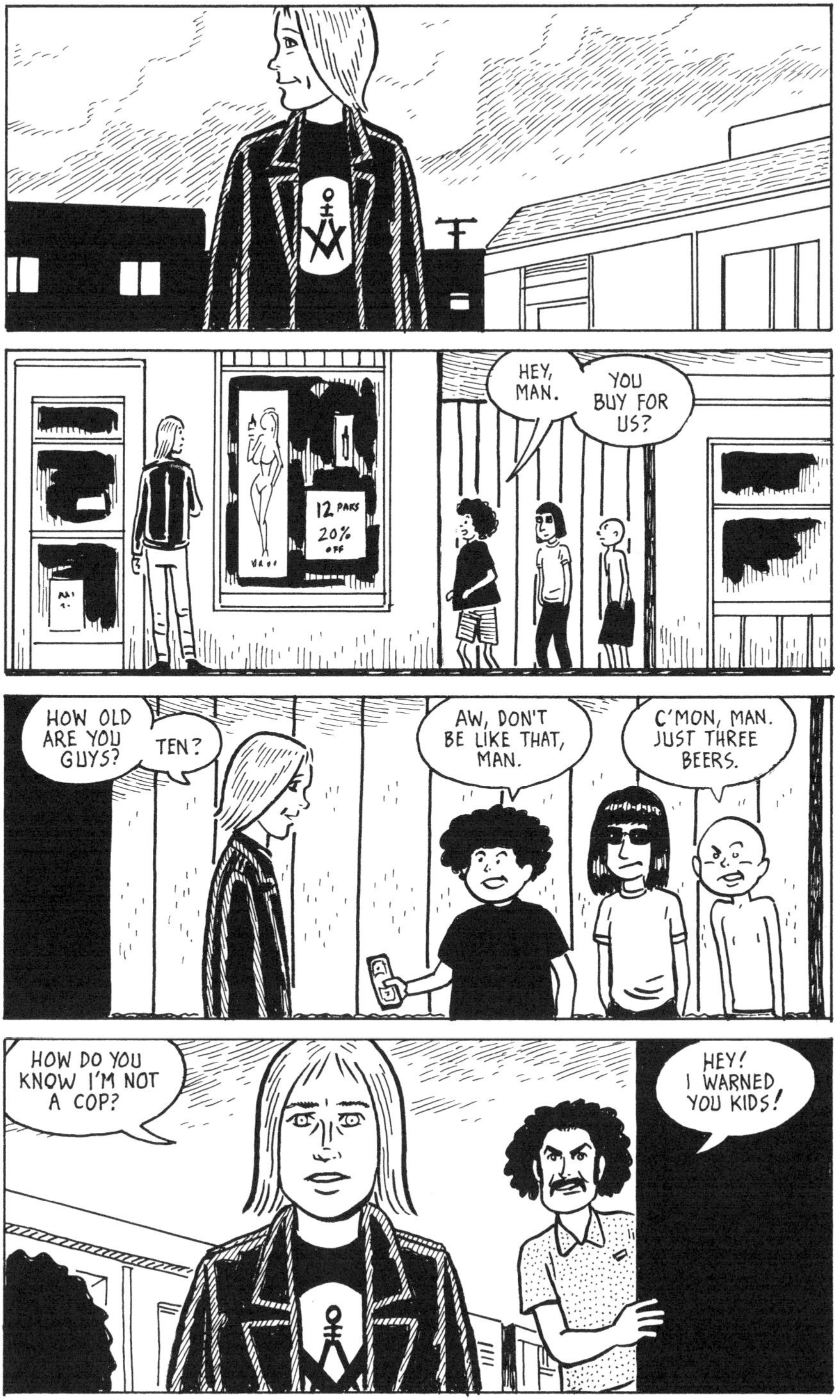
12 PAKS
20%
OFF
HEY, MAN.
YOU BUY FOR US?
HOW OLD ARE YOU GUYS?
TEN?
AW, DON'T BE LIKE THAT, MAN.
C'MON, MAN. JUST THREE BEERS.
HOW DO YOU KNOW I'M NOT A COP?
HEY! I WARNED YOU KIDS!

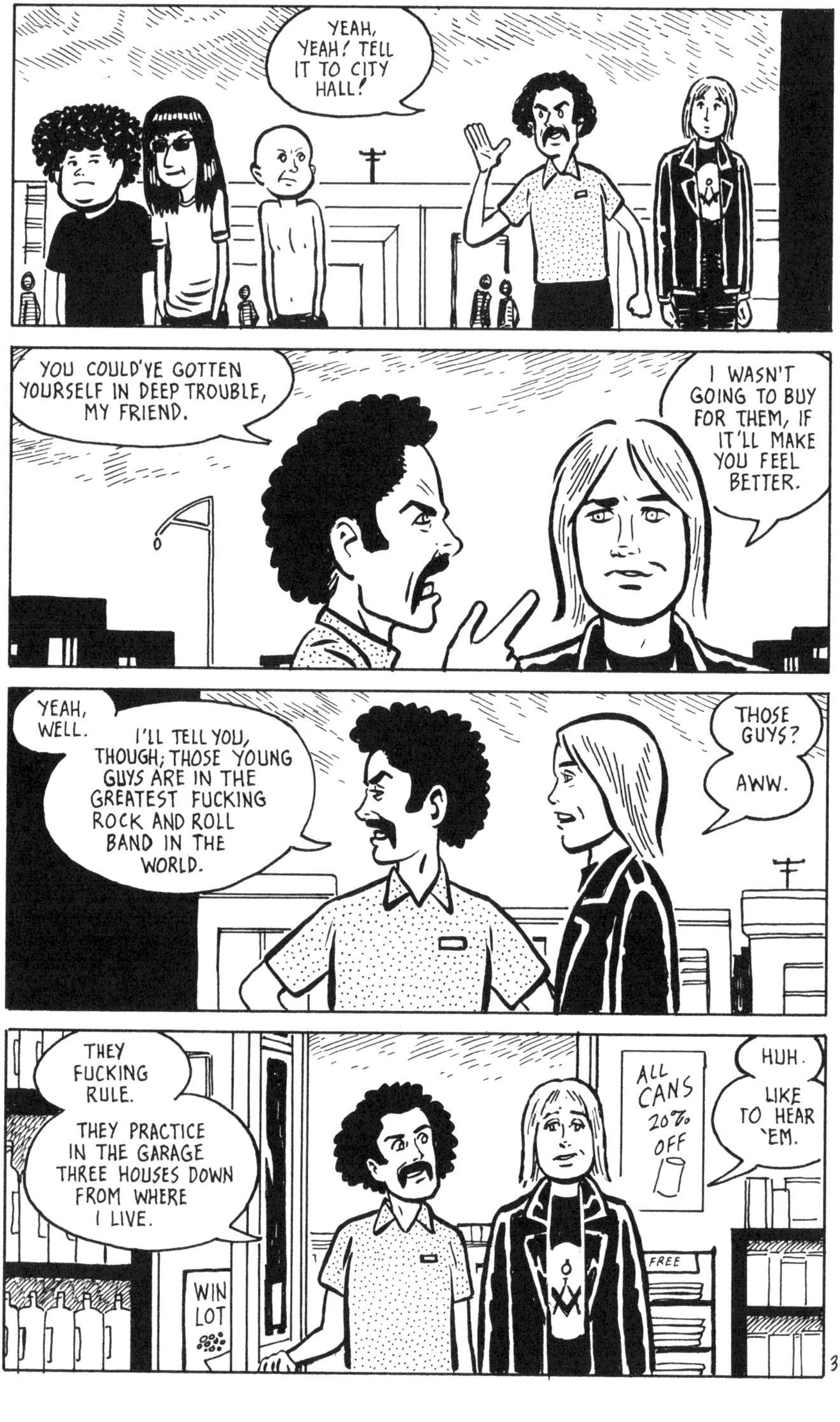
YEAH, YEAH! TELL IT TO CITY HALL!
YOU COULD'VE GOTTEN YOURSELF IN DEEP TROUBLE, MY FRIEND.
I WASN'T GOING TO BUY FOR THEM, IF IT'LL MAKE YOU FEEL BETTER.
YEAH, WELL.
I'LL TELL YOU, THOUGH; THOSE YOUNG GUYS ARE IN THE GREATEST FUCKING ROCK AND ROLL BAND IN THE WORLD.
THOSE GUYS?
AWW.
THEY FUCKING RULE.
THEY PRACTICE IN THE GARAGE THREE HOUSES DOWN FROM WHERE I LIVE.
ALL CANS 20% OFF
FREE
WIN LOT
HUH.
LIKE TO HEAR 'EM.

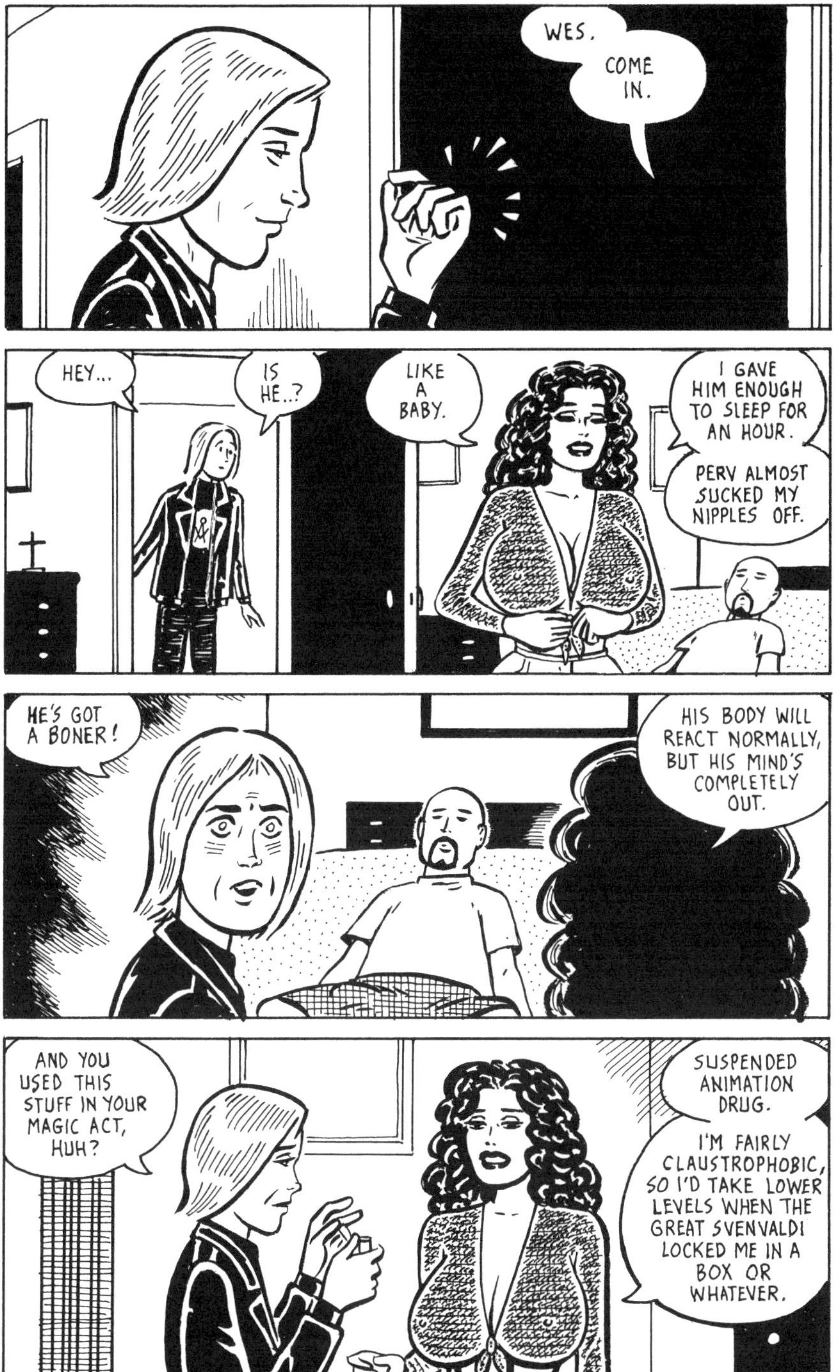
WES.
COME IN.
HEY...
IS HE..?
LIKE A BABY.
I GAVE HIM ENOUGH TO SLEEP FOR AN HOUR.
PERV ALMOST SUCKED MY NIPPLES OFF.
HE'S GOT A BONER!
HIS BODY WILL REACT NORMALLY, BUT HIS MIND'S COMPLETELY OUT.
AND YOU USED THIS STUFF IN YOUR MAGIC ACT, HUH?
SUSPENDED ANIMATION DRUG.
I'M FAIRLY CLAUSTROPHOBIC, SO I'D TAKE LOWER LEVELS WHEN THE GREAT SVENVALDI LOCKED ME IN A BOX OR WHATEVER.

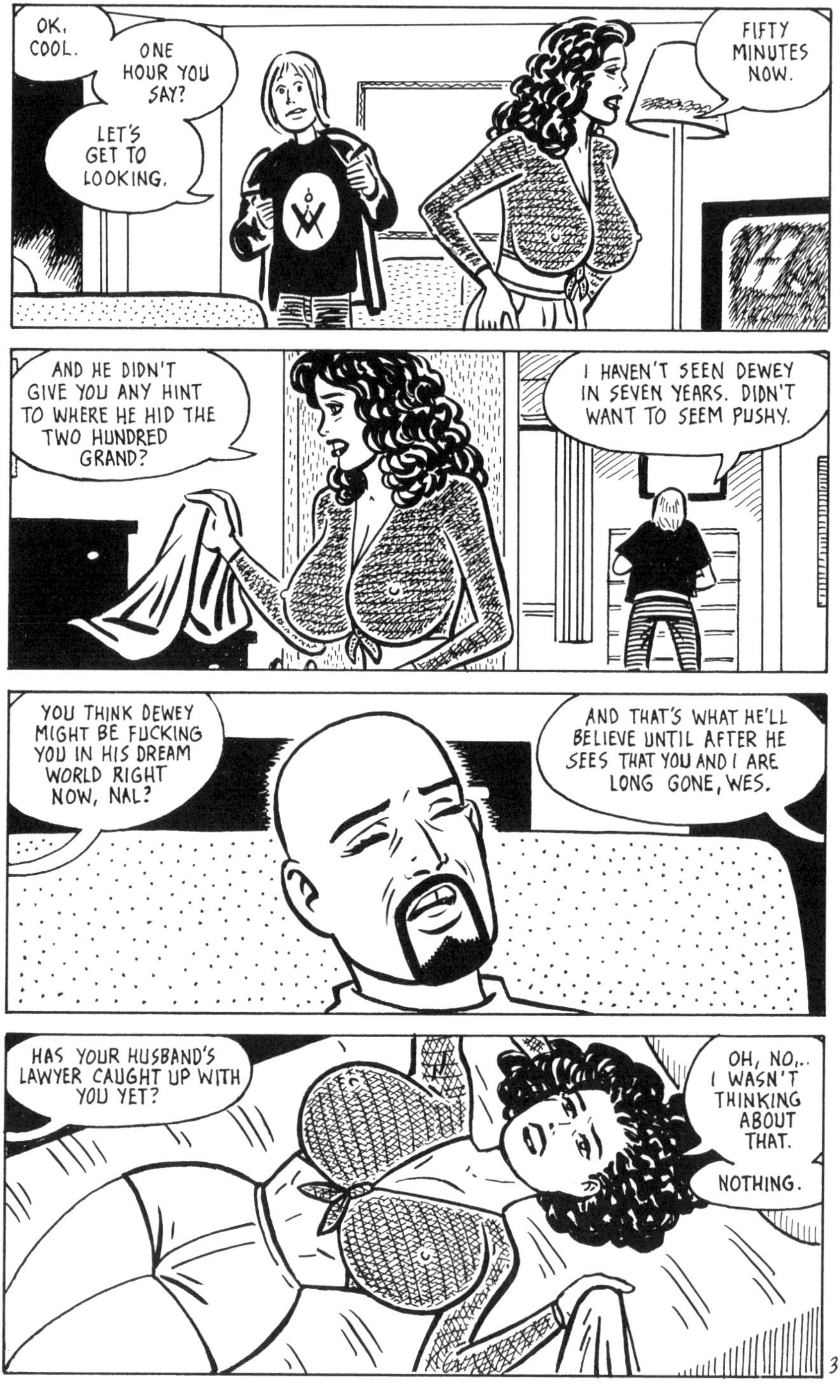
OK. COOL.
ONE HOUR YOU SAY?
LET'S GET TO LOOKING.
FIFTY MINUTES NOW.
AND HE DIDN'T GIVE YOU ANY HINT TO WHERE HE HID THE TWO HUNDRED GRAND?
I HAVEN'T SEEN DEWEY IN SEVEN YEARS. DIDN'T WANT TO SEEM PUSHY.
YOU THINK DEWEY MIGHT BE FUCKING YOU IN HIS DREAM WORLD RIGHT NOW, NAL?
AND THAT'S WHAT HE'LL BELIEVE UNTIL AFTER HE SEES THAT YOU AND I ARE LONG GONE, WES.
HAS YOUR HUSBAND'S LAWYER CAUGHT UP WITH YOU YET?
OH, NO... I WASN'T THINKING ABOUT THAT.
NOTHING.

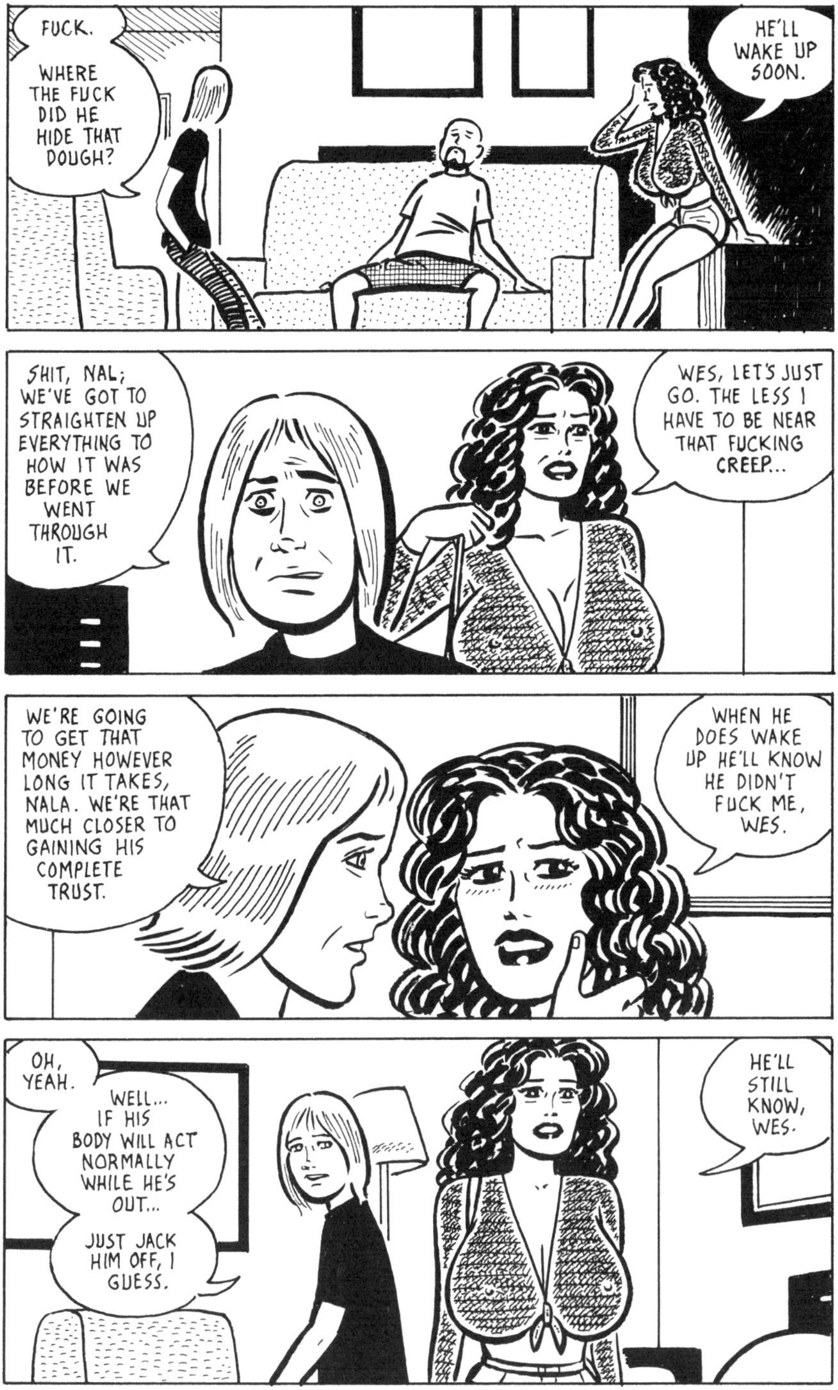
FUCK.
WHERE THE FUCK DID HE HIDE THAT DOUGH?
HE'LL WAKE UP SOON.
SHIT, NAL; WE'VE GOT TO STRAIGHTEN UP EVERYTHING TO HOW IT WAS BEFORE WE WENT THROUGH IT.
WES, LET'S JUST GO. THE LESS I HAVE TO BE NEAR THAT FUCKING CREEP...
WE'RE GOING TO GET THAT MONEY HOWEVER LONG IT TAKES, NALA. WE'RE THAT MUCH CLOSER TO GAINING HIS COMPLETE TRUST.
WHEN HE DOES WAKE UP HE'LL KNOW HE DIDN'T FUCK ME, WES.
OH, YEAH.
WELL... IF HIS BODY WILL ACT NORMALLY WHILE HE'S OUT...
JUST JACK HIM OFF, I GUESS.
HE'LL STILL KNOW, WES.

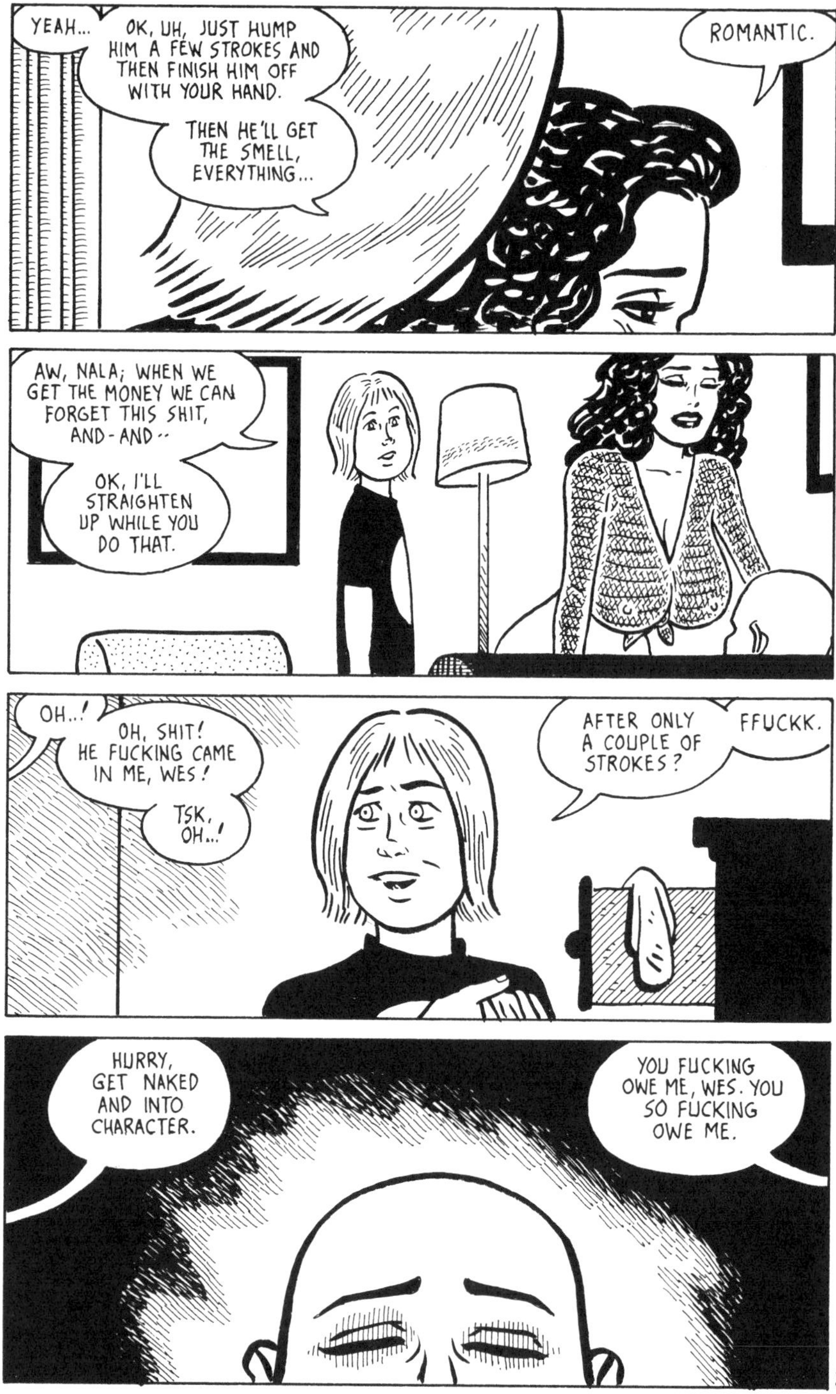
YEAH...
OK, UH, JUST HUMP HIM A FEW STROKES AND THEN FINISH HIM OFF WITH YOUR HAND.
THEN HE'LL GET THE SMELL, EVERYTHING...
ROMANTIC.
AW, NALA; WHEN WE GET THE MONEY WE CAN FORGET THIS SHIT, AND-AND--
OK, I'LL STRAIGHTEN UP WHILE YOU DO THAT.
OH..!
OH, SHIT! HE FUCKING CAME IN ME, WES!
TSK, OH..!
AFTER ONLY A COUPLE OF STROKES?
FFUCKK.
HURRY, GET NAKED AND INTO CHARACTER.
YOU FUCKING OWE ME, WES. YOU SO FUCKING OWE ME.

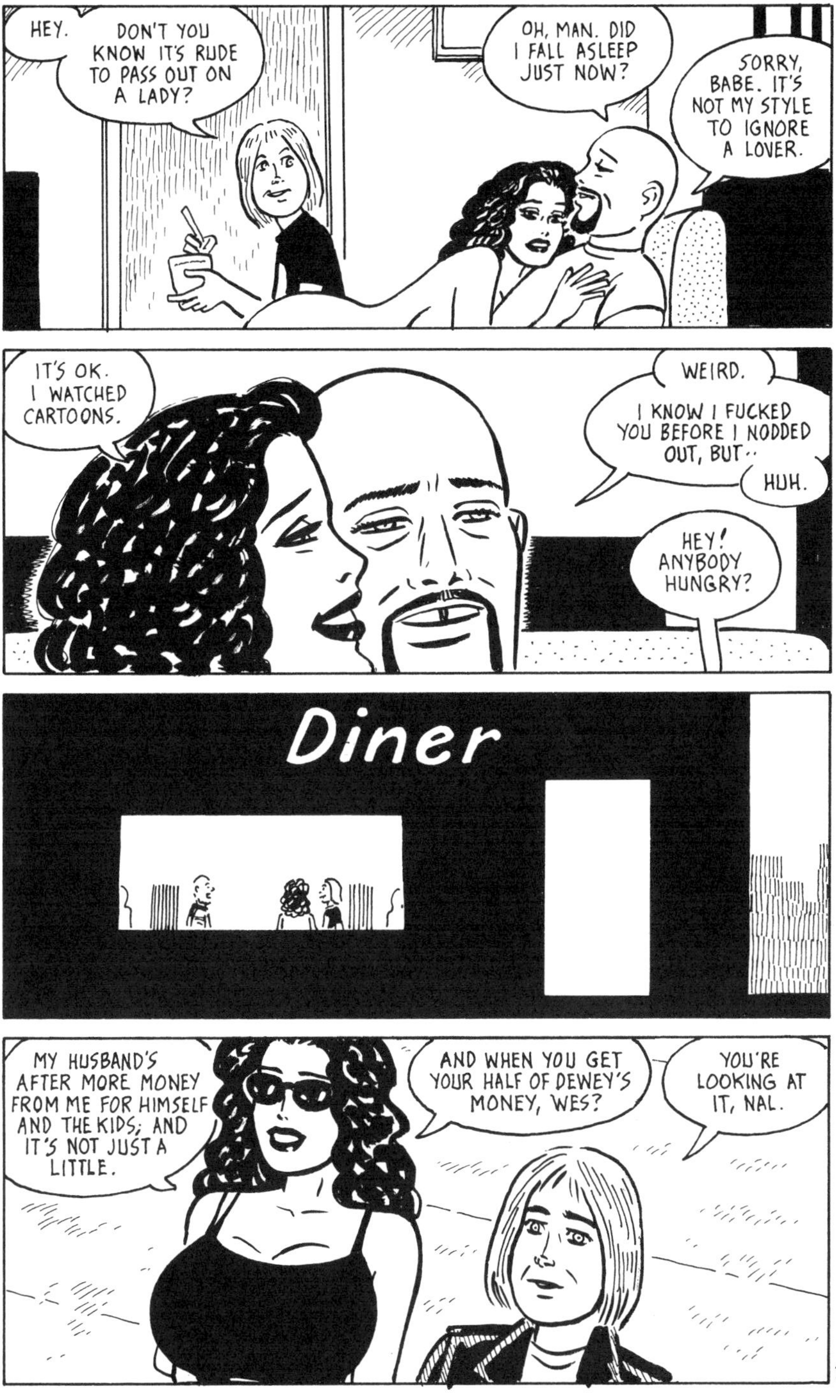
HEY.
DON'T YOU KNOW IT'S RUDE TO PASS OUT ON A LADY?
OH, MAN. DID I FALL ASLEEP JUST NOW?
SORRY, BABE. IT'S NOT MY STYLE TO IGNORE A LOVER.
IT'S OK. I WATCHED CARTOONS.
WEIRD.
I KNOW I FUCKED YOU BEFORE I NODDED OUT, BUT..
HUH.
HEY! ANYBODY HUNGRY?
Diner
MY HUSBAND'S AFTER MORE MONEY FROM ME FOR HIMSELF AND THE KIDS; AND IT'S NOT JUST A LITTLE.
AND WHEN YOU GET YOUR HALF OF DEWEY'S MONEY, WES?
YOU'RE LOOKING AT IT, NAL.

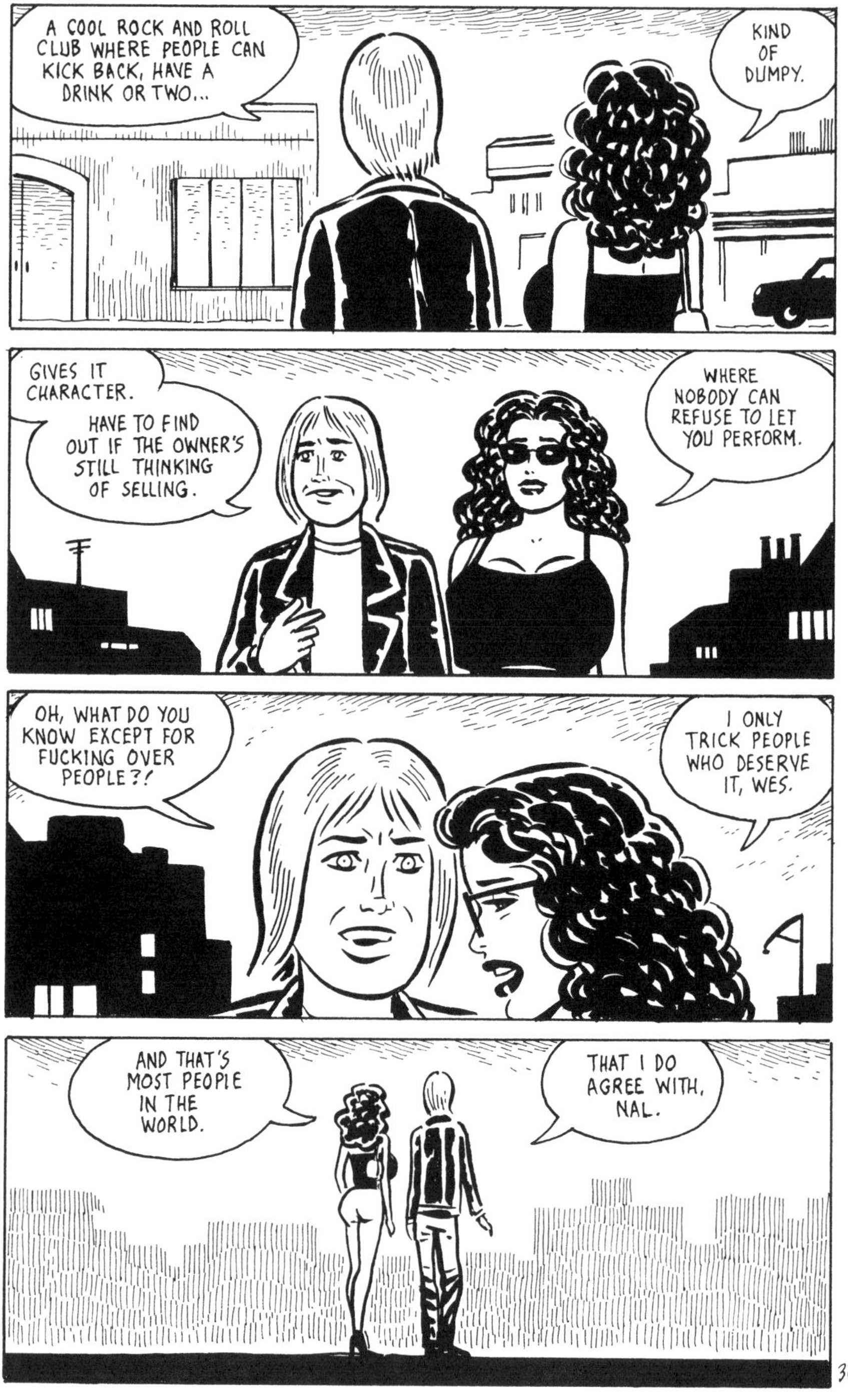
A COOL ROCK AND ROLL CLUB WHERE PEOPLE CAN KICK BACK, HAVE A DRINK OR TWO...
KIND OF DUMPY.
GIVES IT CHARACTER.
HAVE TO FIND OUT IF THE OWNER'S STILL THINKING OF SELLING.
WHERE NOBODY CAN REFUSE TO LET YOU PERFORM.
OH, WHAT DO YOU KNOW EXCEPT FOR FUCKING OVER PEOPLE?!
I ONLY TRICK PEOPLE WHO DESERVE IT, WES.
AND THAT'S MOST PEOPLE IN THE WORLD.
THAT I DO AGREE WITH, NAL.

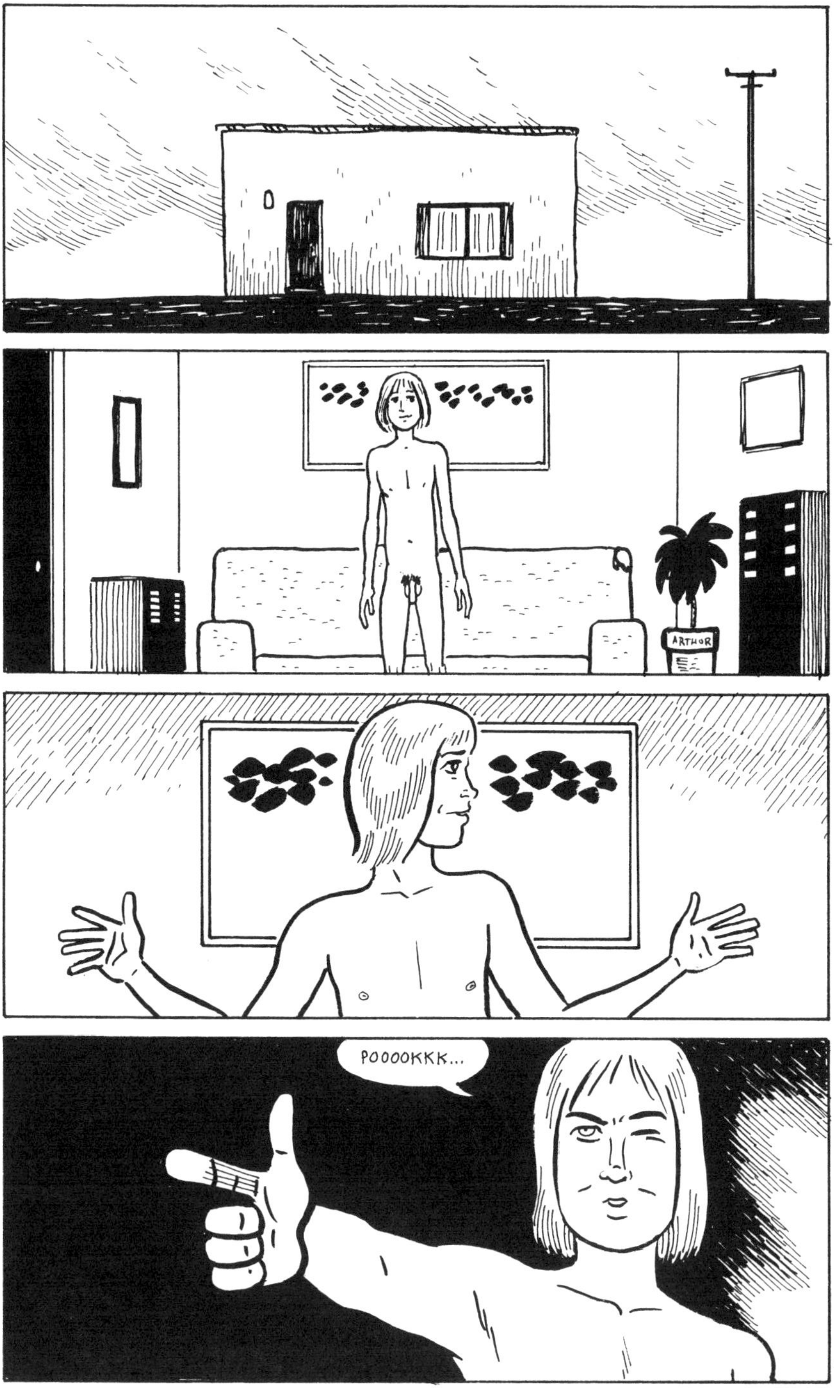
ARTHOR
POOOOKKK...

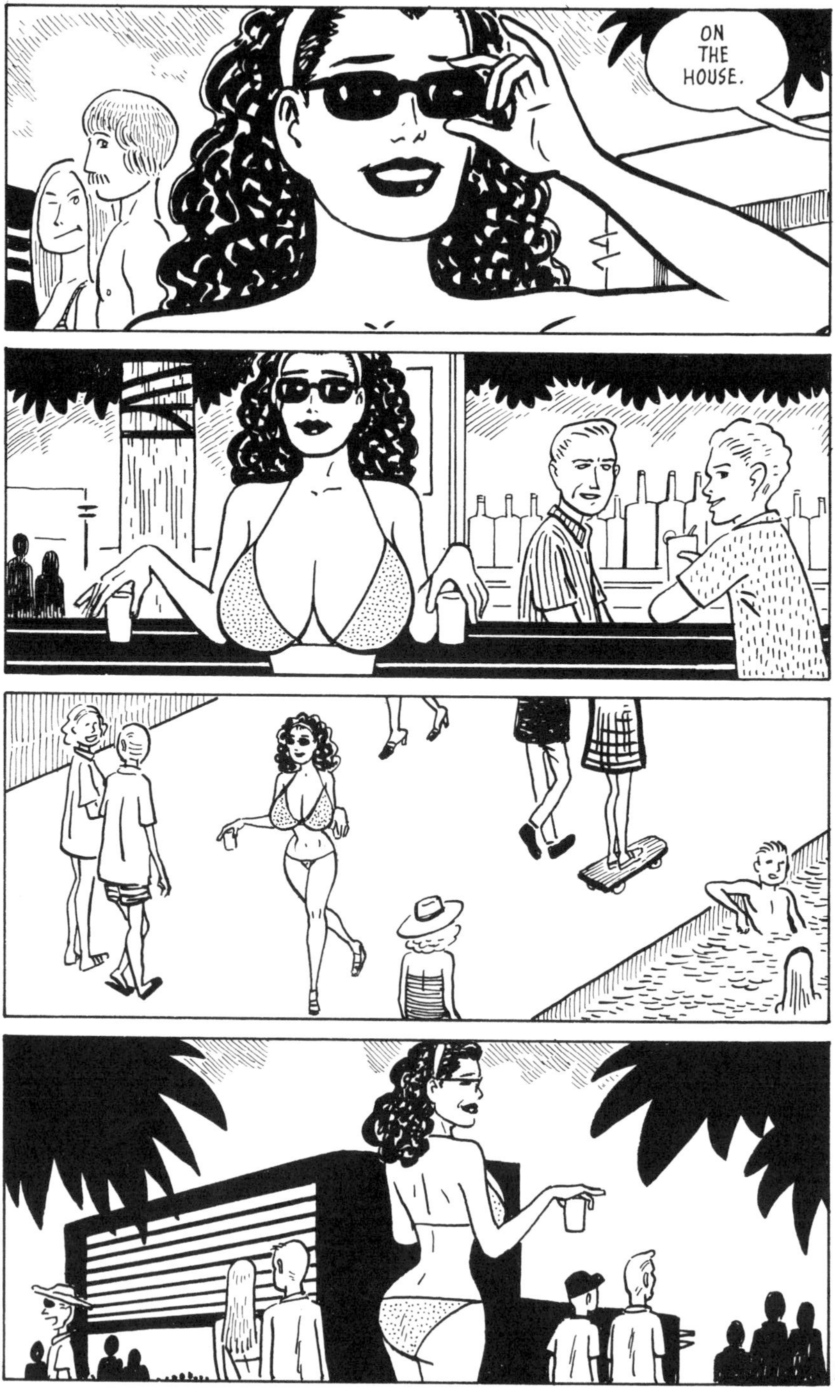
ON THE HOUSE.

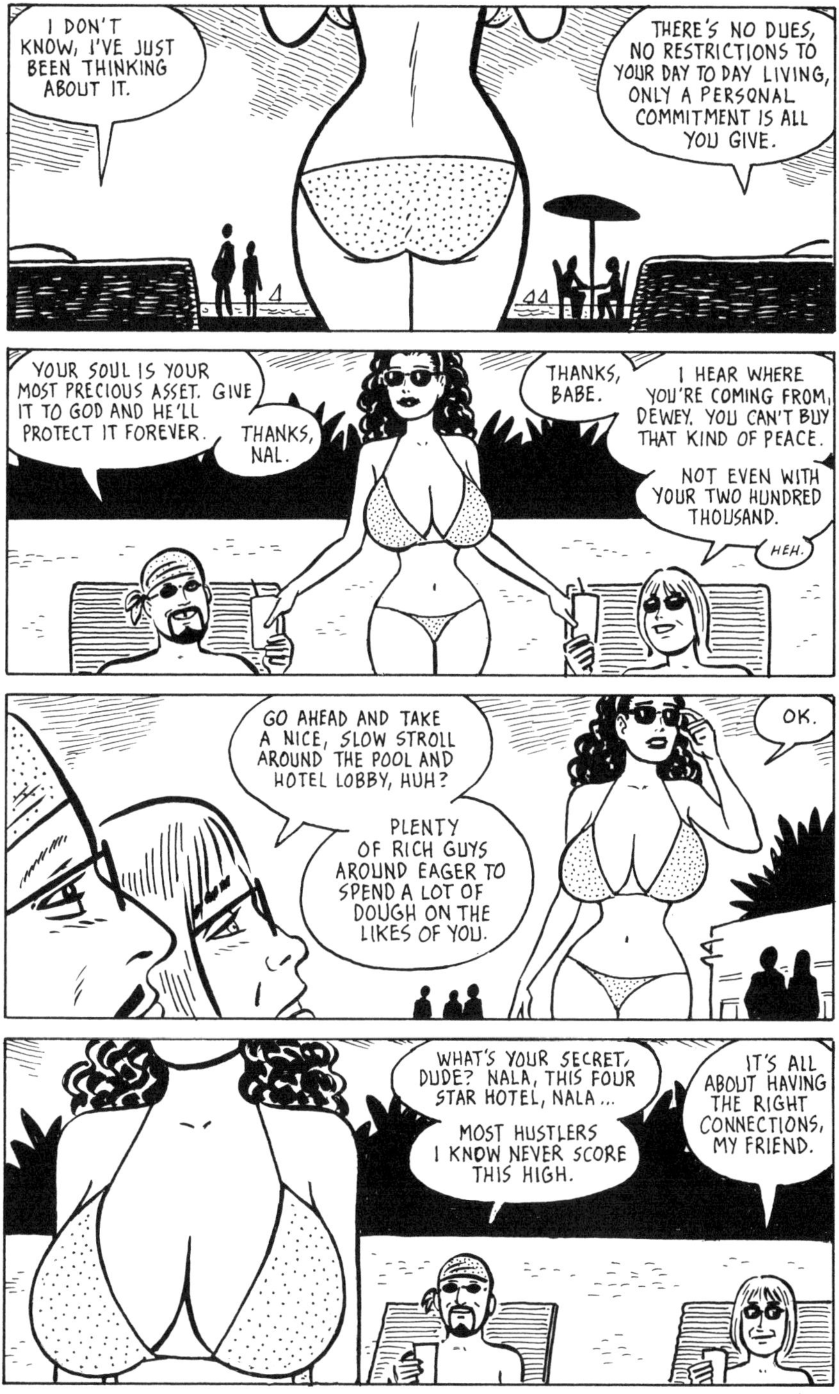

I DON'T KNOW, I'VE JUST BEEN THINKING ABOUT IT.
THERE'S NO DUES, NO RESTRICTIONS TO YOUR DAY TO DAY LIVING, ONLY A PERSONAL COMMITMENT IS ALL YOU GIVE.
YOUR SOUL IS YOUR MOST PRECIOUS ASSET. GIVE IT TO GOD AND HE'LL PROTECT IT FOREVER.
THANKS, NAL.
THANKS, BABE.
I HEAR WHERE YOU'RE COMING FROM, DEWEY. YOU CAN'T BUY THAT KIND OF PEACE.
NOT EVEN WITH YOUR TWO HUNDRED THOUSAND.
HEH.
GO AHEAD AND TAKE A NICE, SLOW STROLL AROUND THE POOL AND HOTEL LOBBY, HUH?
PLENTY OF RICH GUYS AROUND EAGER TO SPEND A LOT OF DOUGH ON THE LIKES OF YOU.
OK.
WHAT'S YOUR SECRET, DUDE? NALA, THIS FOUR STAR HOTEL, NALA...
MOST HUSTLERS I KNOW NEVER SCORE THIS HIGH.
IT'S ALL ABOUT HAVING THE RIGHT CONNECTIONS, MY FRIEND.

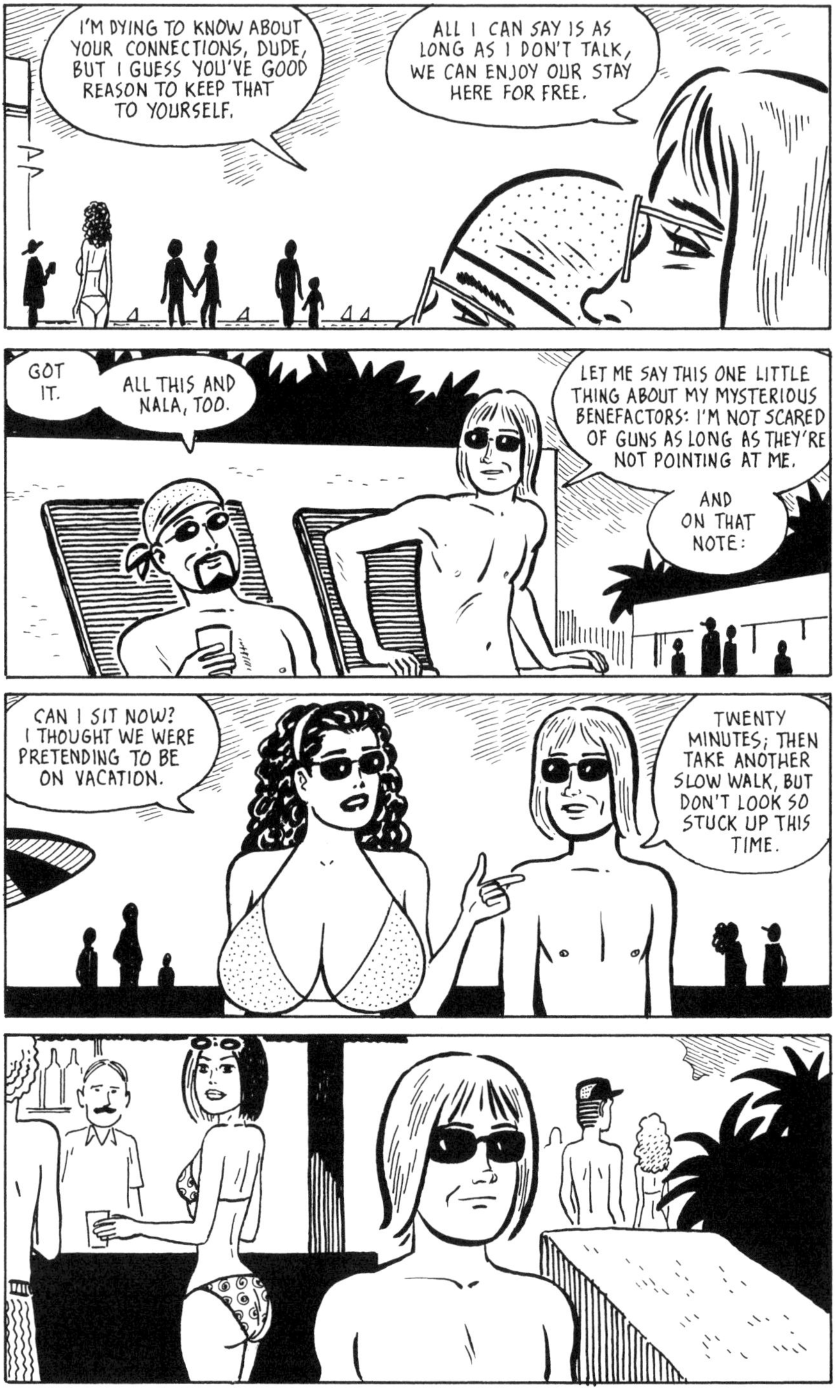
I'M DYING TO KNOW ABOUT YOUR CONNECTIONS, DUDE, BUT I GUESS YOU'VE GOOD REASON TO KEEP THAT TO YOURSELF.
ALL I CAN SAY IS AS LONG AS I DON'T TALK, WE CAN ENJOY OUR STAY HERE FOR FREE.
GOT IT.
ALL THIS AND NALA, TOO.
LET ME SAY THIS ONE LITTLE THING ABOUT MY MYSTERIOUS BENEFACTORS: I'M NOT SCARED OF GUNS AS LONG AS THEY'RE NOT POINTING AT ME.
AND ON THAT NOTE:
CAN I SIT NOW? I THOUGHT WE WERE PRETENDING TO BE ON VACATION.
TWENTY MINUTES; THEN TAKE ANOTHER SLOW WALK, BUT DON'T LOOK SO STUCK UP THIS TIME.

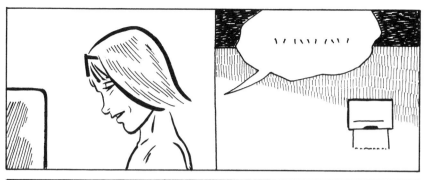

CLASSIC NUMBER. YOU'LL HAVE IT STUCK IN YOUR HEAD YOUR WHOLE TIME HERE.

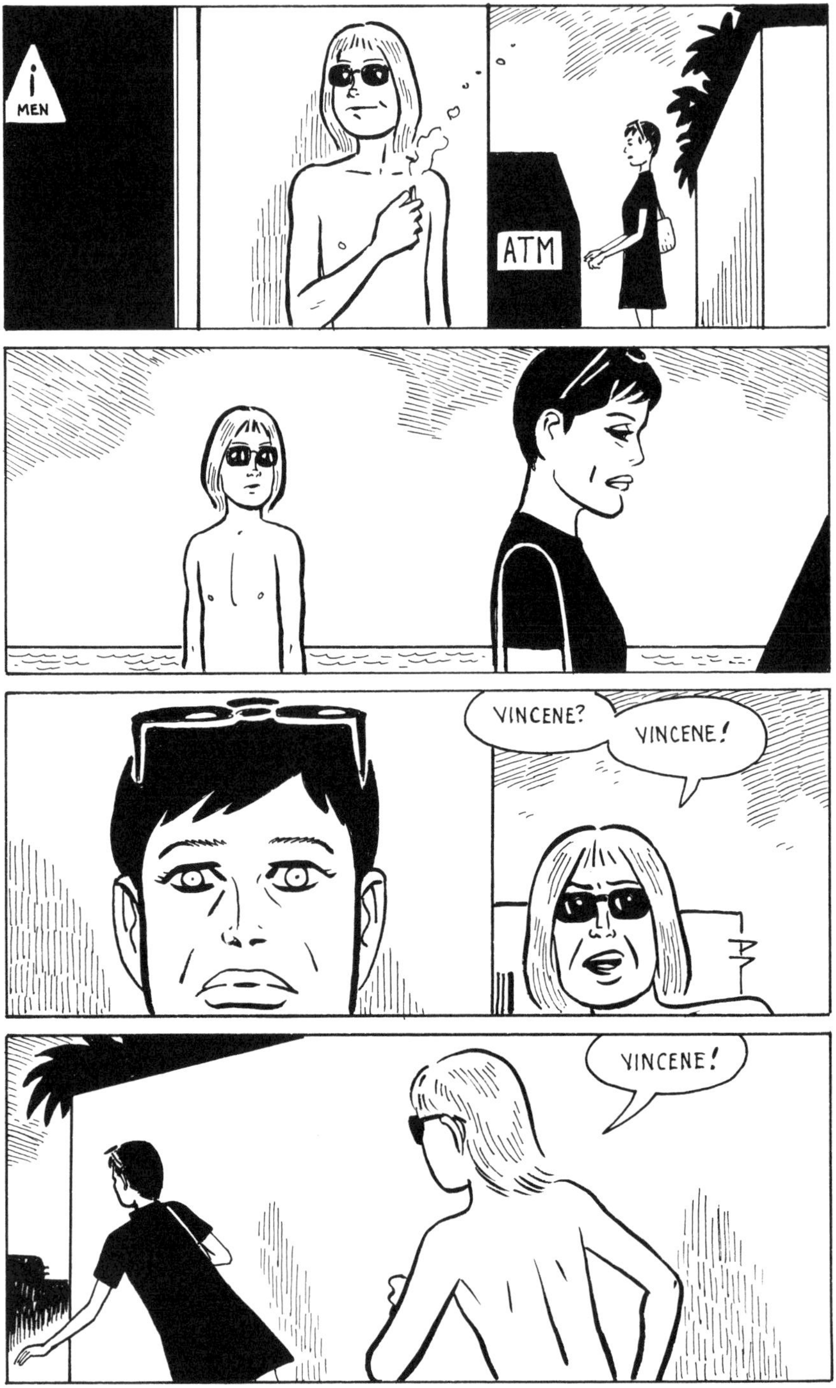
MEN
ATM
VINCENE?
VINCENE!
VINCENE!

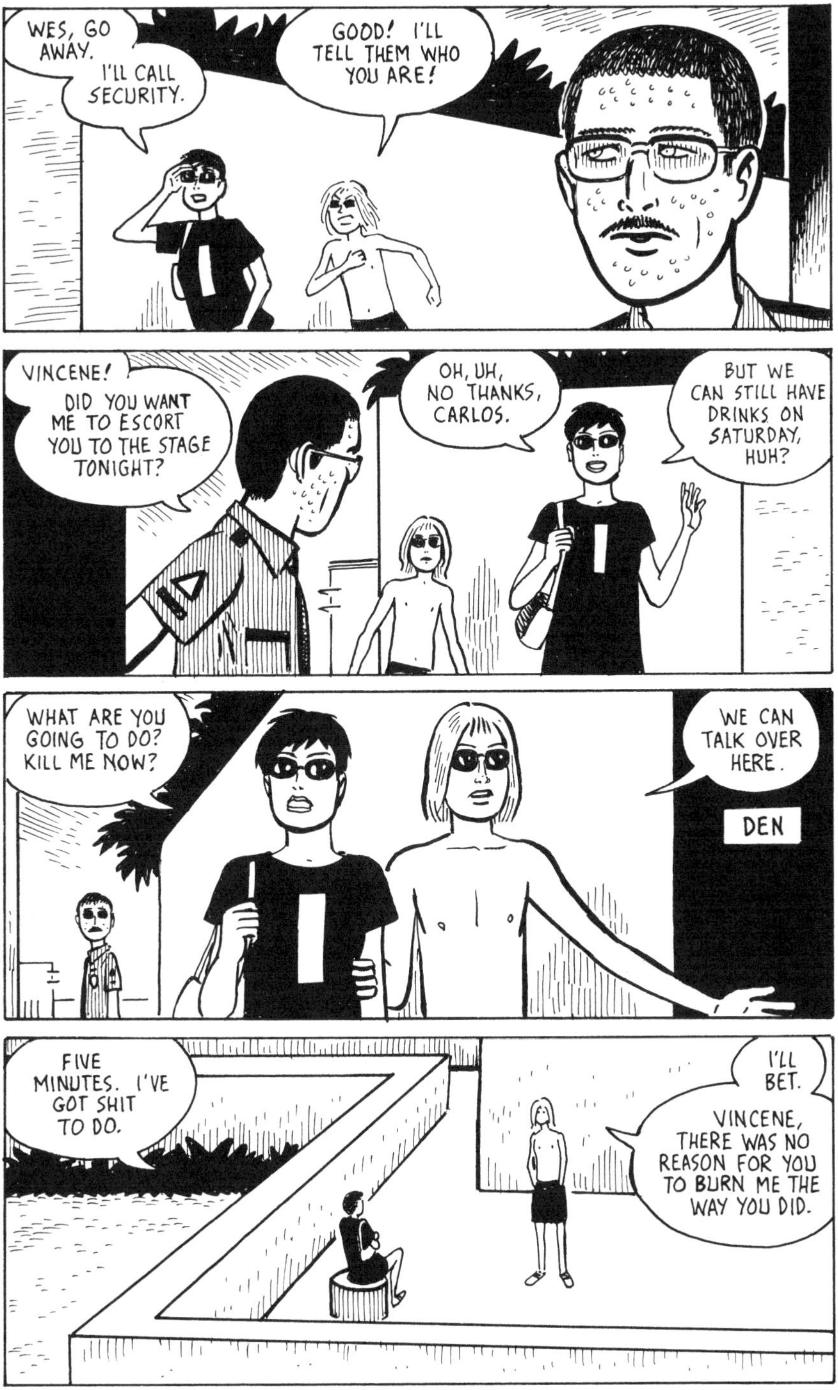
WES, GO AWAY.
I'LL CALL SECURITY.
GOOD! I'LL TELL THEM WHO YOU ARE!
VINCENE!
DID YOU WANT ME TO ESCORT YOU TO THE STAGE TONIGHT?
OH, UH, NO THANKS, CARLOS.
BUT WE CAN STILL HAVE DRINKS ON SATURDAY, HUH?
WHAT ARE YOU GOING TO DO? KILL ME NOW?
WE CAN TALK OVER HERE.
DEN
FIVE MINUTES. I'VE GOT SHIT TO DO.
I'LL BET.
VINCENE, THERE WAS NO REASON FOR YOU TO BURN ME THE WAY YOU DID.

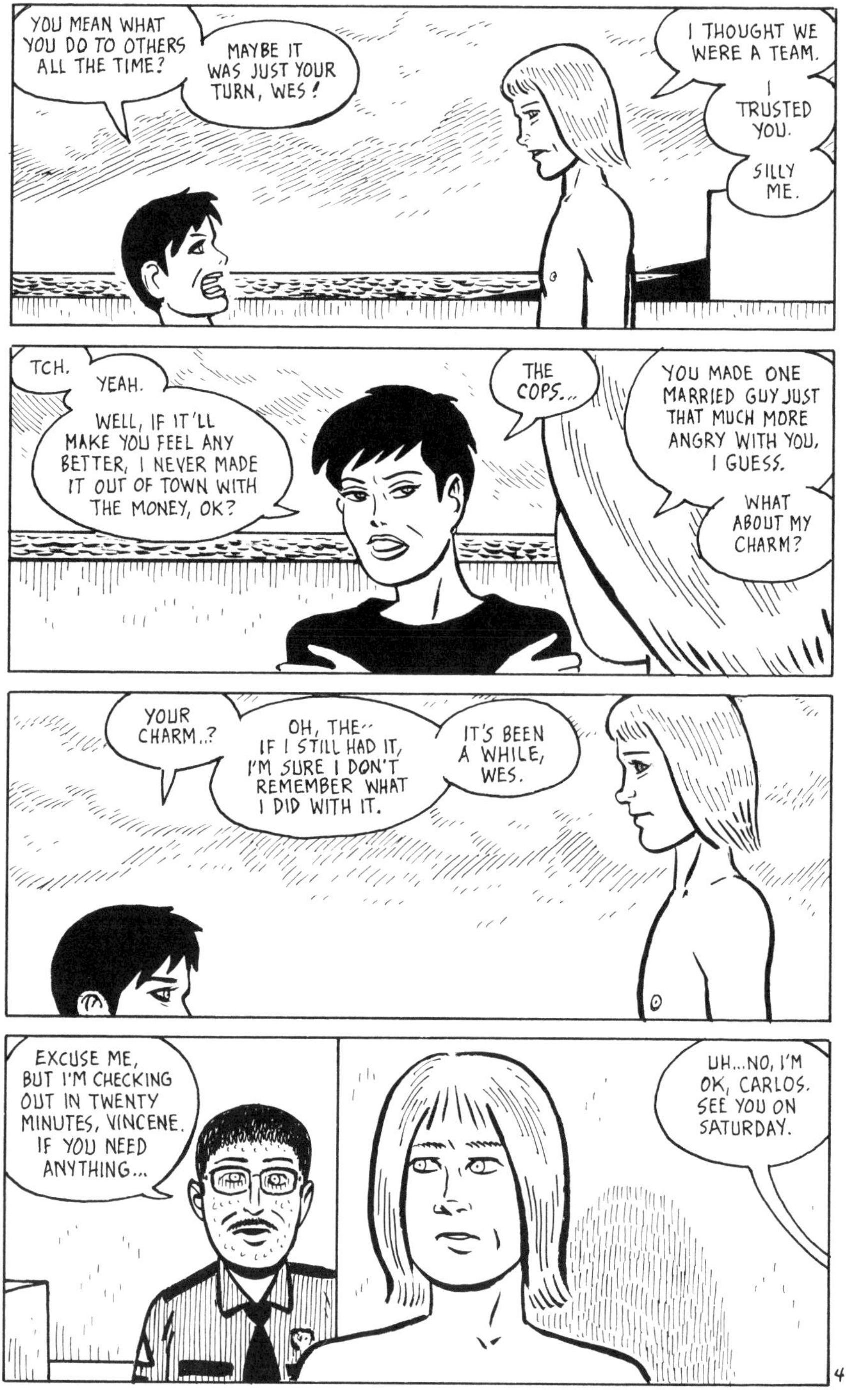
YOU MEAN WHAT YOU DO TO OTHERS ALL THE TIME?
MAYBE IT WAS JUST YOUR TURN, WES!
I THOUGHT WE WERE A TEAM.
I TRUSTED YOU.
SILLY ME.
TCH.
YEAH.
WELL, IF IT'LL MAKE YOU FEEL ANY BETTER, I NEVER MADE IT OUT OF TOWN WITH THE MONEY, OK?
THE COPS...
YOU MADE ONE MARRIED GUY JUST THAT MUCH MORE ANGRY WITH YOU, I GUESS.
WHAT ABOUT MY CHARM?
YOUR CHARM..?
OH, THE-- IF I STILL HAD IT, I'M SURE I DON'T REMEMBER WHAT I DID WITH IT.
IT'S BEEN A WHILE, WES.
EXCUSE ME, BUT I'M CHECKING OUT IN TWENTY MINUTES, VINCENE. IF YOU NEED ANYTHING...
UH...NO, I'M OK, CARLOS. SEE YOU ON SATURDAY.

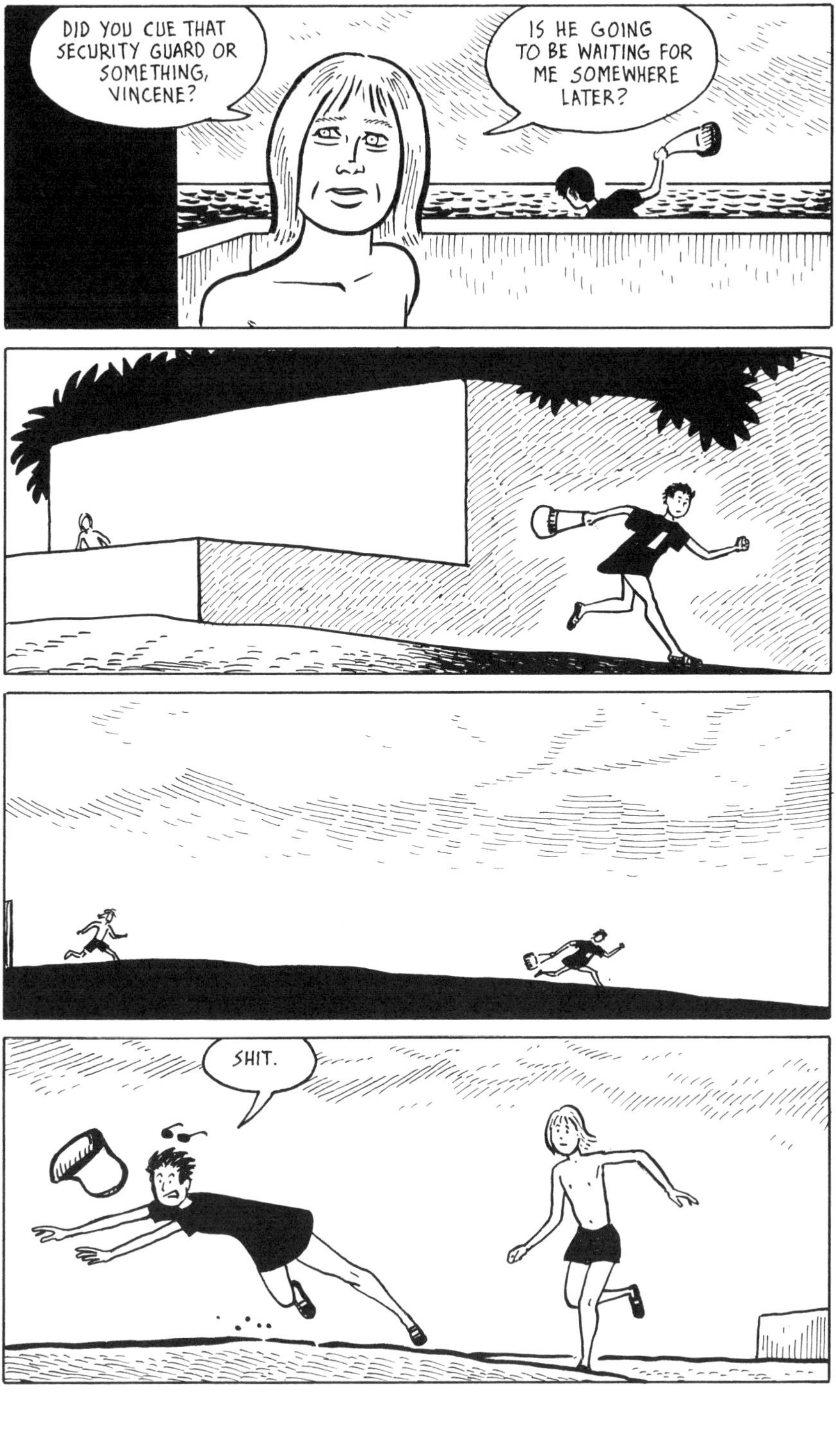
DID YOU CUE THAT SECURITY GUARD OR SOMETHING, VINCENE?
IS HE GOING TO BE WAITING FOR ME SOMEWHERE LATER?
SHIT.

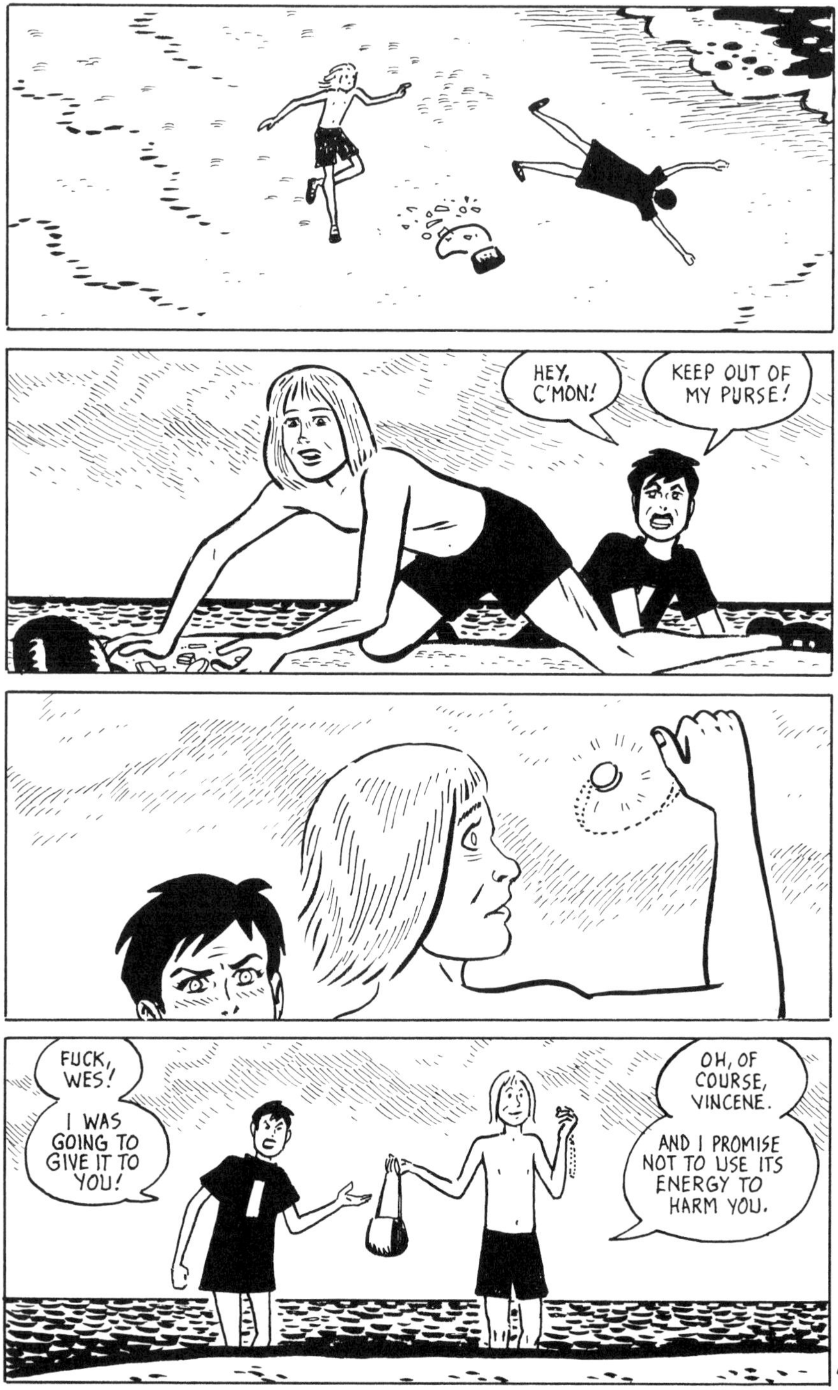
HEY, C'MON!
KEEP OUT OF MY PURSE!
FUCK, WES!
I WAS GOING TO GIVE IT TO YOU!
OH, OF COURSE, VINCENE.
AND I PROMISE NOT TO USE ITS ENERGY TO HARM YOU.

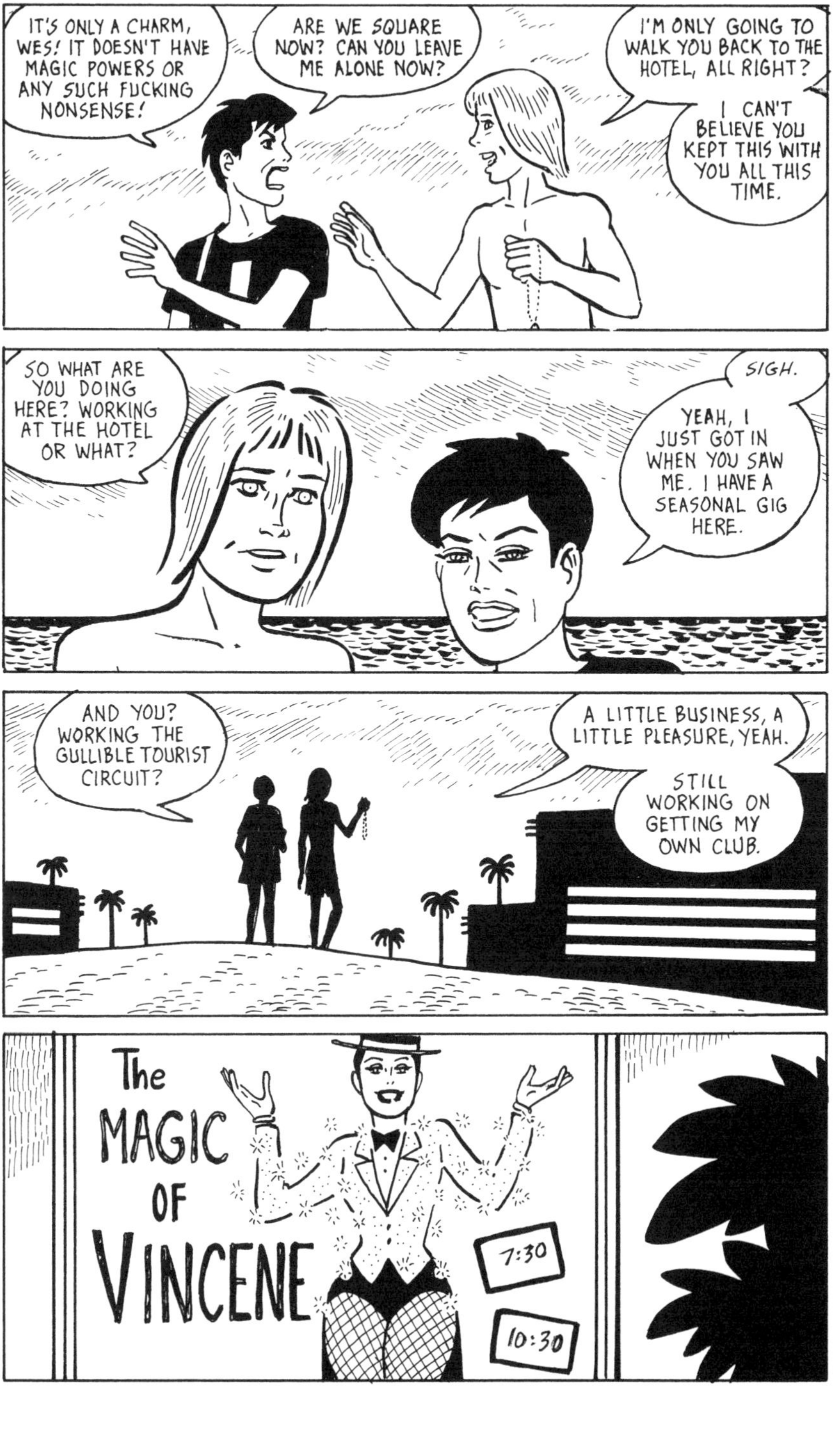
IT'S ONLY A CHARM, WES! IT DOESN'T HAVE MAGIC POWERS OR ANY SUCH FUCKING NONSENSE!
ARE WE SQUARE NOW? CAN YOU LEAVE ME ALONE NOW?
I'M ONLY GOING TO WALK YOU BACK TO THE HOTEL, ALL RIGHT?
I CAN'T BELIEVE YOU KEPT THIS WITH YOU ALL THIS TIME.
SO WHAT ARE YOU DOING HERE? WORKING AT THE HOTEL OR WHAT?
SIGH.
YEAH, I JUST GOT IN WHEN YOU SAW ME. I HAVE A SEASONAL GIG HERE.
AND YOU? WORKING THE GULLIBLE TOURIST CIRCUIT?
A LITTLE BUSINESS, A LITTLE PLEASURE, YEAH.
STILL WORKING ON GETTING MY OWN CLUB.
The MAGIC OF VINCENE
7:30
10:30

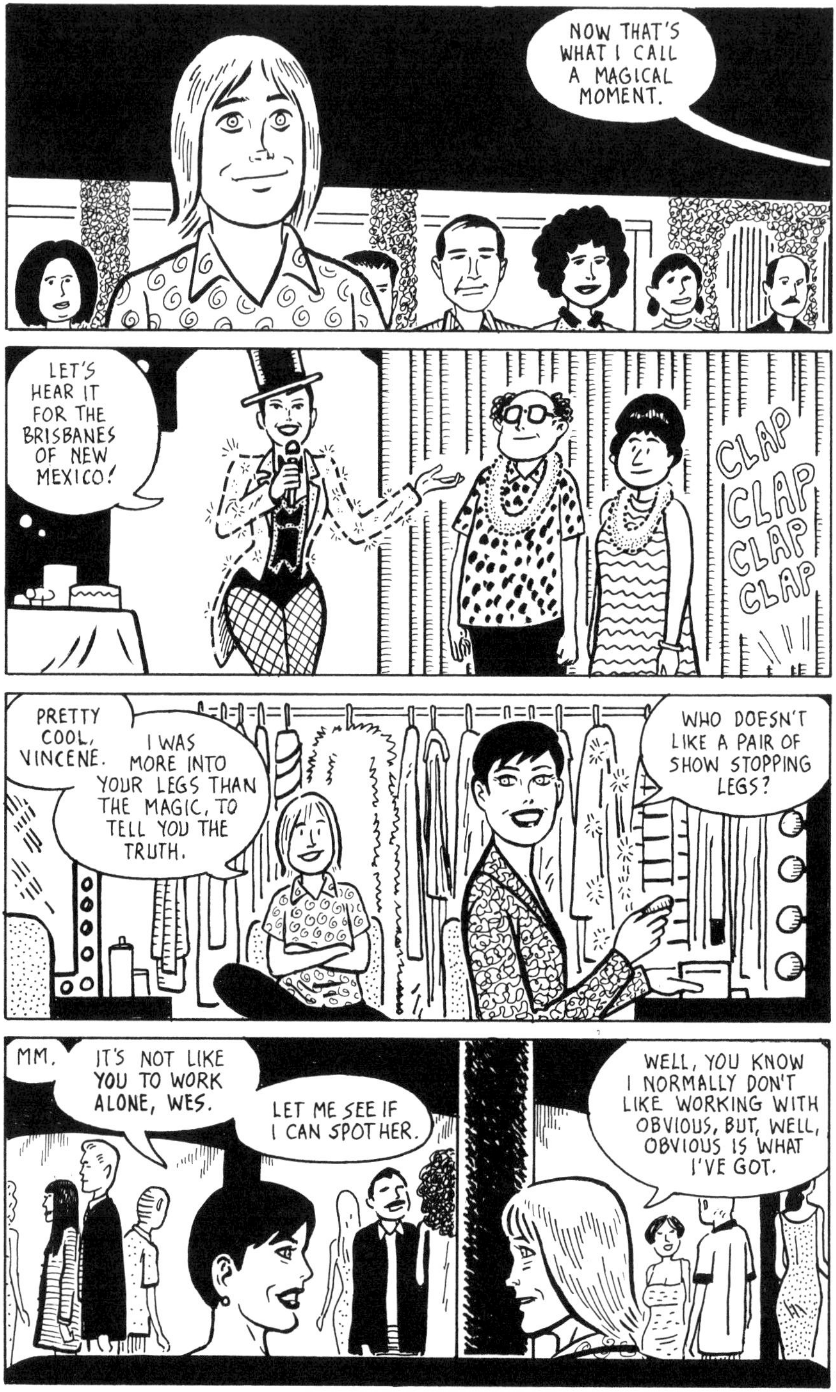

NOW THAT'S WHAT I CALL A MAGICAL MOMENT.
LET'S HEAR IT FOR THE BRISBANES OF NEW MEXICO!
CLAP CLAP CLAP CLAP
PRETTY COOL, VINCENE.
I WAS MORE INTO YOUR LEGS THAN THE MAGIC, TO TELL YOU THE TRUTH.
WHO DOESN'T LIKE A PAIR OF SHOW STOPPING LEGS?
MM.
IT'S NOT LIKE YOU TO WORK ALONE, WES.
LET ME SEE IF I CAN SPOT HER.
WELL, YOU KNOW I NORMALLY DON'T LIKE WORKING WITH OBVIOUS, BUT, WELL, OBVIOUS IS WHAT I'VE GOT.

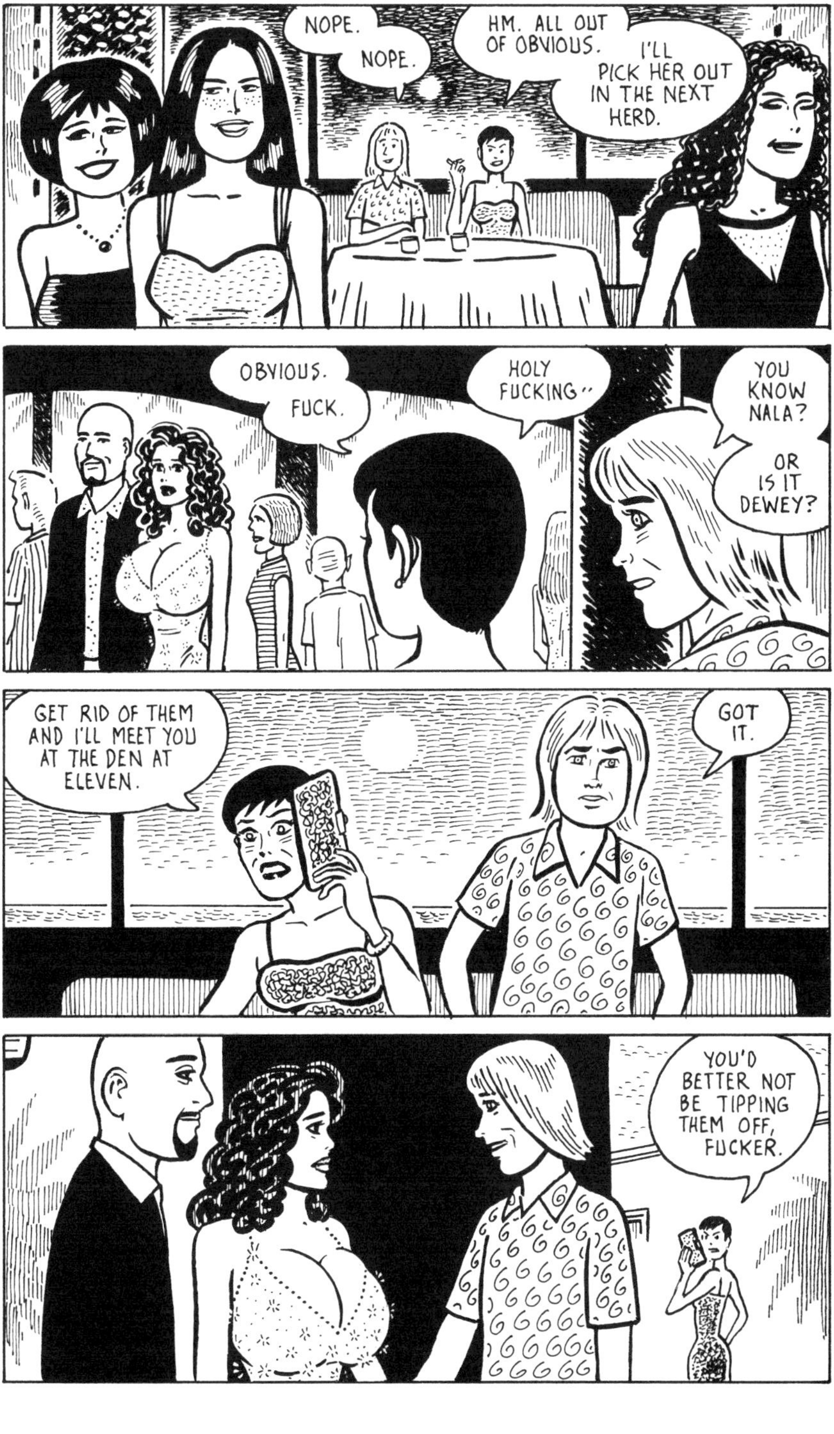
NOPE.
NOPE.
HM. ALL OUT OF OBVIOUS.
I'LL PICK HER OUT IN THE NEXT HERD.
OBVIOUS.
FUCK.
HOLY FUCKING..
YOU KNOW NALA?
OR IS IT DEWEY?
GET RID OF THEM AND I'LL MEET YOU AT THE DEN AT ELEVEN.
GOT IT.
YOU'D BETTER NOT BE TIPPING THEM OFF, FUCKER.

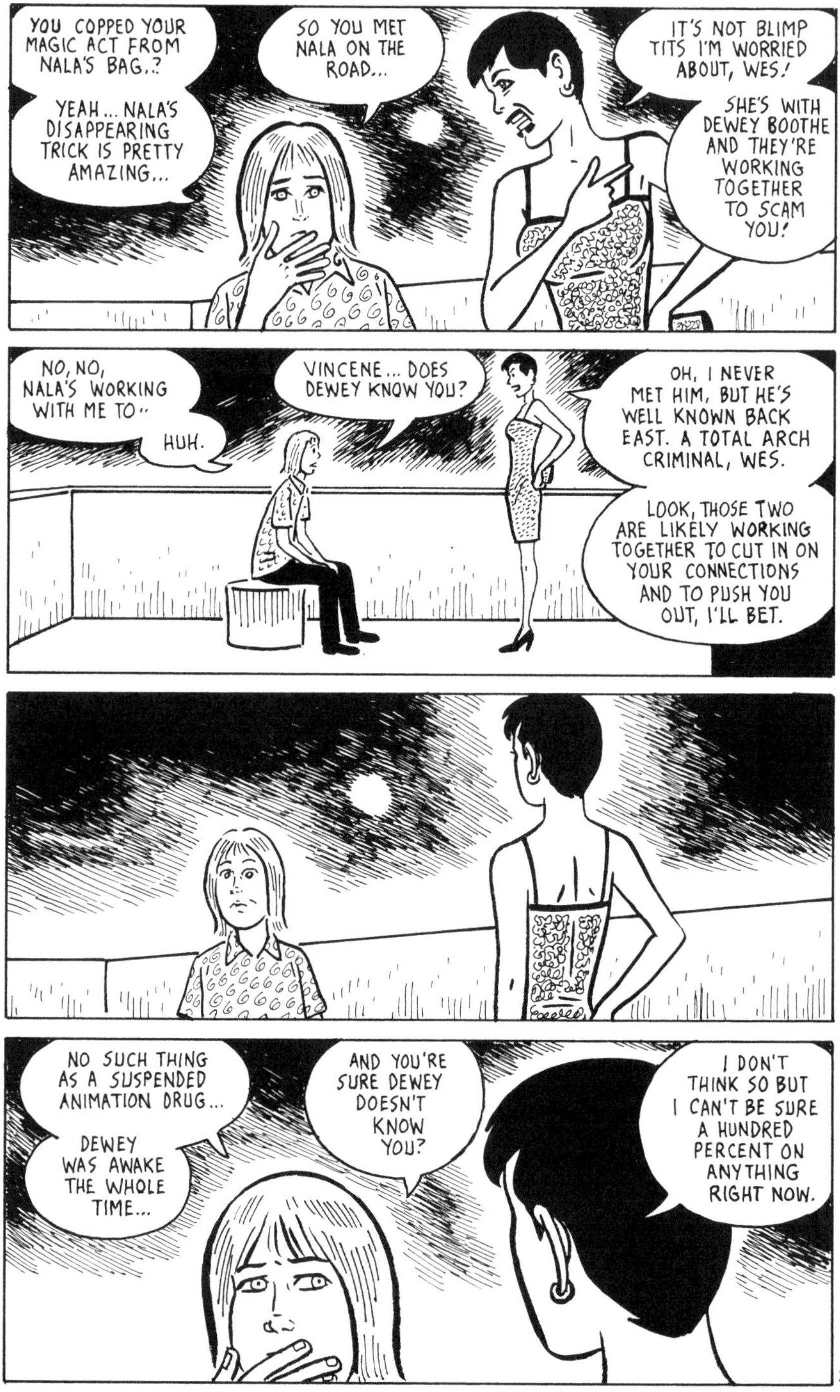
YOU COPPED YOUR MAGIC ACT FROM NALA'S BAG..?
YEAH... NALA'S DISAPPEARING TRICK IS PRETTY AMAZING...
SO YOU MET NALA ON THE ROAD...
IT'S NOT BLIMP TITS I'M WORRIED ABOUT, WES!
SHE'S WITH DEWEY BOOTHE AND THEY'RE WORKING TOGETHER TO SCAM YOU!
NO, NO, NALA'S WORKING WITH ME TO..
HUH.
VINCENE... DOES DEWEY KNOW YOU?
OH, I NEVER MET HIM, BUT HE'S WELL KNOWN BACK EAST. A TOTAL ARCH CRIMINAL, WES.
LOOK, THOSE TWO ARE LIKELY WORKING TOGETHER TO CUT IN ON YOUR CONNECTIONS AND TO PUSH YOU OUT, I'LL BET.
NO SUCH THING AS A SUSPENDED ANIMATION DRUG...
DEWEY WAS AWAKE THE WHOLE TIME...
AND YOU'RE SURE DEWEY DOESN'T KNOW YOU?
I DON'T THINK SO BUT I CAN'T BE SURE A HUNDRED PERCENT ON ANYTHING RIGHT NOW.

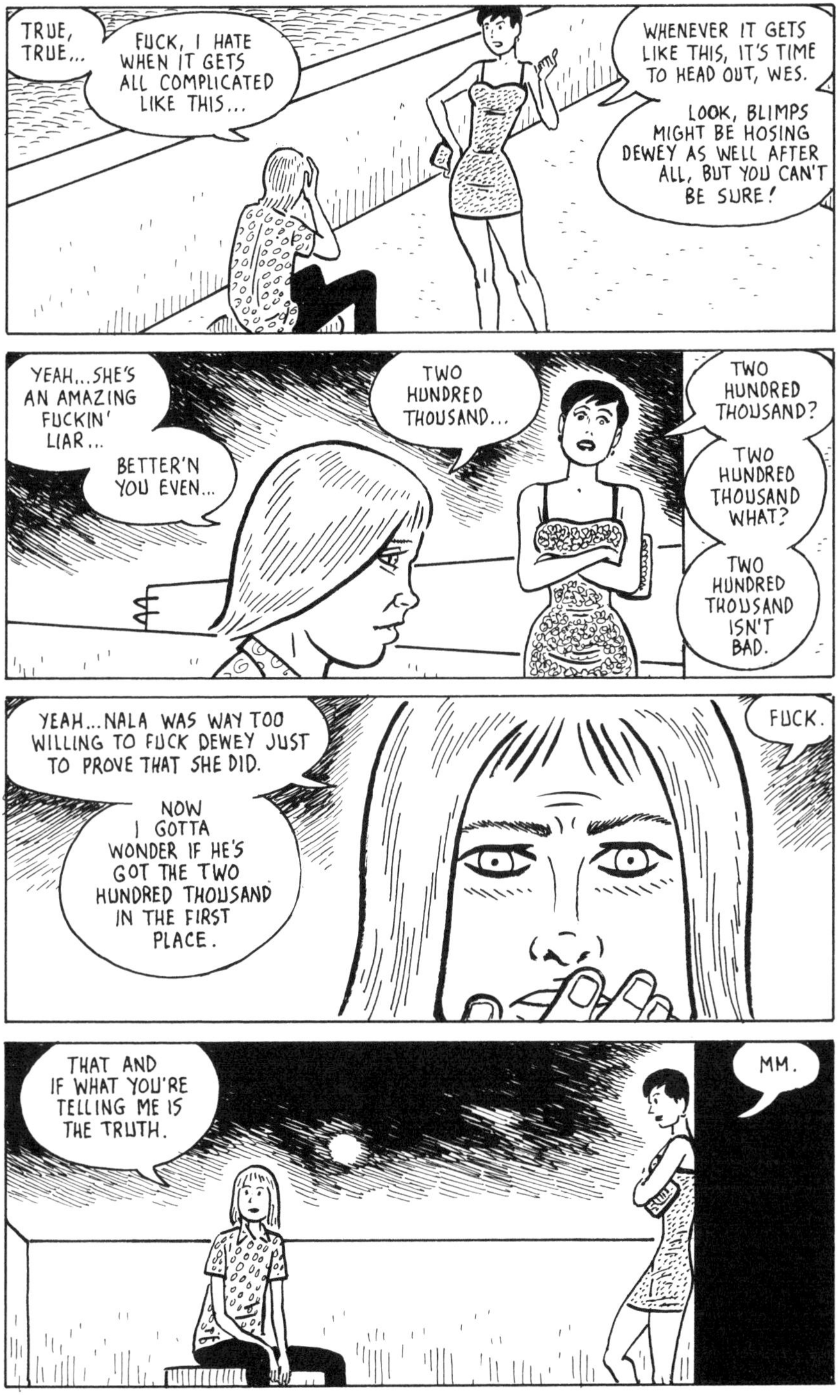
TRUE, TRUE...
FUCK, I HATE WHEN IT GETS ALL COMPLICATED LIKE THIS...
WHENEVER IT GETS LIKE THIS, IT'S TIME TO HEAD OUT, WES.
LOOK, BLIMPS MIGHT BE HOSING DEWEY AS WELL AFTER ALL, BUT YOU CAN'T BE SURE!
YEAH...SHE'S AN AMAZING FUCKIN' LIAR...
BETTER'N YOU EVEN...
TWO HUNDRED THOUSAND...
TWO HUNDRED THOUSAND?
TWO HUNDRED THOUSAND WHAT?
TWO HUNDRED THOUSAND ISN'T BAD.
YEAH...NALA WAS WAY TOO WILLING TO FUCK DEWEY JUST TO PROVE THAT SHE DID.
NOW I GOTTA WONDER IF HE'S GOT THE TWO HUNDRED THOUSAND IN THE FIRST PLACE.
FUCK.
THAT AND IF WHAT YOU'RE TELLING ME IS THE TRUTH.
MM.

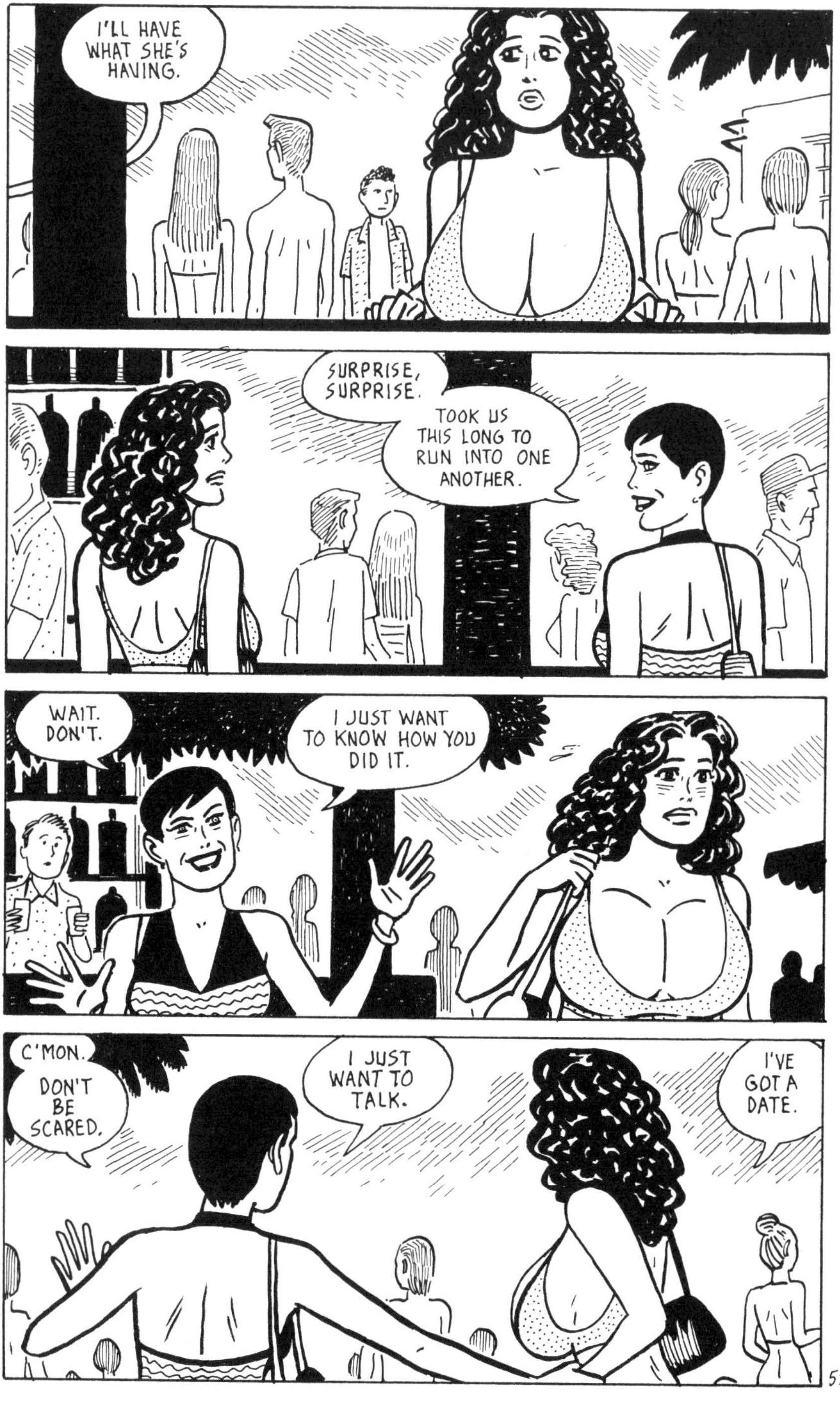
I'LL HAVE WHAT SHE'S HAVING.
SURPRISE, SURPRISE.
TOOK US THIS LONG TO RUN INTO ONE ANOTHER.
WAIT. DON'T.
I JUST WANT TO KNOW HOW YOU DID IT.
C'MON.
DON'T BE SCARED.
I JUST WANT TO TALK.
I'VE GOT A DATE.

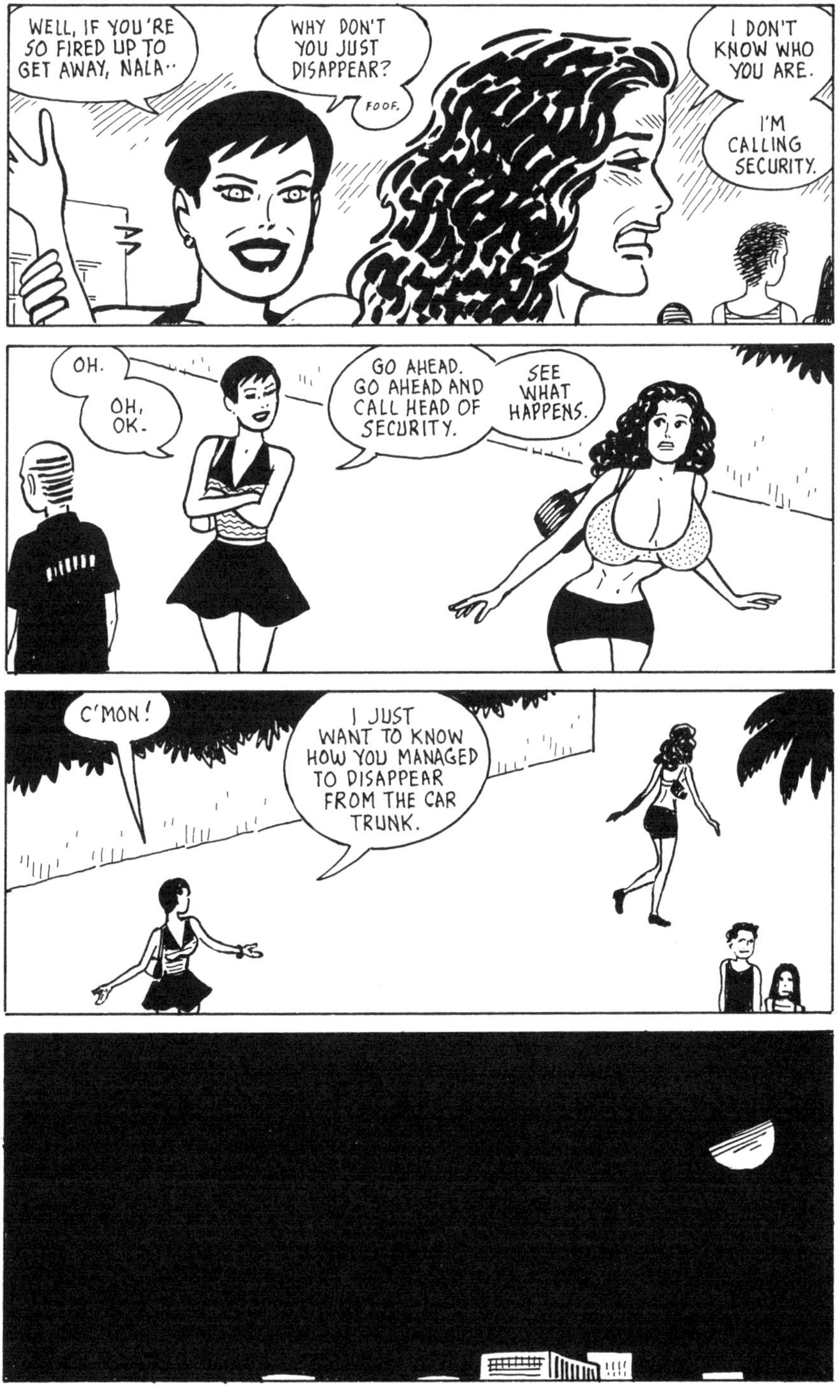
WELL, IF YOU'RE SO FIRED UP TO GET AWAY, NALA..
WHY DON'T YOU JUST DISAPPEAR?
FOOF.
I DON'T KNOW WHO YOU ARE.
I'M CALLING SECURITY.
OH.
OH, OK.
GO AHEAD. GO AHEAD AND CALL HEAD OF SECURITY.
SEE WHAT HAPPENS.
C'MON!
I JUST WANT TO KNOW HOW YOU MANAGED TO DISAPPEAR FROM THE CAR TRUNK.

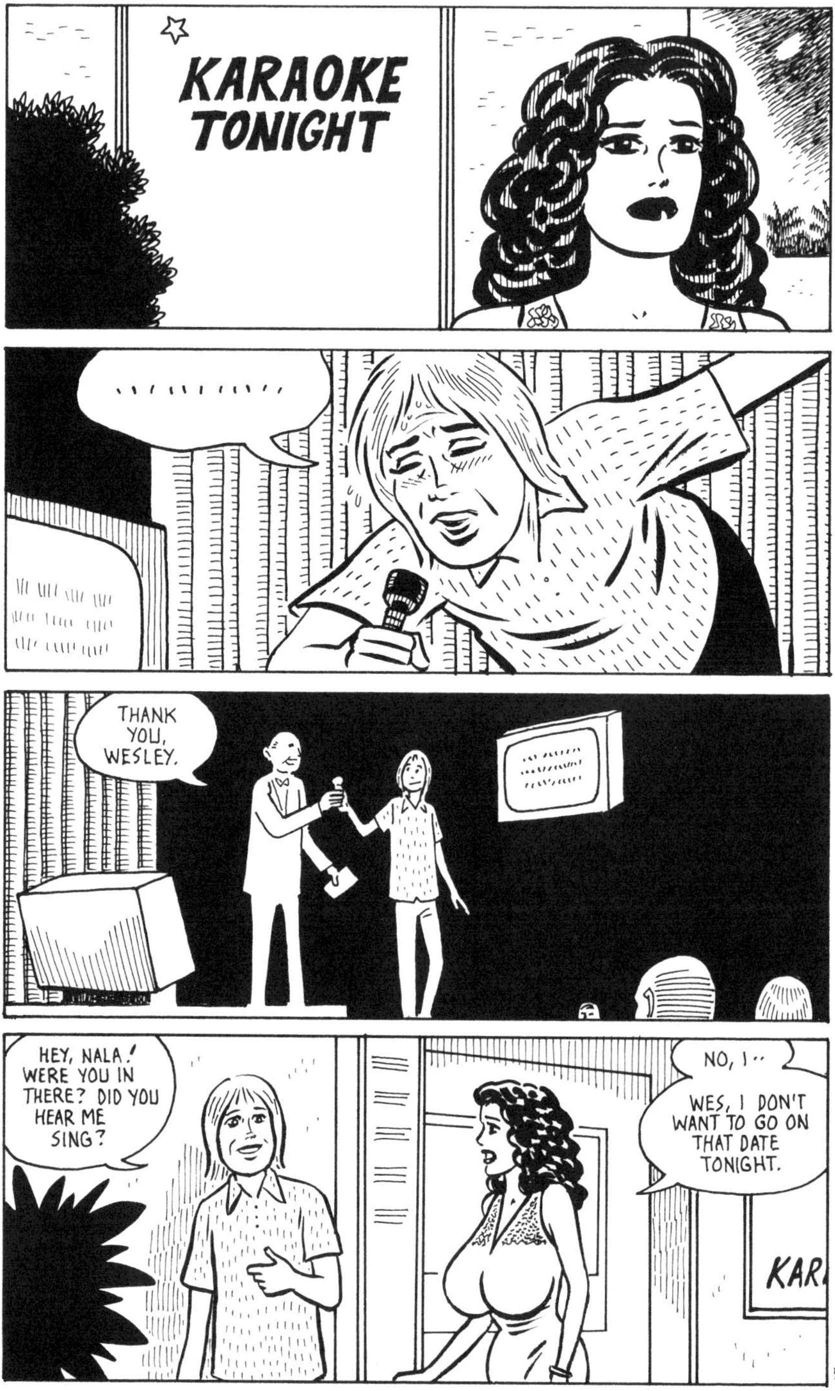
KARAOKE TONIGHT
THANK YOU, WESLEY.
HEY, NALA! WERE YOU IN THERE? DID YOU HEAR ME SING?
NO, I ..
WES, I DON'T WANT TO GO ON THAT DATE TONIGHT.
KAR

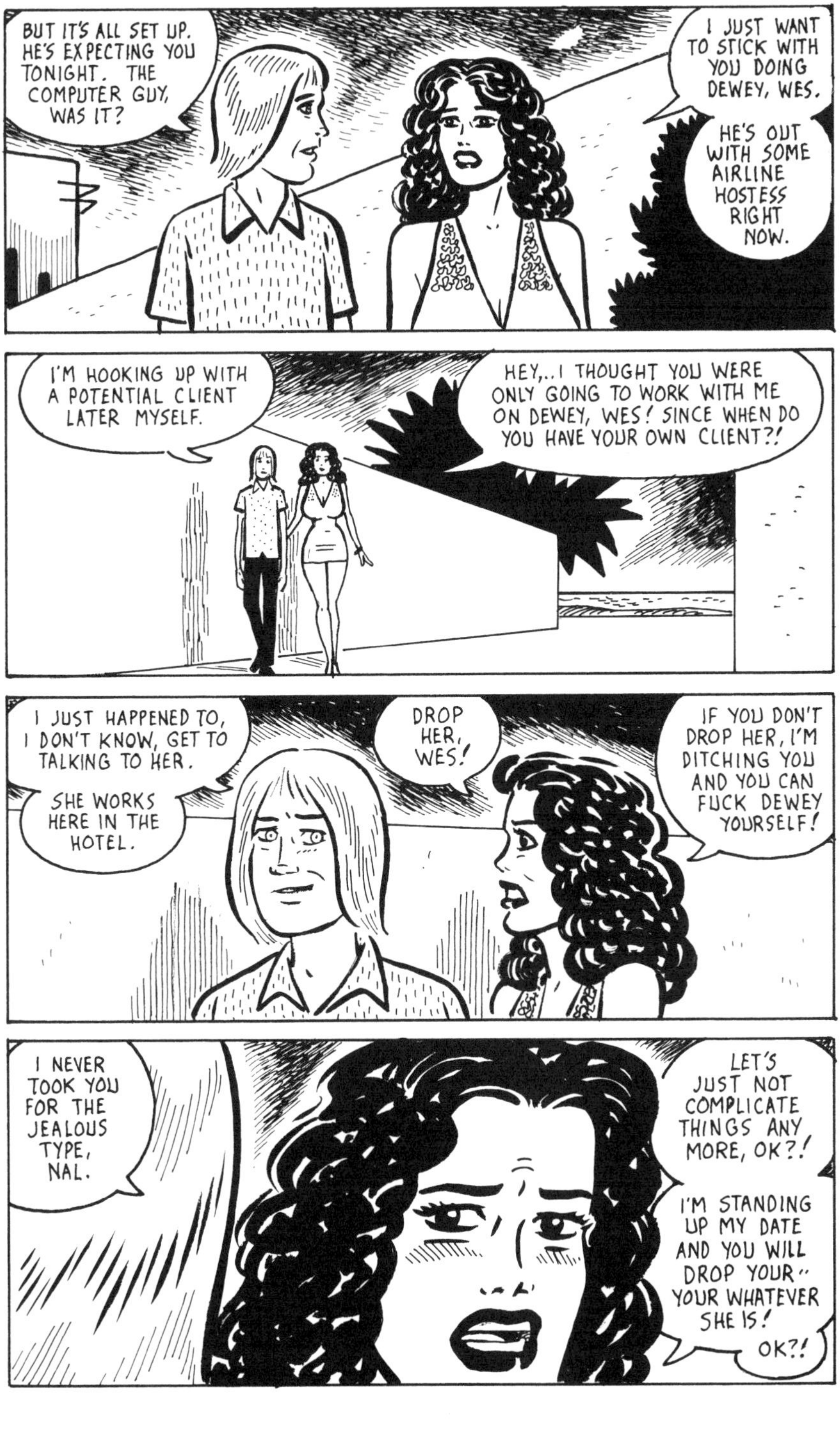
BUT IT'S ALL SET UP. HE'S EXPECTING YOU TONIGHT. THE COMPUTER GUY, WAS IT?
I JUST WANT TO STICK WITH YOU DOING DEWEY, WES.
HE'S OUT WITH SOME AIRLINE HOSTESS RIGHT NOW.
I'M HOOKING UP WITH A POTENTIAL CLIENT LATER MYSELF.
HEY,..I THOUGHT YOU WERE ONLY GOING TO WORK WITH ME ON DEWEY, WES! SINCE WHEN DO YOU HAVE YOUR OWN CLIENT?!
I JUST HAPPENED TO, I DON'T KNOW, GET TO TALKING TO HER.
SHE WORKS HERE IN THE HOTEL.
DROP HER, WES!
IF YOU DON'T DROP HER, I'M DITCHING YOU AND YOU CAN FUCK DEWEY YOURSELF!
I NEVER TOOK YOU FOR THE JEALOUS TYPE, NAL.
LET'S JUST NOT COMPLICATE THINGS ANY MORE, OK?!
I'M STANDING UP MY DATE AND YOU WILL DROP YOUR.. YOUR WHATEVER SHE IS!
OK?!

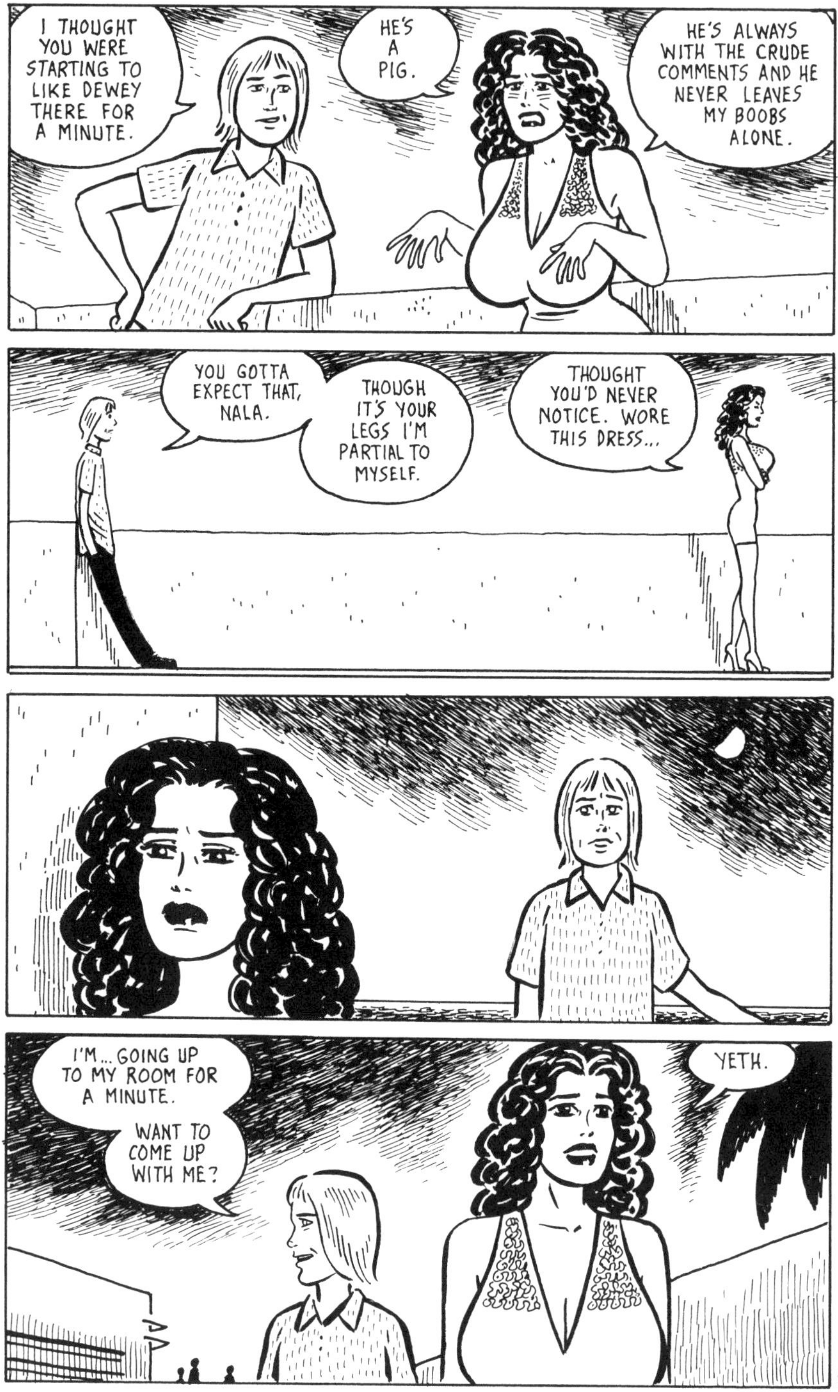
I THOUGHT YOU WERE STARTING TO LIKE DEWEY THERE FOR A MINUTE.
HE'S A PIG.
HE'S ALWAYS WITH THE CRUDE COMMENTS AND HE NEVER LEAVES MY BOOBS ALONE.
YOU GOTTA EXPECT THAT, NALA.
THOUGH IT'S YOUR LEGS I'M PARTIAL TO MYSELF.
THOUGHT YOU'D NEVER NOTICE. WORE THIS DRESS...
I'M... GOING UP TO MY ROOM FOR A MINUTE.
WANT TO COME UP WITH ME?
YETH.

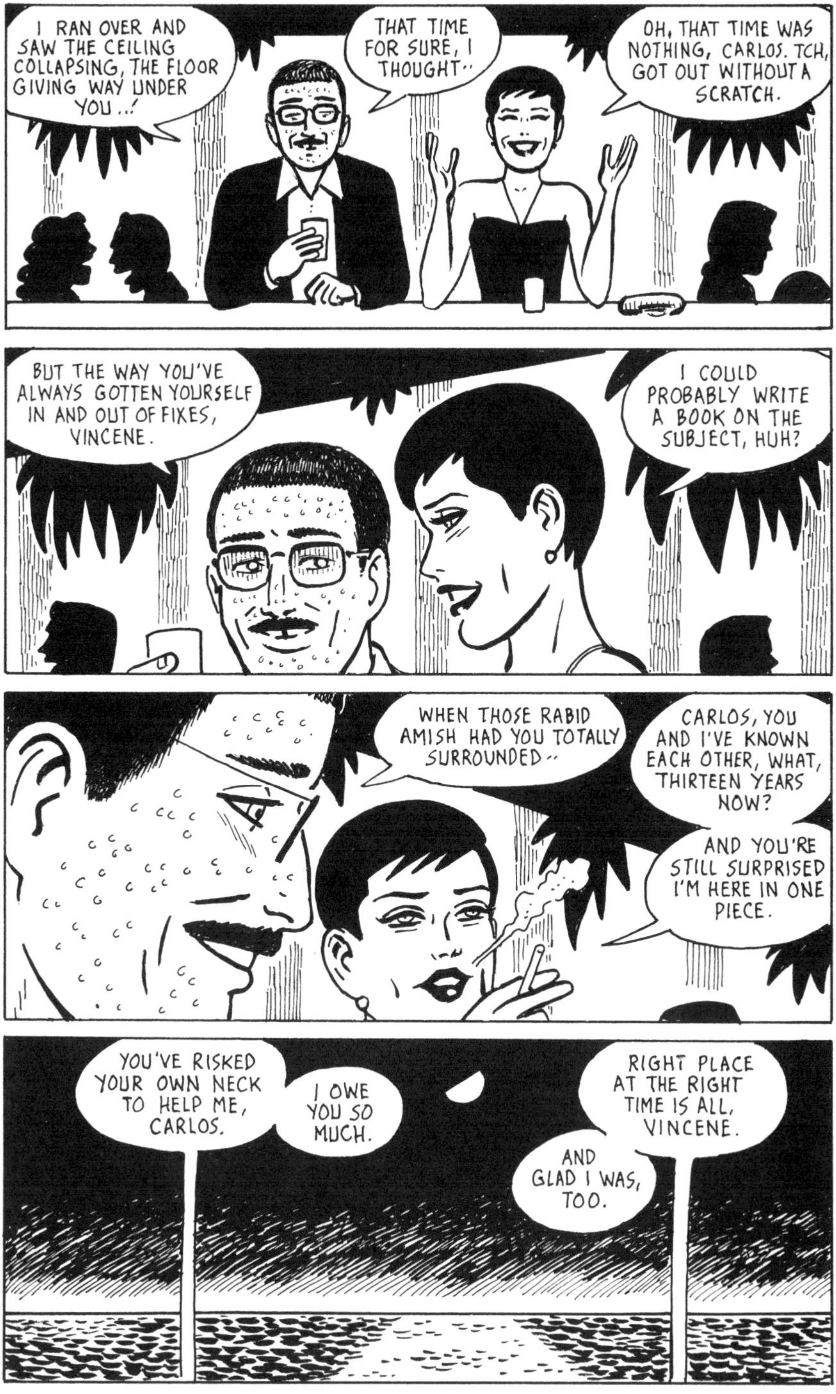
I RAN OVER AND SAW THE CEILING COLLAPSING, THE FLOOR GIVING WAY UNDER YOU...!
THAT TIME FOR SURE, I THOUGHT..
OH, THAT TIME WAS NOTHING, CARLOS. TCH, GOT OUT WITHOUT A SCRATCH.
BUT THE WAY YOU'VE ALWAYS GOTTEN YOURSELF IN AND OUT OF FIXES, VINCENE.
I COULD PROBABLY WRITE A BOOK ON THE SUBJECT, HUH?
WHEN THOSE RABID AMISH HAD YOU TOTALLY SURROUNDED..
CARLOS, YOU AND I'VE KNOWN EACH OTHER, WHAT, THIRTEEN YEARS NOW?
AND YOU'RE STILL SURPRISED I'M HERE IN ONE PIECE.
YOU'VE RISKED YOUR OWN NECK TO HELP ME, CARLOS.
I OWE YOU SO MUCH.
RIGHT PLACE AT THE RIGHT TIME IS ALL, VINCENE.
AND GLAD I WAS, TOO.

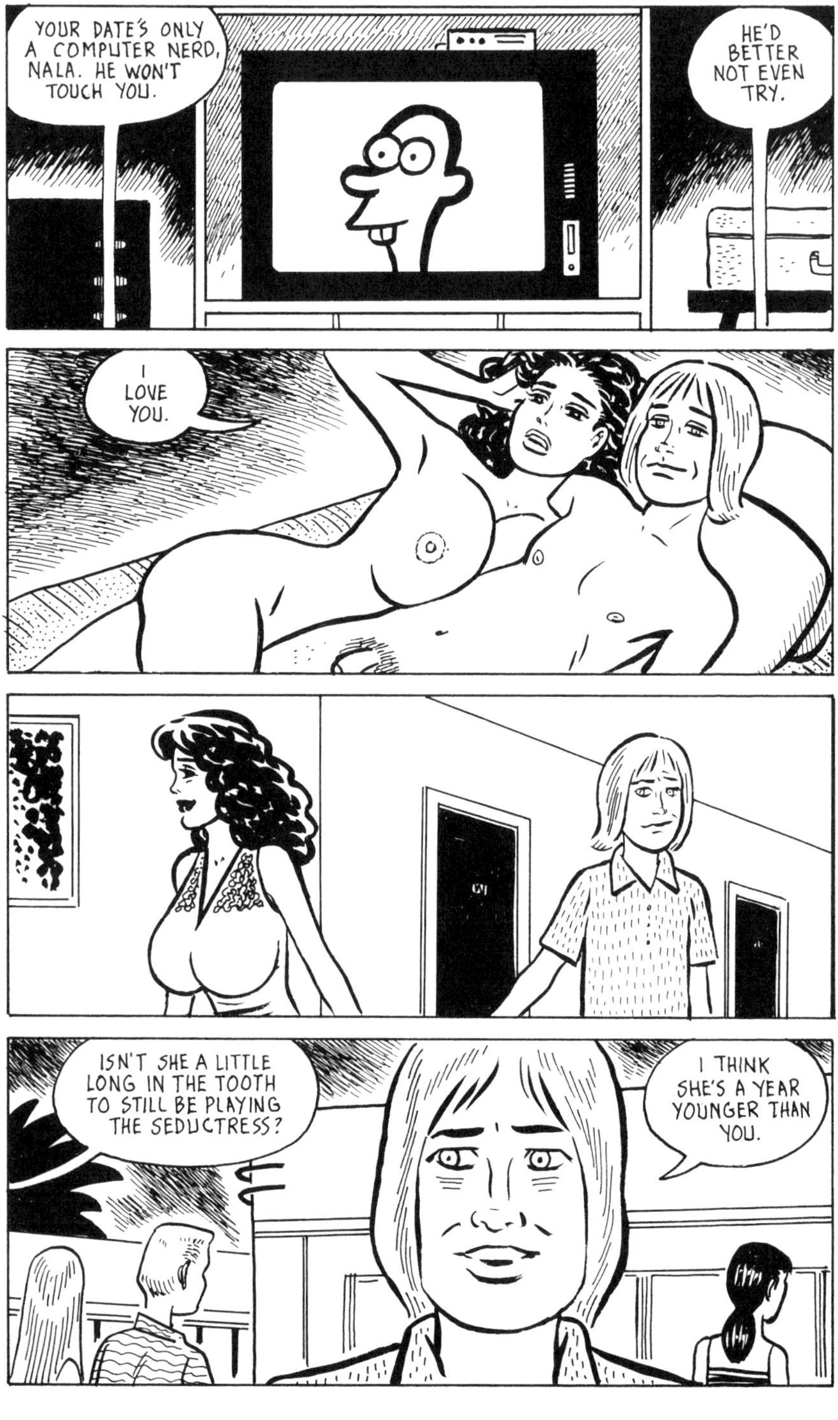
YOUR DATE'S ONLY A COMPUTER NERD, NALA. HE WON'T TOUCH YOU.
HE'D BETTER NOT EVEN TRY.
I LOVE YOU.
ISN'T SHE A LITTLE LONG IN THE TOOTH TO STILL BE PLAYING THE SEDUCTRESS?
I THINK SHE'S A YEAR YOUNGER THAN YOU.

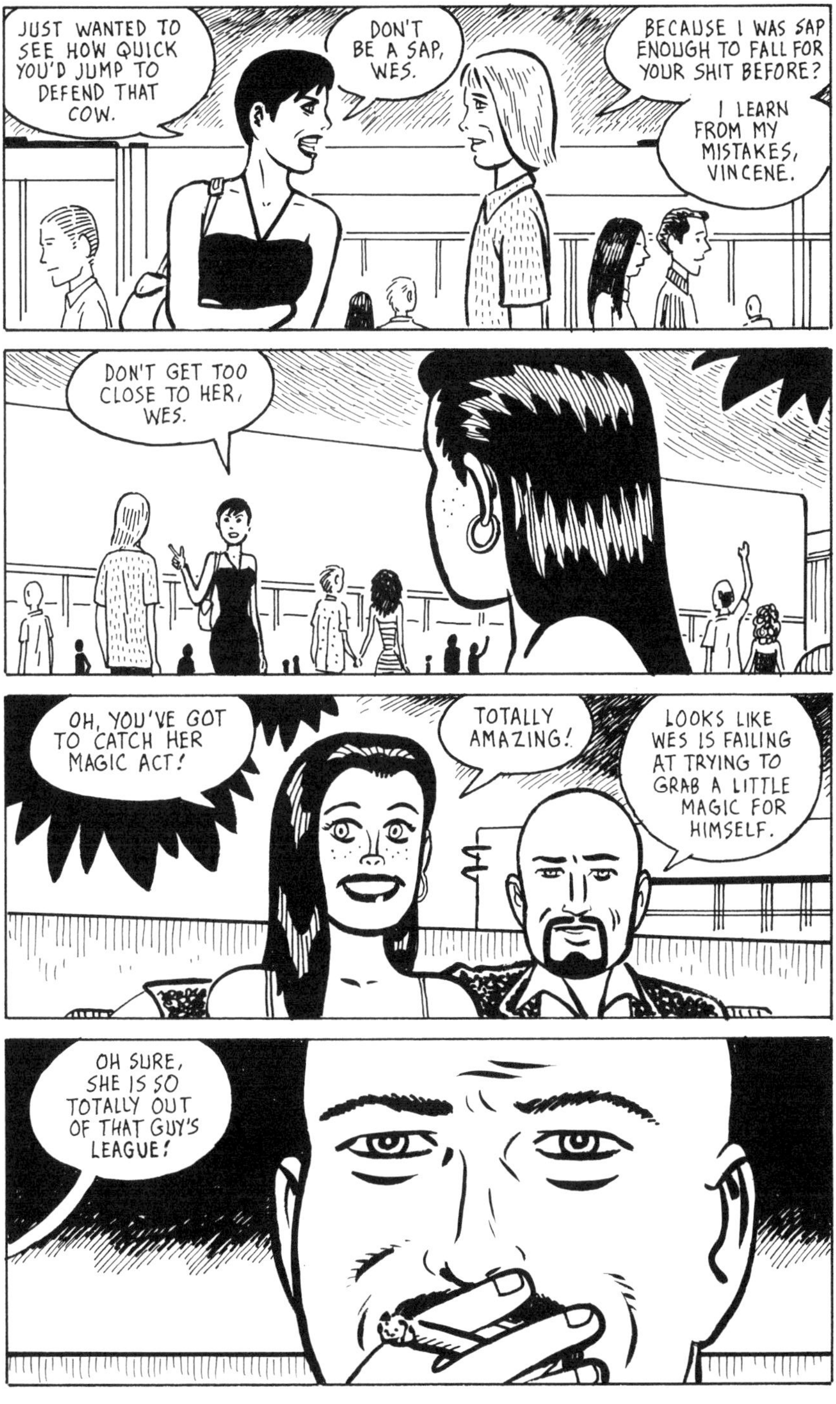
JUST WANTED TO SEE HOW QUICK YOU'D JUMP TO DEFEND THAT COW.
DON'T BE A SAP, WES.
BECAUSE I WAS SAP ENOUGH TO FALL FOR YOUR SHIT BEFORE?
I LEARN FROM MY MISTAKES, VINCENE.
DON'T GET TOO CLOSE TO HER, WES.
OH, YOU'VE GOT TO CATCH HER MAGIC ACT!
TOTALLY AMAZING!
LOOKS LIKE WES IS FAILING AT TRYING TO GRAB A LITTLE MAGIC FOR HIMSELF.
OH SURE, SHE IS SO TOTALLY OUT OF THAT GUY'S LEAGUE!

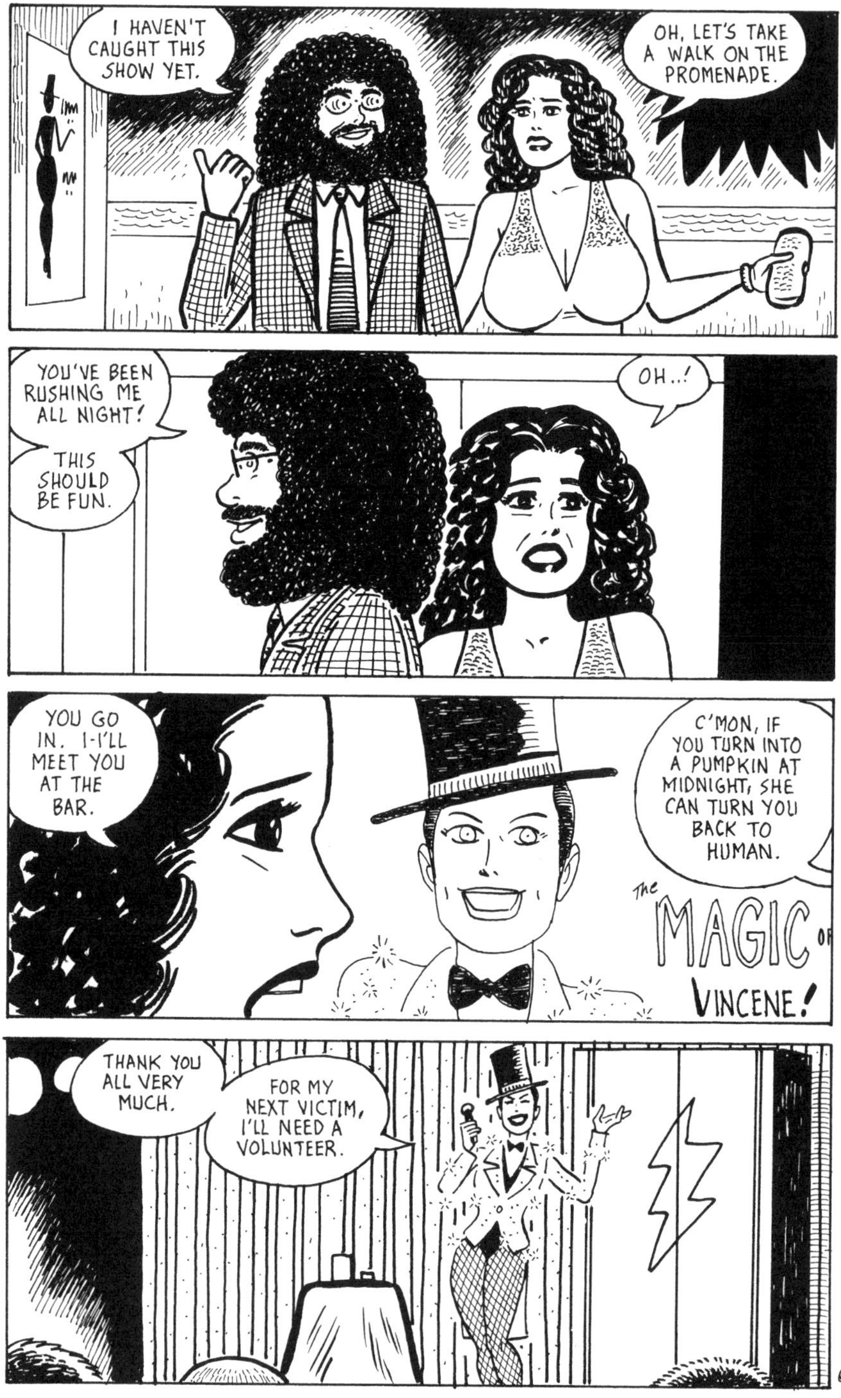
I HAVEN'T CAUGHT THIS SHOW YET.
OH, LET'S TAKE A WALK ON THE PROMENADE.
YOU'VE BEEN RUSHING ME ALL NIGHT!
THIS SHOULD BE FUN.
OH..!
YOU GO IN. I-I'LL MEET YOU AT THE BAR.
C'MON, IF YOU TURN INTO A PUMPKIN AT MIDNIGHT, SHE CAN TURN YOU BACK TO HUMAN.
THE MAGIC OF VINCENE!
THANK YOU ALL VERY MUCH.
FOR MY NEXT VICTIM, I'LL NEED A VOLUNTEER.

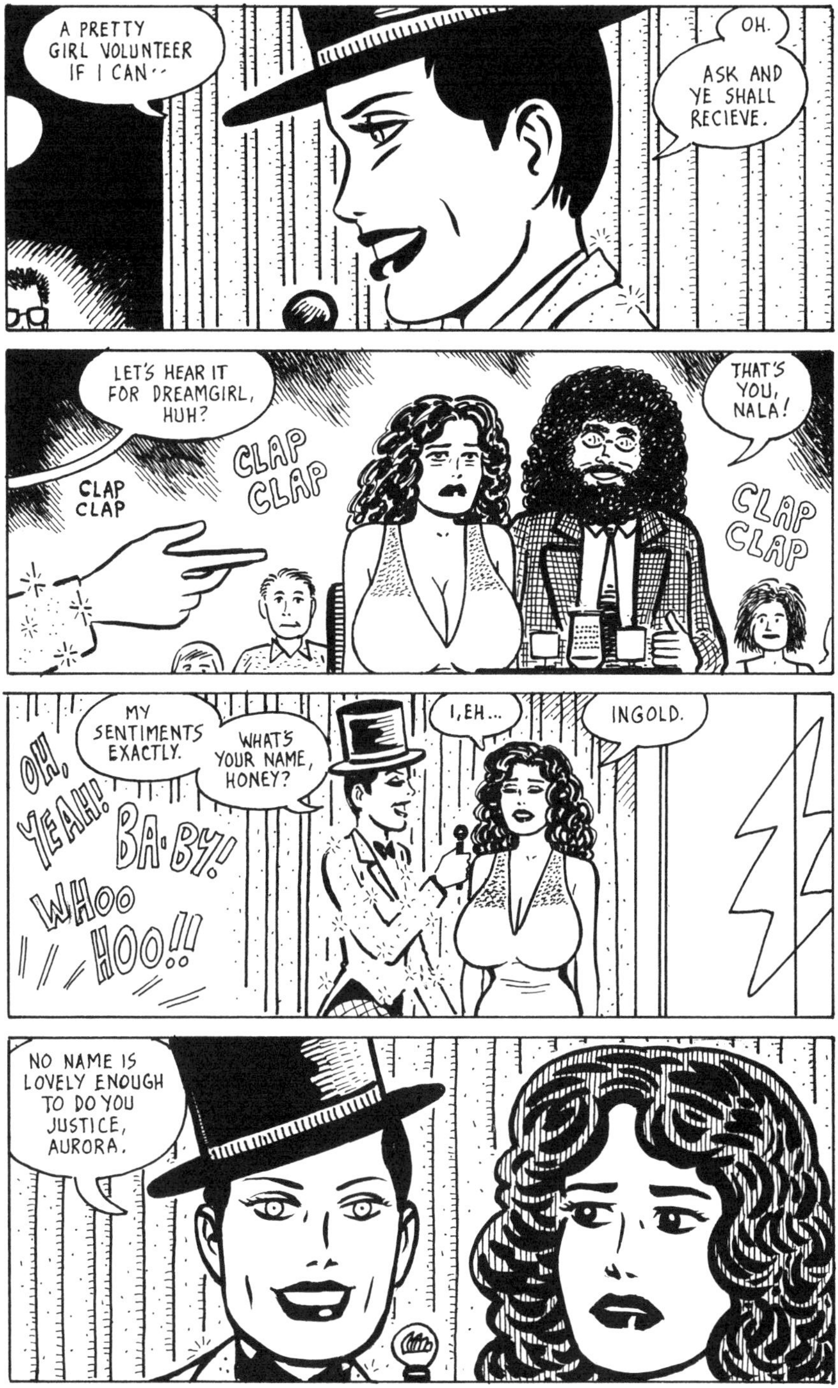
A PRETTY GIRL VOLUNTEER IF I CAN··
OH.
ASK AND YE SHALL RECIEVE.
LET'S HEAR IT FOR DREAMGIRL, HUH?
CLAP CLAP
CLAP CLAP
THAT'S YOU, NALA!
CLAP CLAP
OH, YEAH!
MY SENTIMENTS EXACTLY.
WHAT'S YOUR NAME, HONEY?
BA·BY!
I, EH...
INGOLD.
WHOO HOO!!
NO NAME IS LOVELY ENOUGH TO DO YOU JUSTICE, AURORA.

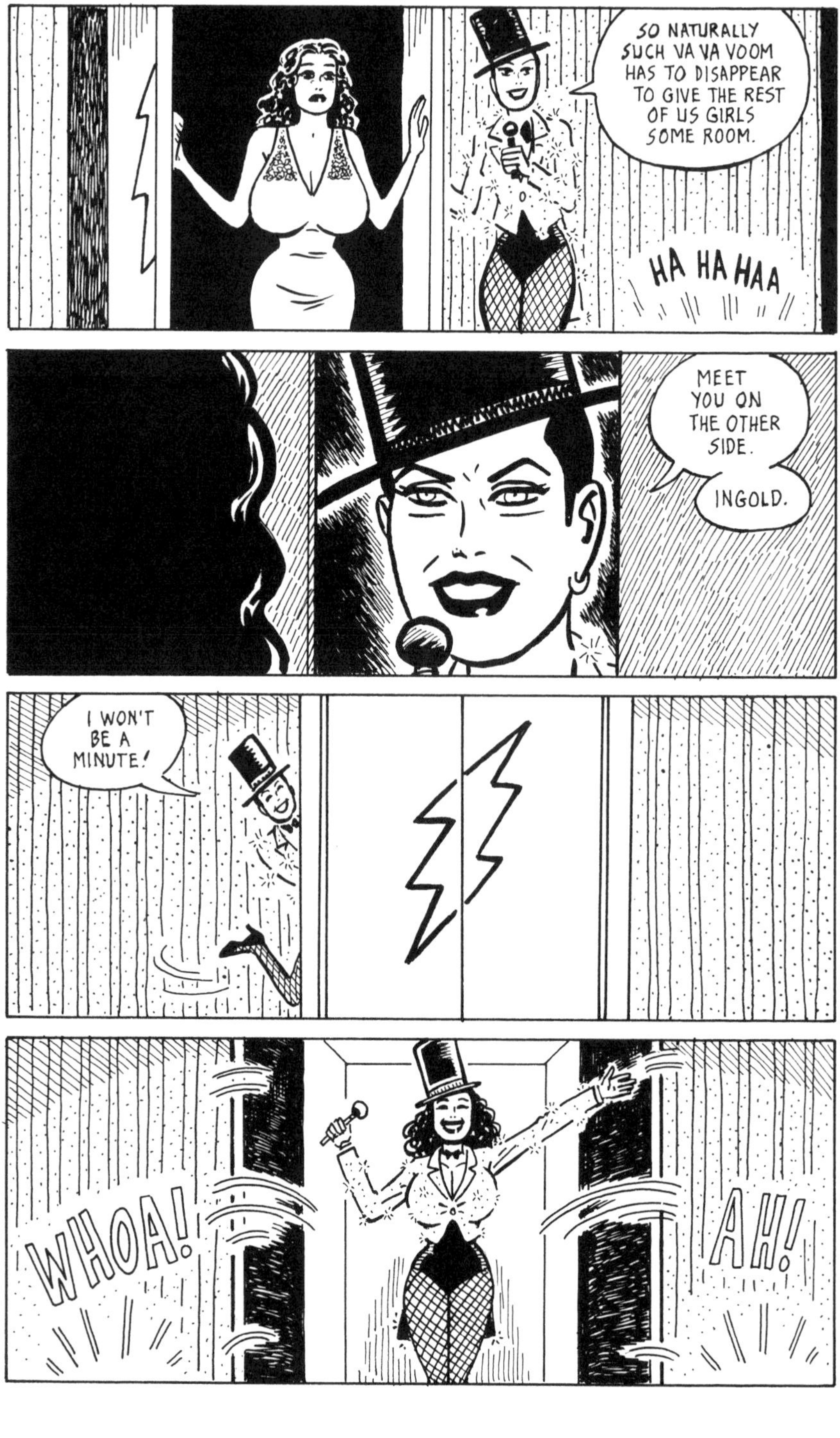
SO NATURALLY SUCH VA VA VOOM HAS TO DISAPPEAR TO GIVE THE REST OF US GIRLS SOME ROOM.
HA HA HAA
MEET YOU ON THE OTHER SIDE.
INGOLD.
I WON'T BE A MINUTE!
WHOA!
AH!

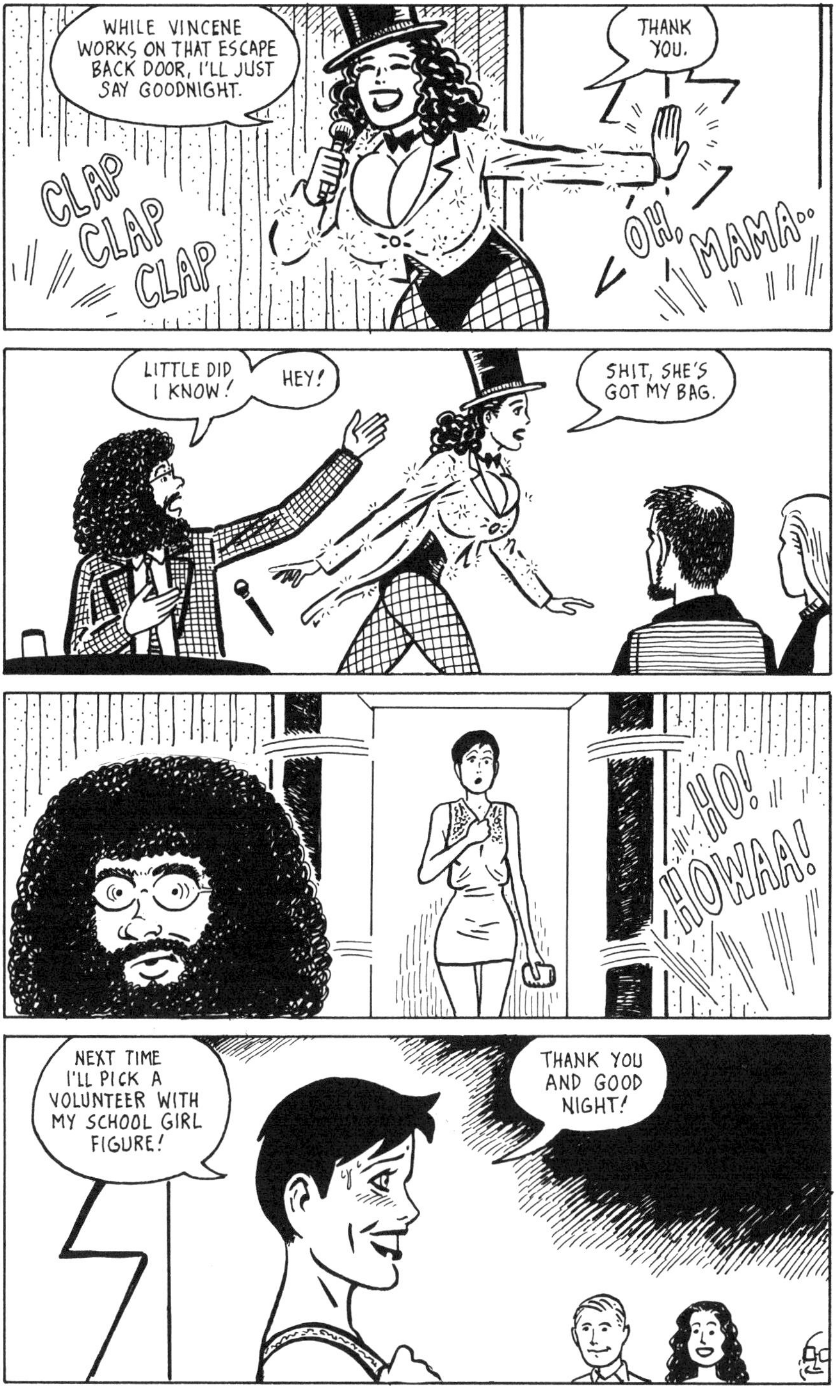
WHILE VINCENE WORKS ON THAT ESCAPE BACK DOOR, I'LL JUST SAY GOODNIGHT.
THANK YOU.
CLAP CLAP CLAP
OH, MAMA..
LITTLE DID I KNOW!
HEY!
SHIT, SHE'S GOT MY BAG.
HO! HOWAA!
NEXT TIME I'LL PICK A VOLUNTEER WITH MY SCHOOL GIRL FIGURE!
THANK YOU AND GOOD NIGHT!

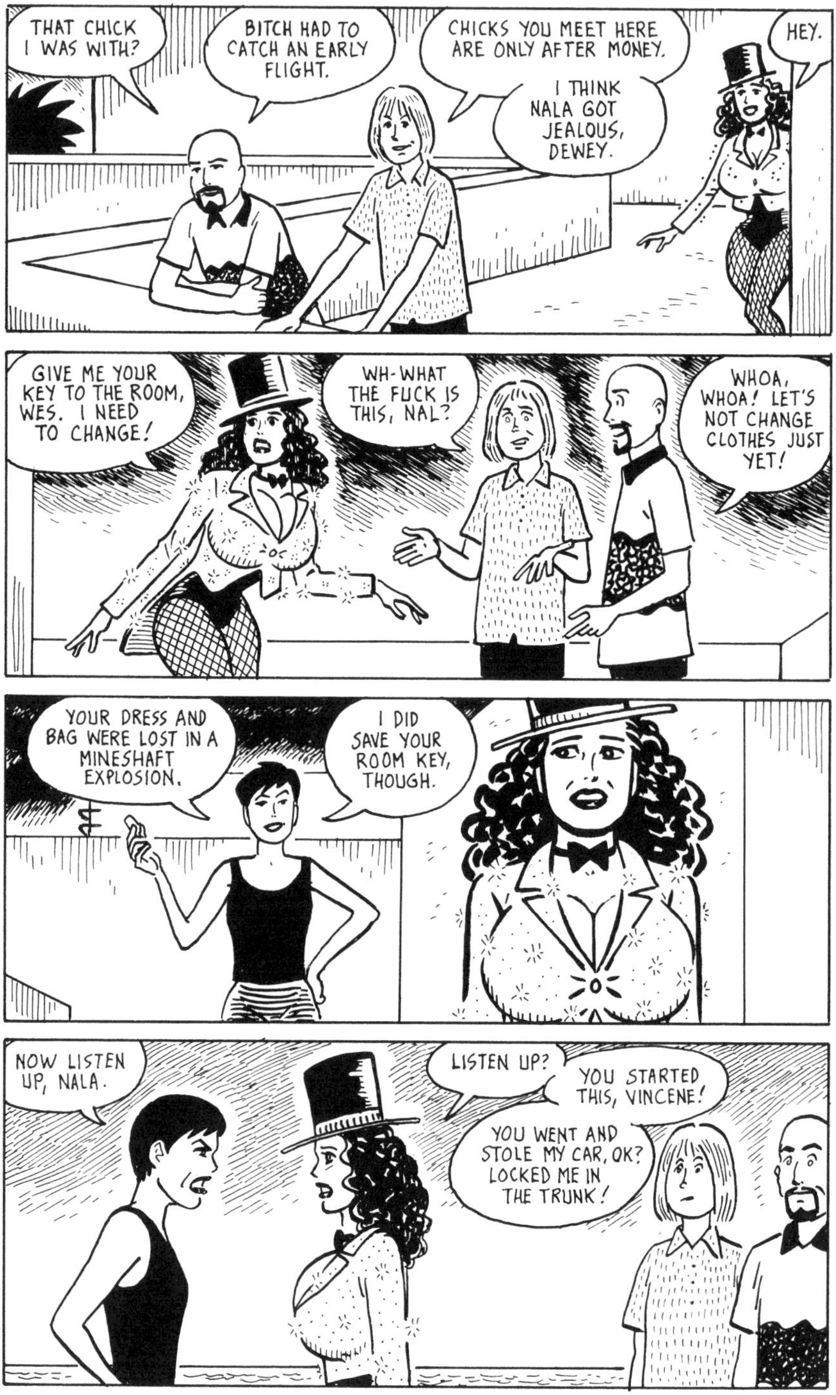
THAT CHICK I WAS WITH?
BITCH HAD TO CATCH AN EARLY FLIGHT.
CHICKS YOU MEET HERE ARE ONLY AFTER MONEY.
I THINK NALA GOT JEALOUS, DEWEY.
HEY.
GIVE ME YOUR KEY TO THE ROOM, WES. I NEED TO CHANGE!
WH-WHAT THE FUCK IS THIS, NAL?
WHOA, WHOA! LET'S NOT CHANGE CLOTHES JUST YET!
YOUR DRESS AND BAG WERE LOST IN A MINESHAFT EXPLOSION.
I DID SAVE YOUR ROOM KEY, THOUGH.
NOW LISTEN UP, NALA.
LISTEN UP?
YOU STARTED THIS, VINCENE!
YOU WENT AND STOLE MY CAR, OK? LOCKED ME IN THE TRUNK!

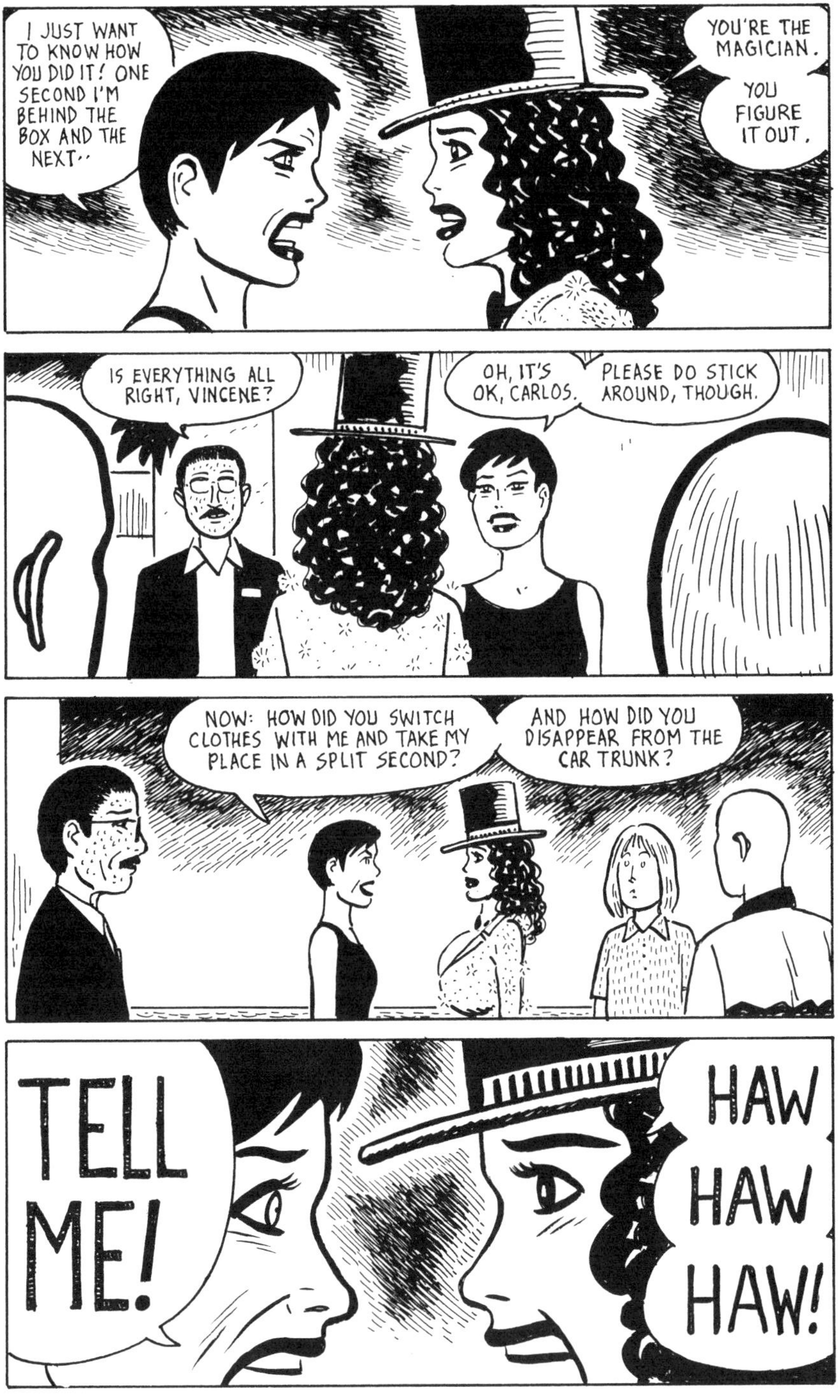

I JUST WANT TO KNOW HOW YOU DID IT! ONE SECOND I'M BEHIND THE BOX AND THE NEXT..
YOU'RE THE MAGICIAN.
YOU FIGURE IT OUT.
IS EVERYTHING ALL RIGHT, VINCENE?
OH, IT'S OK, CARLOS.
PLEASE DO STICK AROUND, THOUGH.
NOW: HOW DID YOU SWITCH CLOTHES WITH ME AND TAKE MY PLACE IN A SPLIT SECOND?
AND HOW DID YOU DISAPPEAR FROM THE CAR TRUNK?
TELL ME!
HAW HAW HAW!

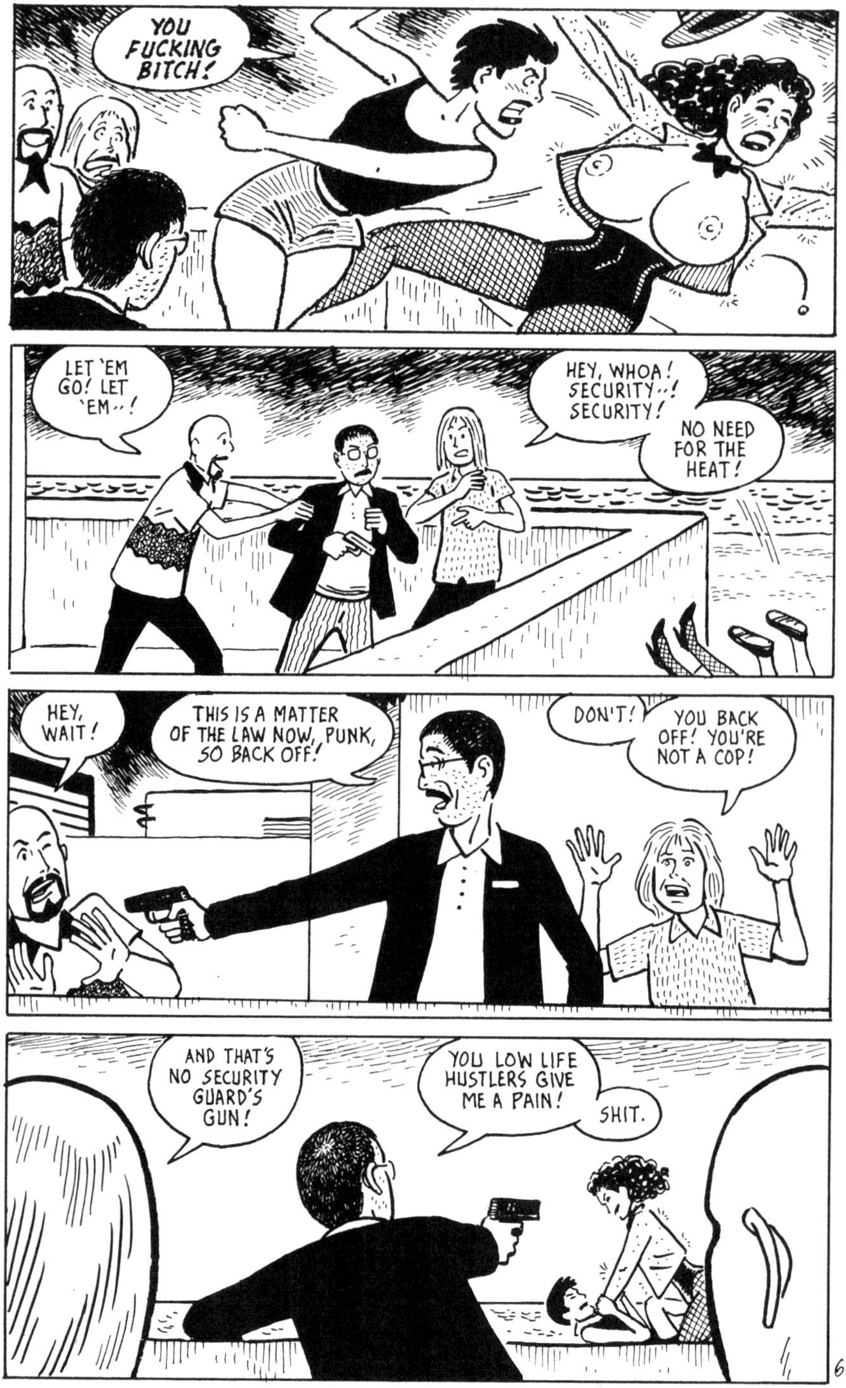

YOU FUCKING BITCH!
LET 'EM GO! LET 'EM..!
HEY, WHOA! SECURITY..! SECURITY!
NO NEED FOR THE HEAT!
HEY, WAIT!
THIS IS A MATTER OF THE LAW NOW, PUNK, SO BACK OFF!
DON'T!
YOU BACK OFF! YOU'RE NOT A COP!
AND THAT'S NO SECURITY GUARD'S GUN!
YOU LOW LIFE HUSTLERS GIVE ME A PAIN!
SHIT.

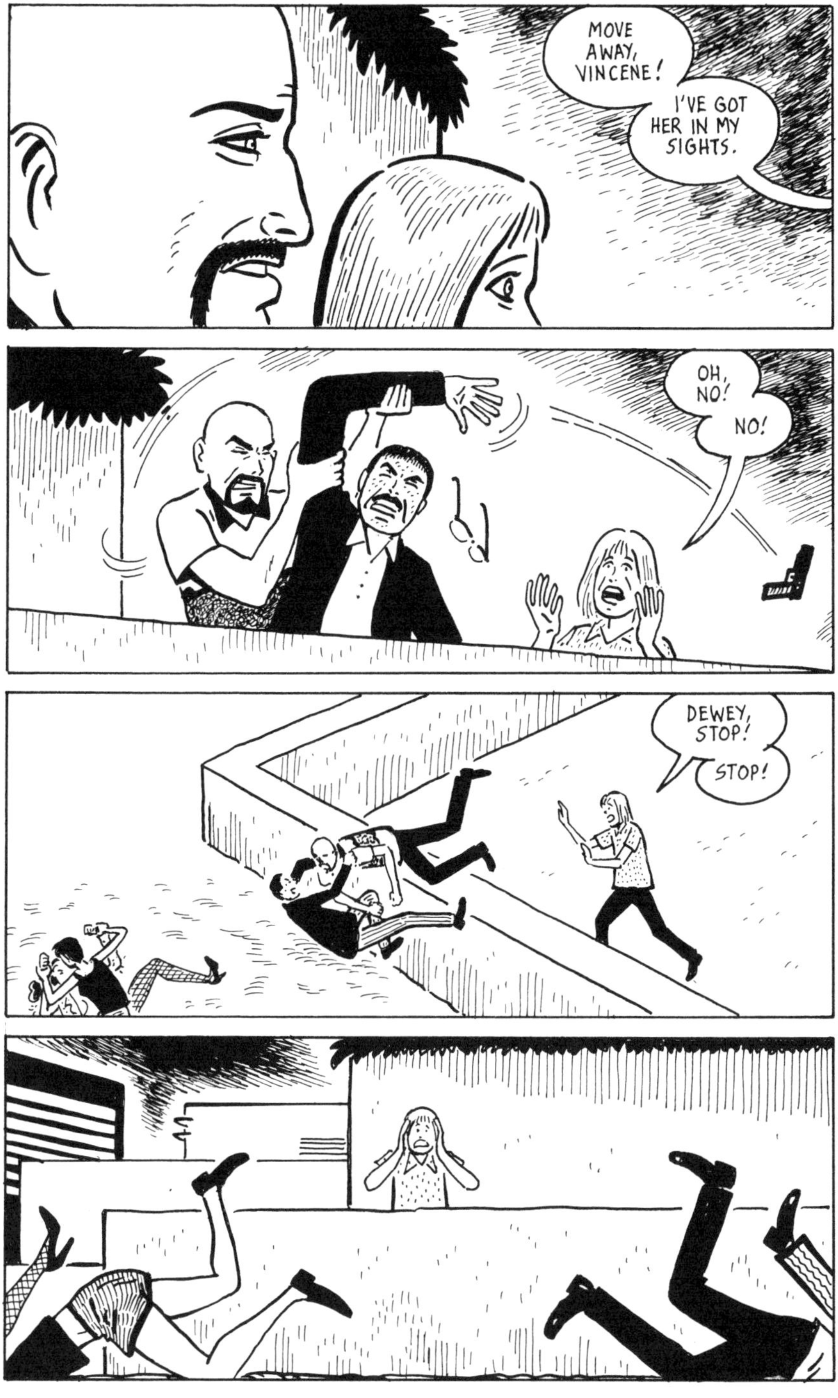
MOVE AWAY, VINCENE!
I'VE GOT HER IN MY SIGHTS.
OH, NO!
NO!
DEWEY, STOP!
STOP!

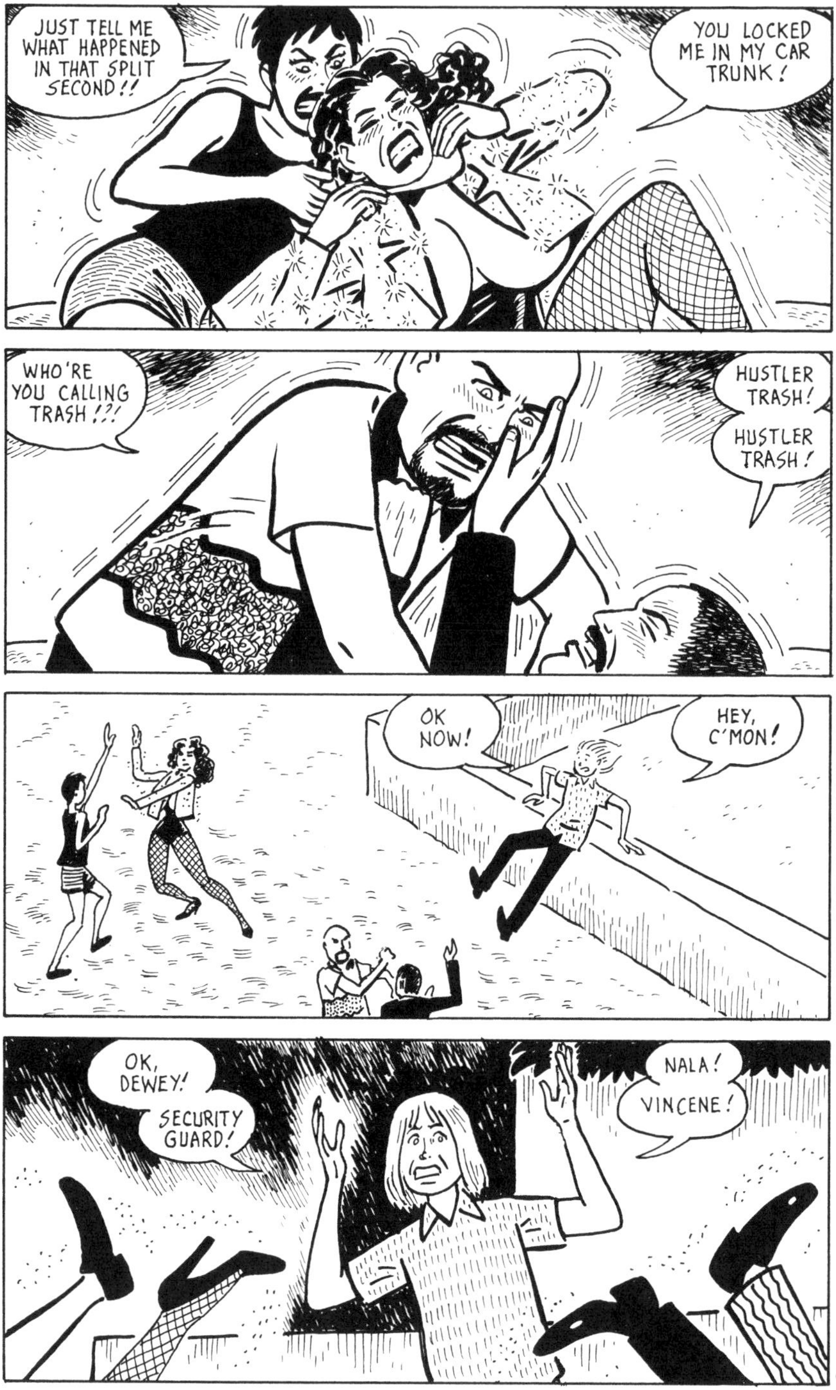
JUST TELL ME WHAT HAPPENED IN THAT SPLIT SECOND!!
YOU LOCKED ME IN MY CAR TRUNK!
WHO'RE YOU CALLING TRASH!?!
HUSTLER TRASH!
HUSTLER TRASH!
OK NOW!
HEY, C'MON!
OK, DEWEY!
SECURITY GUARD!
NALA!
VINCENE!

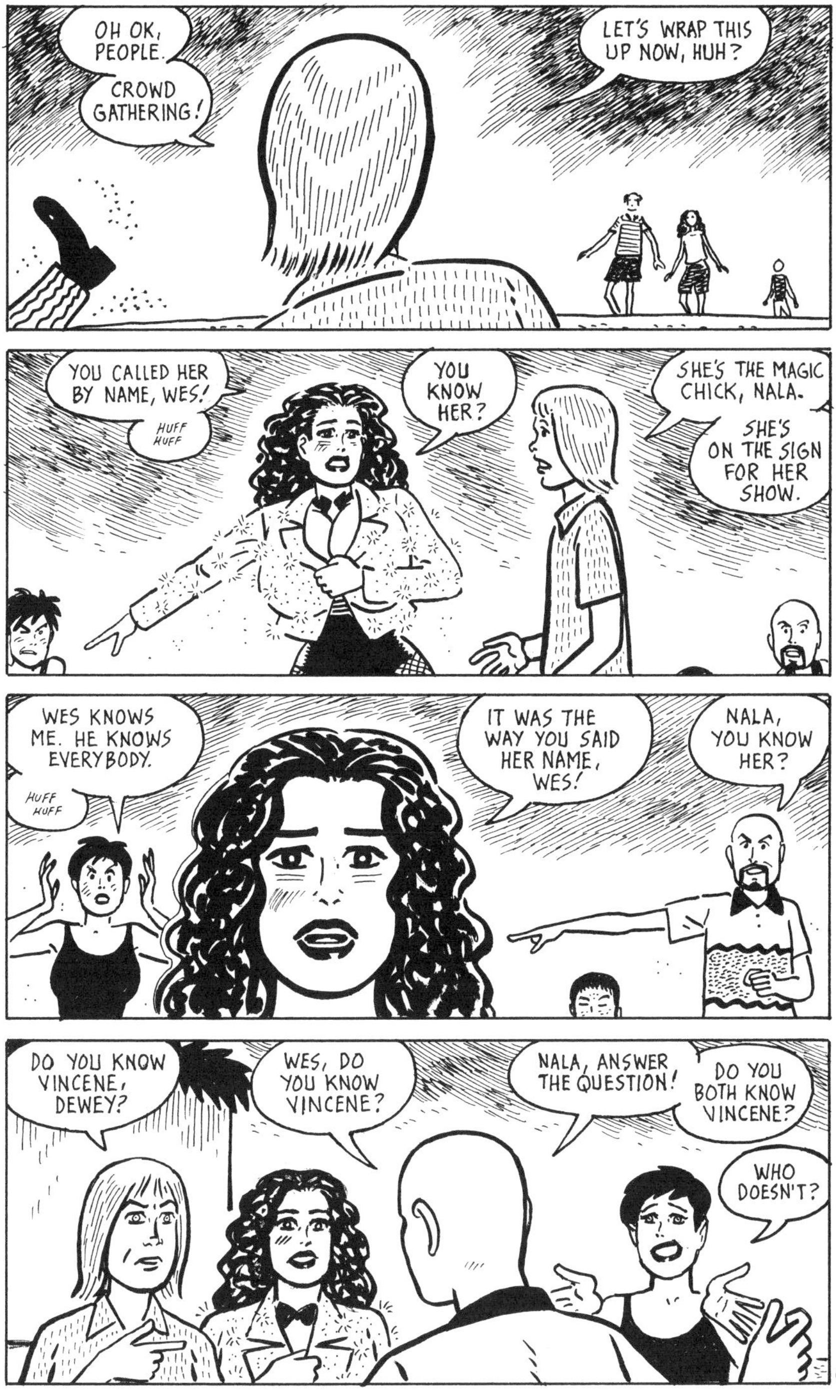
OH OK, PEOPLE.
CROWD GATHERING!
LET'S WRAP THIS UP NOW, HUH?
YOU CALLED HER BY NAME, WES!
HUFF HUFF
YOU KNOW HER?
SHE'S THE MAGIC CHICK, NALA.
SHE'S ON THE SIGN FOR HER SHOW.
WES KNOWS ME. HE KNOWS EVERYBODY.
HUFF HUFF
IT WAS THE WAY YOU SAID HER NAME, WES!
NALA, YOU KNOW HER?
DO YOU KNOW VINCENE, DEWEY?
WES, DO YOU KNOW VINCENE?
NALA, ANSWER THE QUESTION!
DO YOU BOTH KNOW VINCENE?
WHO DOESN'T?

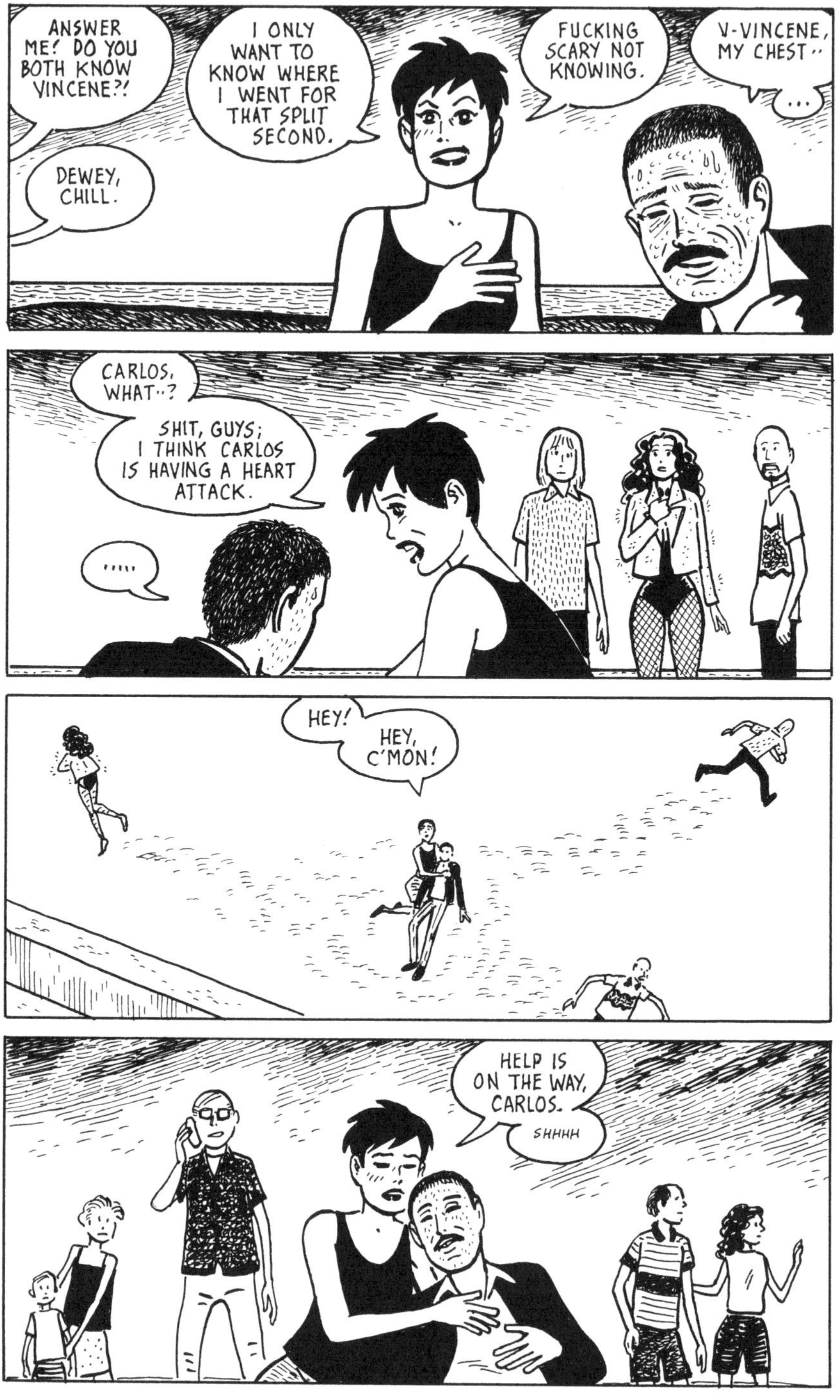
ANSWER ME! DO YOU BOTH KNOW VINCENE?!
DEWEY, CHILL.
I ONLY WANT TO KNOW WHERE I WENT FOR THAT SPLIT SECOND.
FUCKING SCARY NOT KNOWING.
V-VINCENE, MY CHEST..
...
CARLOS, WHAT..?
SHIT, GUYS; I THINK CARLOS IS HAVING A HEART ATTACK.
.....
HEY!
HEY, C'MON!
HELP IS ON THE WAY, CARLOS.
SHHHH

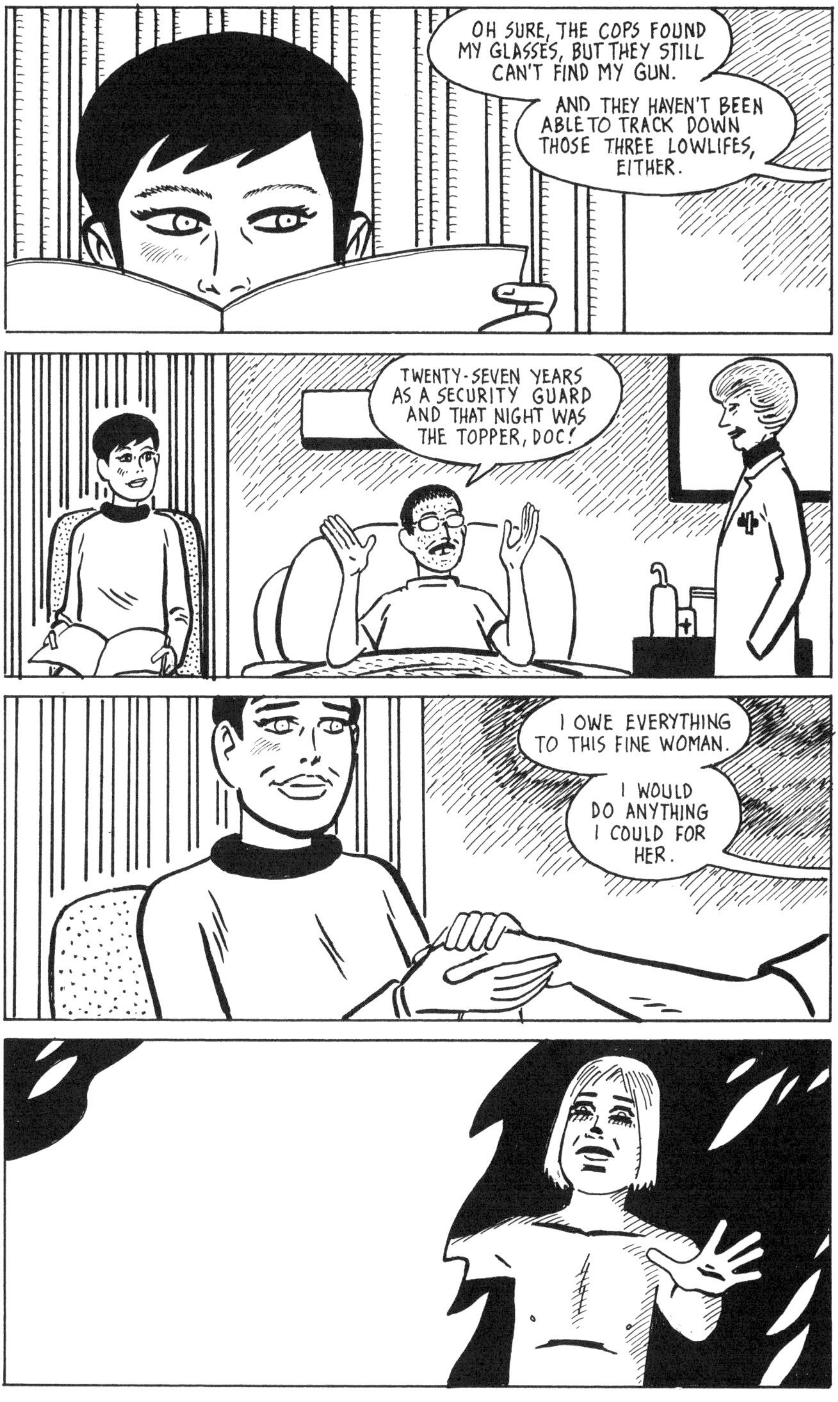
OH SURE, THE COPS FOUND MY GLASSES, BUT THEY STILL CAN'T FIND MY GUN.
AND THEY HAVEN'T BEEN ABLE TO TRACK DOWN THOSE THREE LOWLIFES, EITHER.
TWENTY-SEVEN YEARS AS A SECURITY GUARD AND THAT NIGHT WAS THE TOPPER, DOC!
I OWE EVERYTHING TO THIS FINE WOMAN.
I WOULD DO ANYTHING I COULD FOR HER.

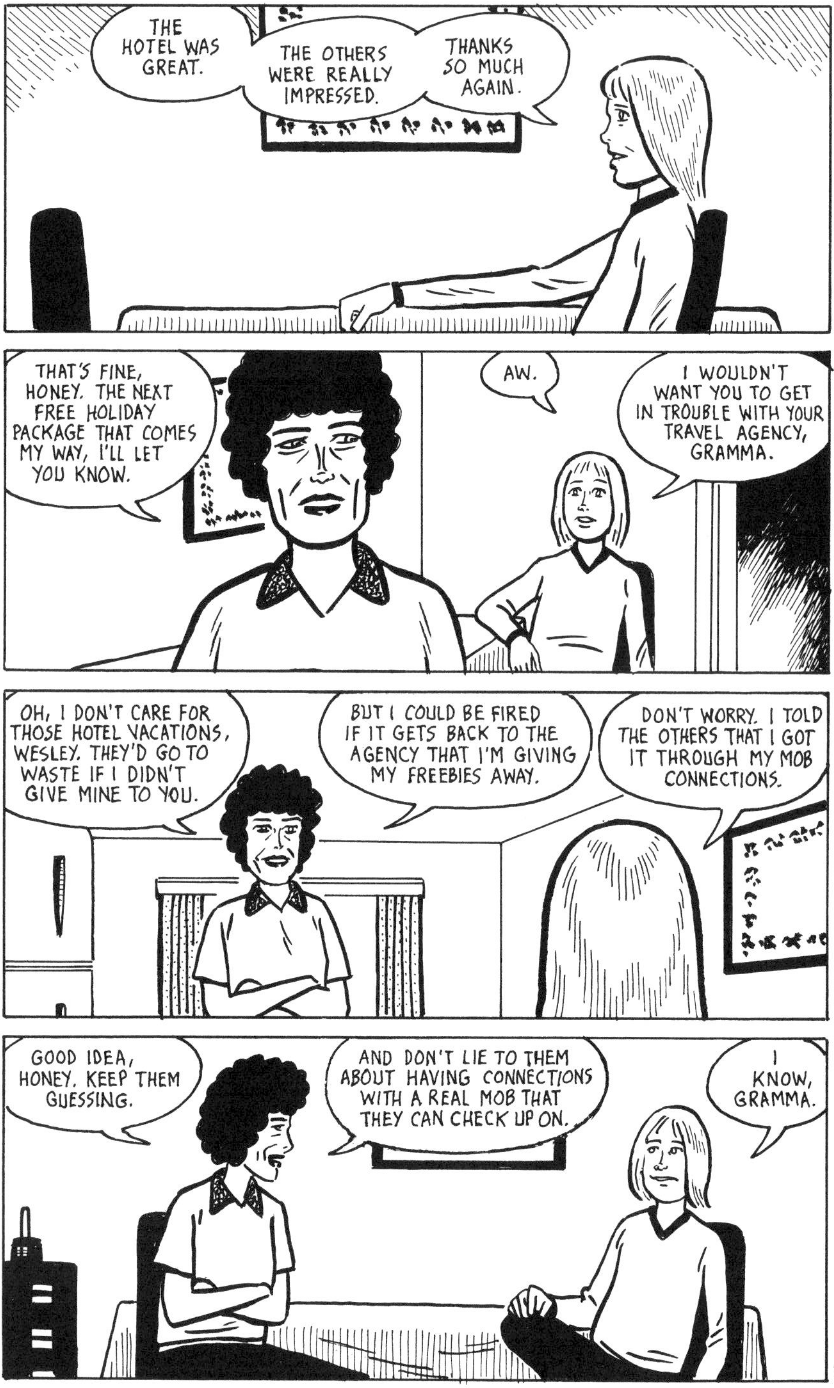
THE HOTEL WAS GREAT.
THE OTHERS WERE REALLY IMPRESSED.
THANKS SO MUCH AGAIN.
THAT'S FINE, HONEY. THE NEXT FREE HOLIDAY PACKAGE THAT COMES MY WAY, I'LL LET YOU KNOW.
AW.
I WOULDN'T WANT YOU TO GET IN TROUBLE WITH YOUR TRAVEL AGENCY, GRAMMA.
OH, I DON'T CARE FOR THOSE HOTEL VACATIONS, WESLEY. THEY'D GO TO WASTE IF I DIDN'T GIVE MINE TO YOU.
BUT I COULD BE FIRED IF IT GETS BACK TO THE AGENCY THAT I'M GIVING MY FREEBIES AWAY.
DON'T WORRY. I TOLD THE OTHERS THAT I GOT IT THROUGH MY MOB CONNECTIONS.
GOOD IDEA, HONEY. KEEP THEM GUESSING.
AND DON'T LIE TO THEM ABOUT HAVING CONNECTIONS WITH A REAL MOB THAT THEY CAN CHECK UP ON.
I KNOW, GRAMMA.

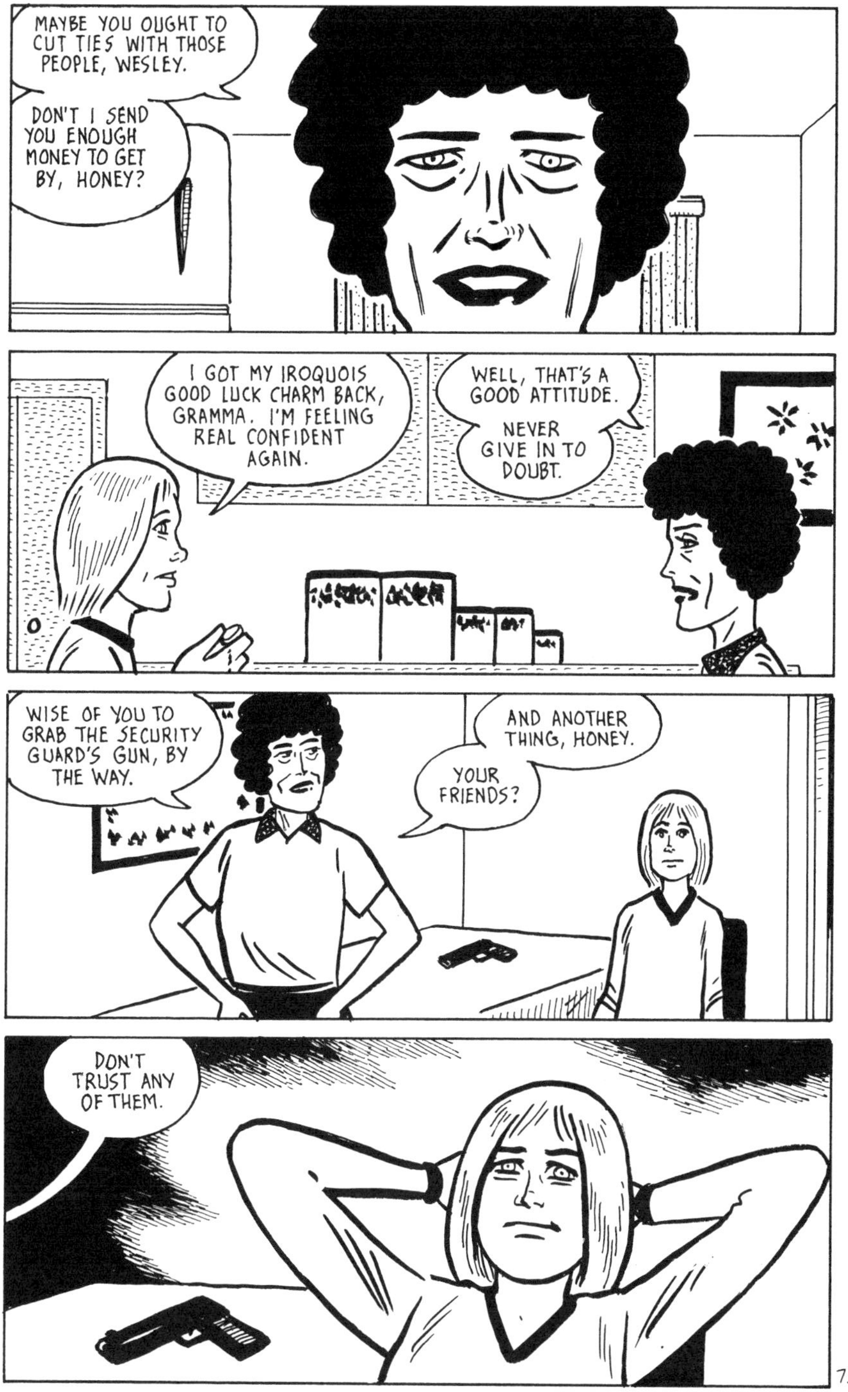
MAYBE YOU OUGHT TO CUT TIES WITH THOSE PEOPLE, WESLEY.
DON'T I SEND YOU ENOUGH MONEY TO GET BY, HONEY?
I GOT MY IROQUOIS GOOD LUCK CHARM BACK, GRAMMA. I'M FEELING REAL CONFIDENT AGAIN.
WELL, THAT'S A GOOD ATTITUDE.
NEVER GIVE IN TO DOUBT.
WISE OF YOU TO GRAB THE SECURITY GUARD'S GUN, BY THE WAY.
AND ANOTHER THING, HONEY.
YOUR FRIENDS?
DON'T TRUST ANY OF THEM.

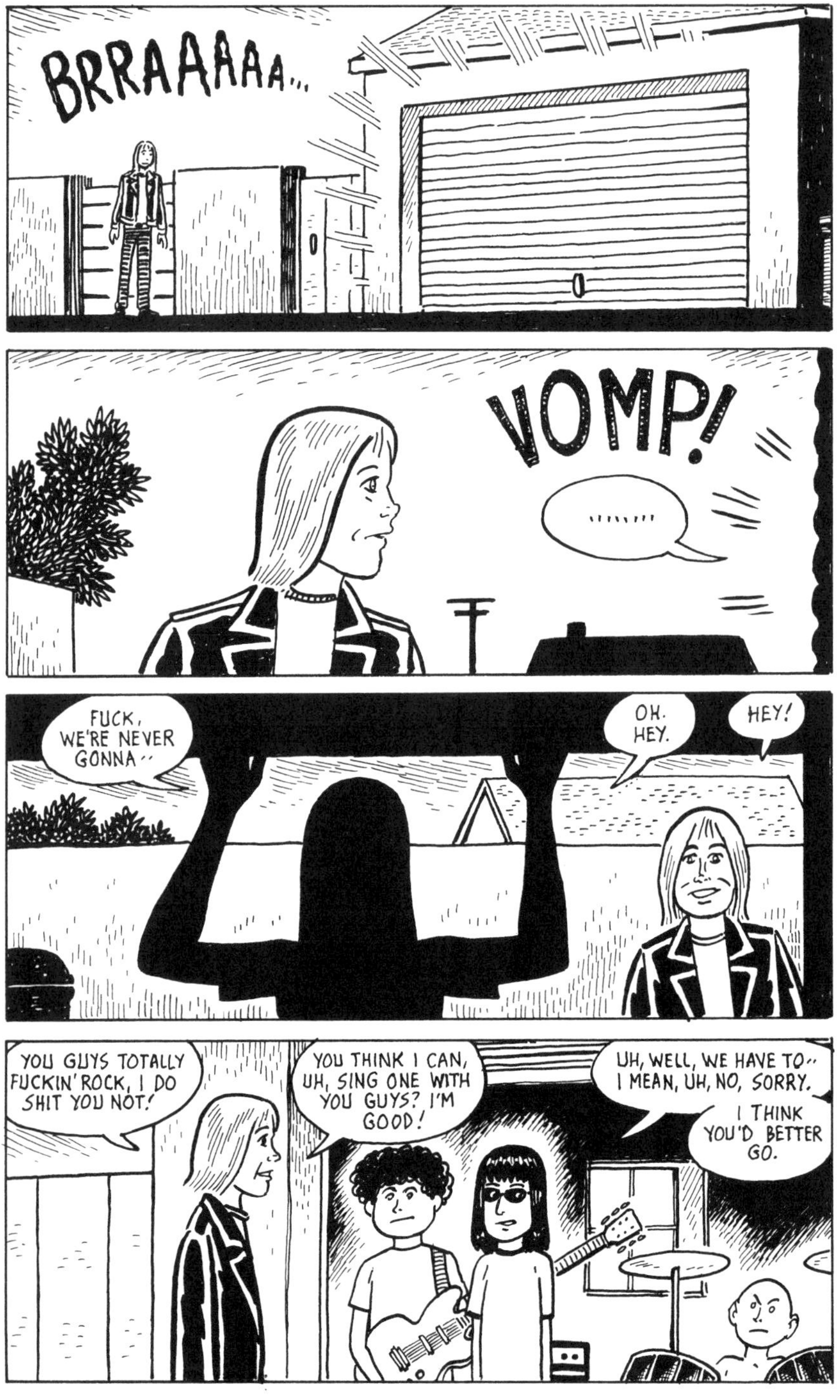
BRRAAAAA...
VOMP!
...,,,,,,
FUCK, WE'RE NEVER GONNA..
OH. HEY.
HEY!
YOU GUYS TOTALLY FUCKIN' ROCK, I DO SHIT YOU NOT!
YOU THINK I CAN, UH, SING ONE WITH YOU GUYS? I'M GOOD!
UH, WELL, WE HAVE TO.. I MEAN, UH, NO, SORRY.
I THINK YOU'D BETTER GO.

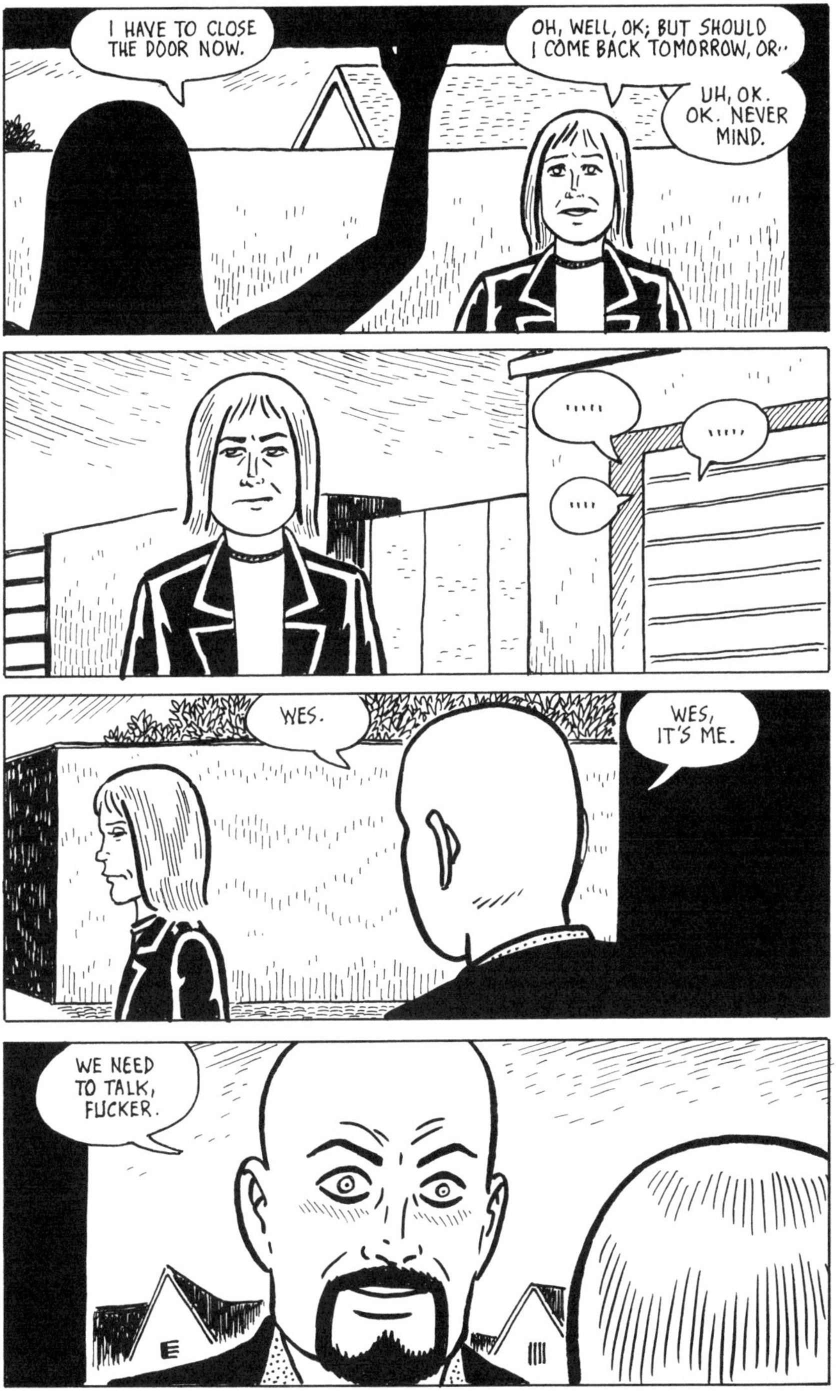
I HAVE TO CLOSE THE DOOR NOW.
OH, WELL, OK; BUT SHOULD I COME BACK TOMORROW, OR..
UH, OK. OK. NEVER MIND.
.....
.....
....
WES.
WES, IT'S ME.
WE NEED TO TALK, FUCKER.

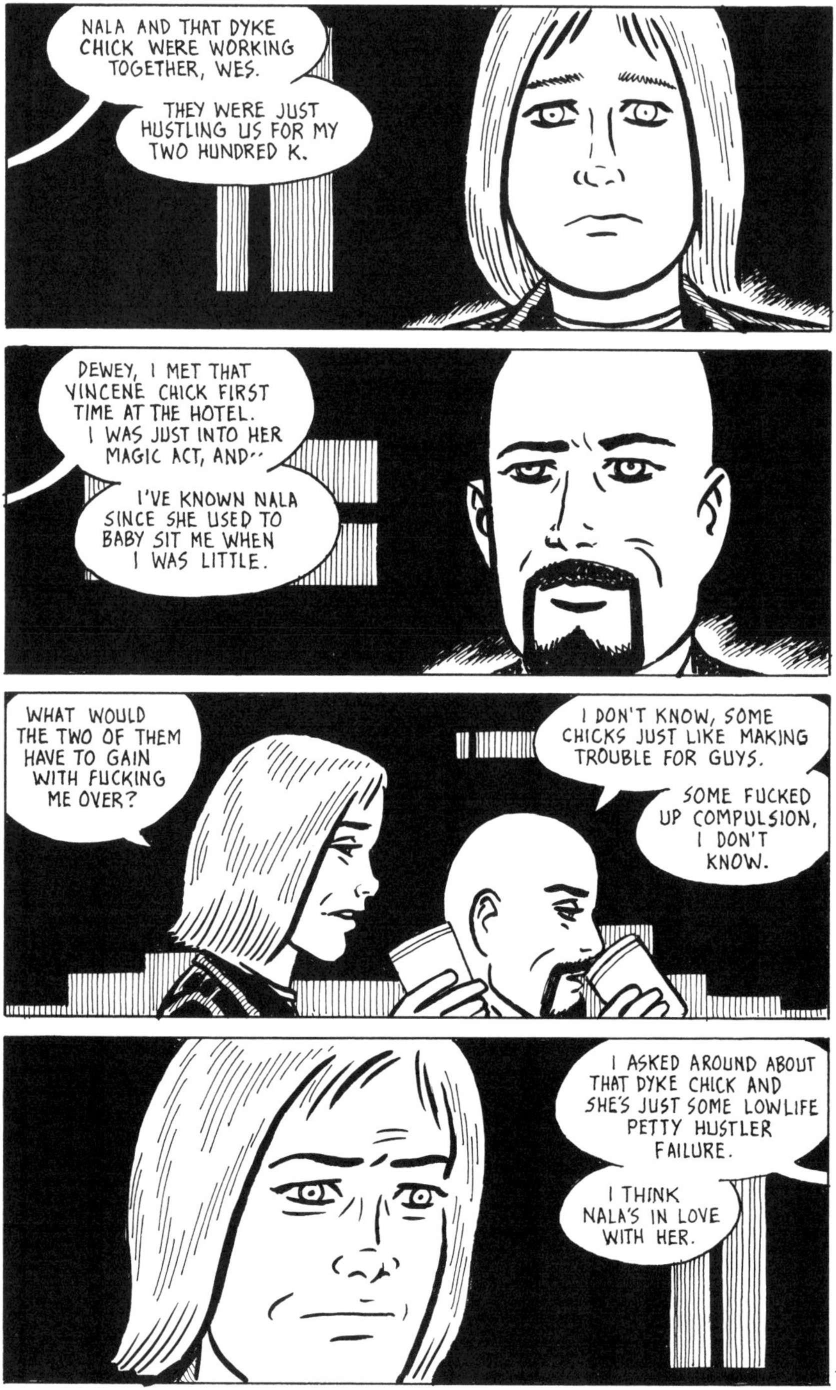
NALA AND THAT DYKE CHICK WERE WORKING TOGETHER, WES.
THEY WERE JUST HUSTLING US FOR MY TWO HUNDRED K.
DEWEY, I MET THAT VINCENE CHICK FIRST TIME AT THE HOTEL. I WAS JUST INTO HER MAGIC ACT, AND--
I'VE KNOWN NALA SINCE SHE USED TO BABY SIT ME WHEN I WAS LITTLE.
WHAT WOULD THE TWO OF THEM HAVE TO GAIN WITH FUCKING ME OVER?
I DON'T KNOW, SOME CHICKS JUST LIKE MAKING TROUBLE FOR GUYS.
SOME FUCKED UP COMPULSION, I DON'T KNOW.
I ASKED AROUND ABOUT THAT DYKE CHICK AND SHE'S JUST SOME LOWLIFE PETTY HUSTLER FAILURE.
I THINK NALA'S IN LOVE WITH HER.

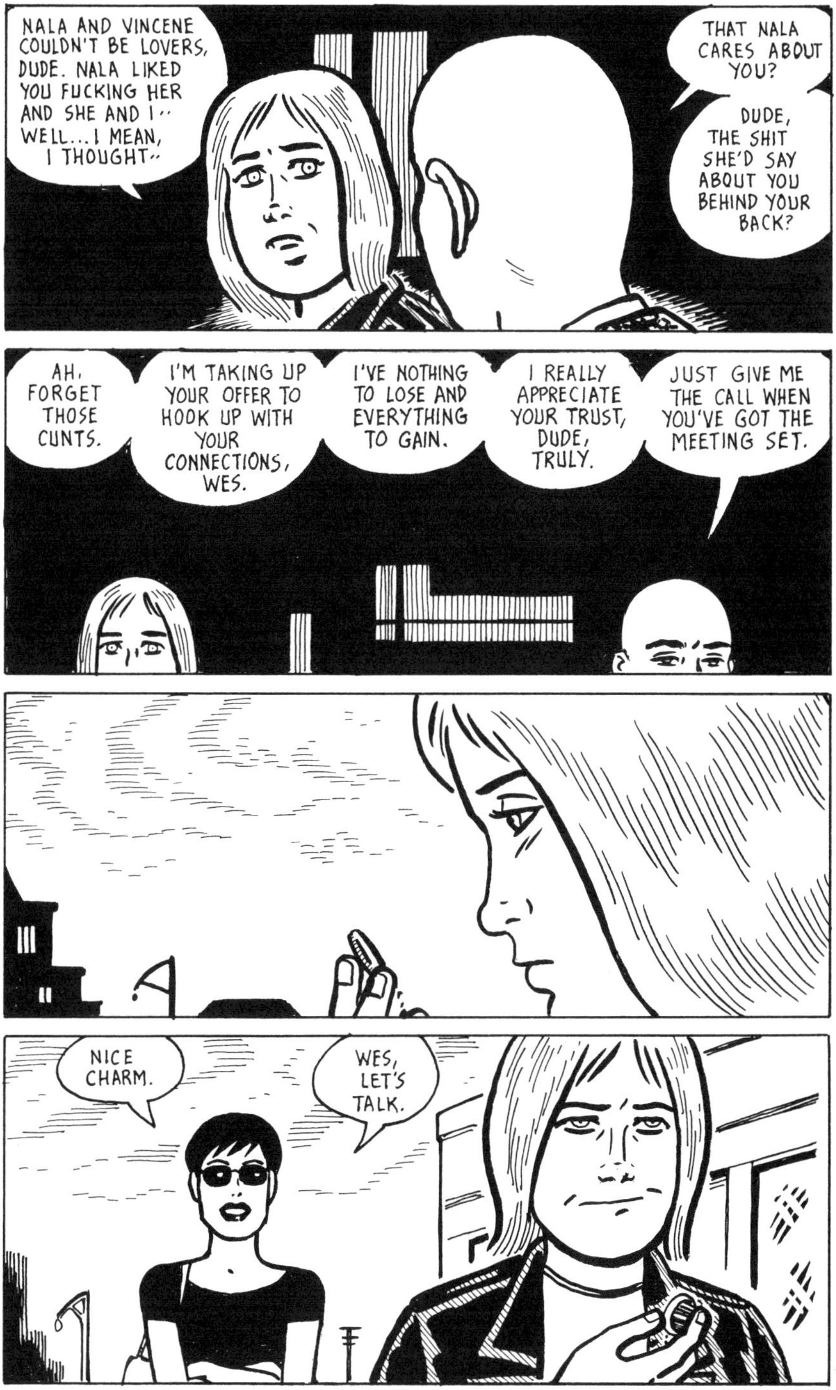
NALA AND VINCENE COULDN'T BE LOVERS, DUDE. NALA LIKED YOU FUCKING HER AND SHE AND I.. WELL... I MEAN, I THOUGHT..
THAT NALA CARES ABOUT YOU?
DUDE, THE SHIT SHE'D SAY ABOUT YOU BEHIND YOUR BACK?
AH, FORGET THOSE CUNTS.
I'M TAKING UP YOUR OFFER TO HOOK UP WITH YOUR CONNECTIONS, WES.
I'VE NOTHING TO LOSE AND EVERYTHING TO GAIN.
I REALLY APPRECIATE YOUR TRUST, DUDE, TRULY.
JUST GIVE ME THE CALL WHEN YOU'VE GOT THE MEETING SET.
NICE CHARM.
WES, LET'S TALK.

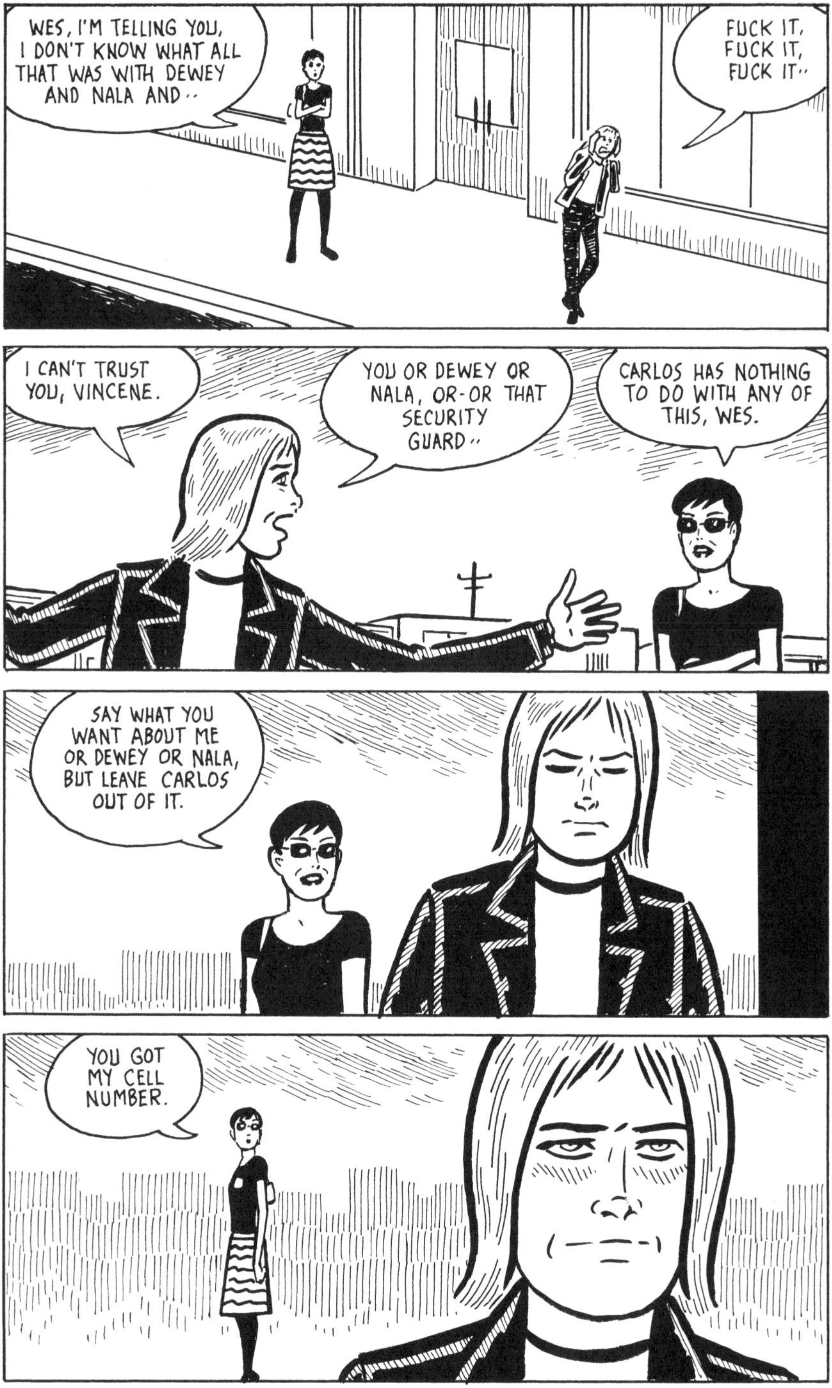
WES, I'M TELLING YOU, I DON'T KNOW WHAT ALL THAT WAS WITH DEWEY AND NALA AND..
FUCK IT, FUCK IT, FUCK IT..
I CAN'T TRUST YOU, VINCENE.
YOU OR DEWEY OR NALA, OR-OR THAT SECURITY GUARD..
CARLOS HAS NOTHING TO DO WITH ANY OF THIS, WES.
SAY WHAT YOU WANT ABOUT ME OR DEWEY OR NALA, BUT LEAVE CARLOS OUT OF IT.
YOU GOT MY CELL NUMBER.

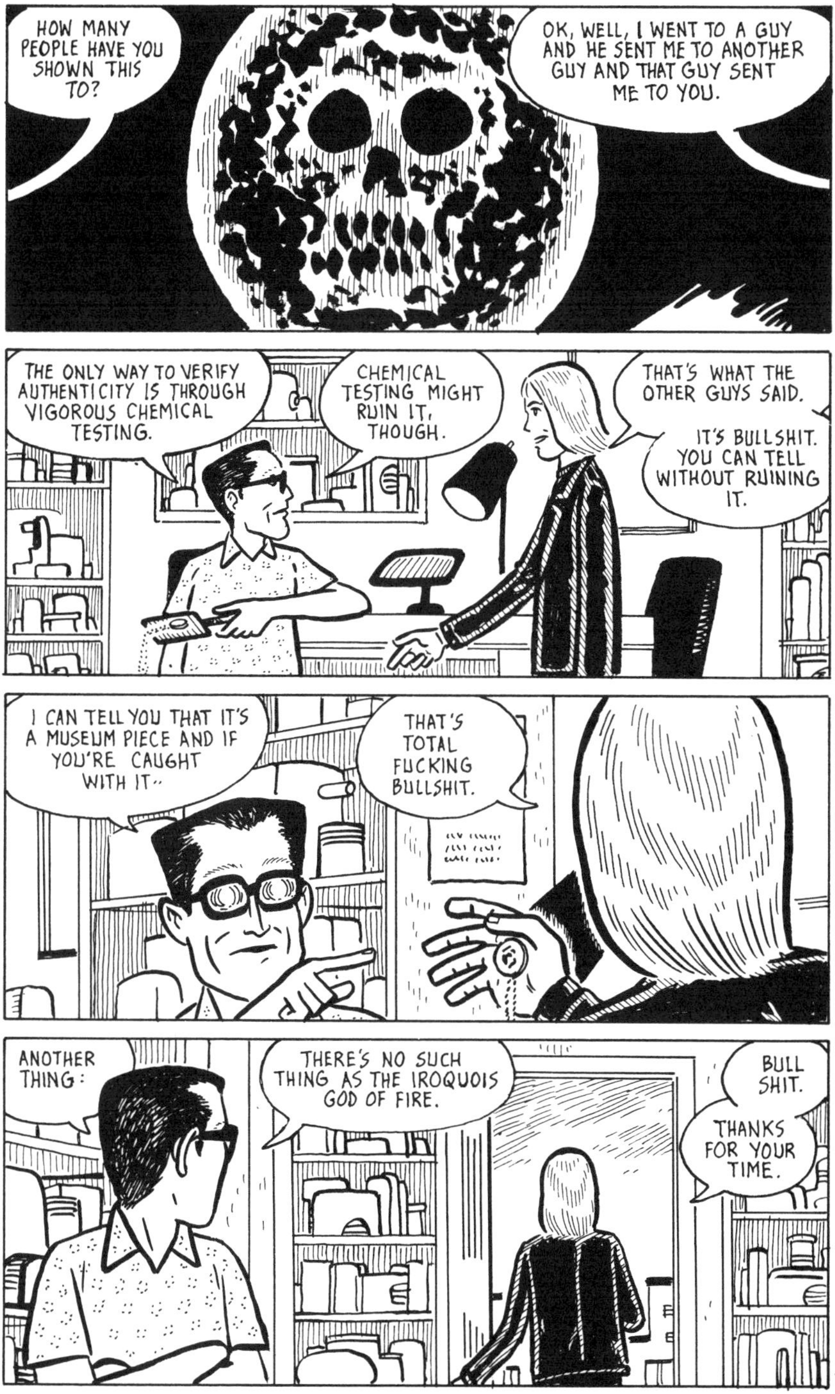
HOW MANY PEOPLE HAVE YOU SHOWN THIS TO?
OK, WELL, I WENT TO A GUY AND HE SENT ME TO ANOTHER GUY AND THAT GUY SENT ME TO YOU.
THE ONLY WAY TO VERIFY AUTHENTICITY IS THROUGH VIGOROUS CHEMICAL TESTING.
CHEMICAL TESTING MIGHT RUIN IT, THOUGH.
THAT'S WHAT THE OTHER GUYS SAID.
IT'S BULLSHIT. YOU CAN TELL WITHOUT RUINING IT.
I CAN TELL YOU THAT IT'S A MUSEUM PIECE AND IF YOU'RE CAUGHT WITH IT..
THAT'S TOTAL FUCKING BULLSHIT.
ANOTHER THING:
THERE'S NO SUCH THING AS THE IROQUOIS GOD OF FIRE.
BULL SHIT.
THANKS FOR YOUR TIME.

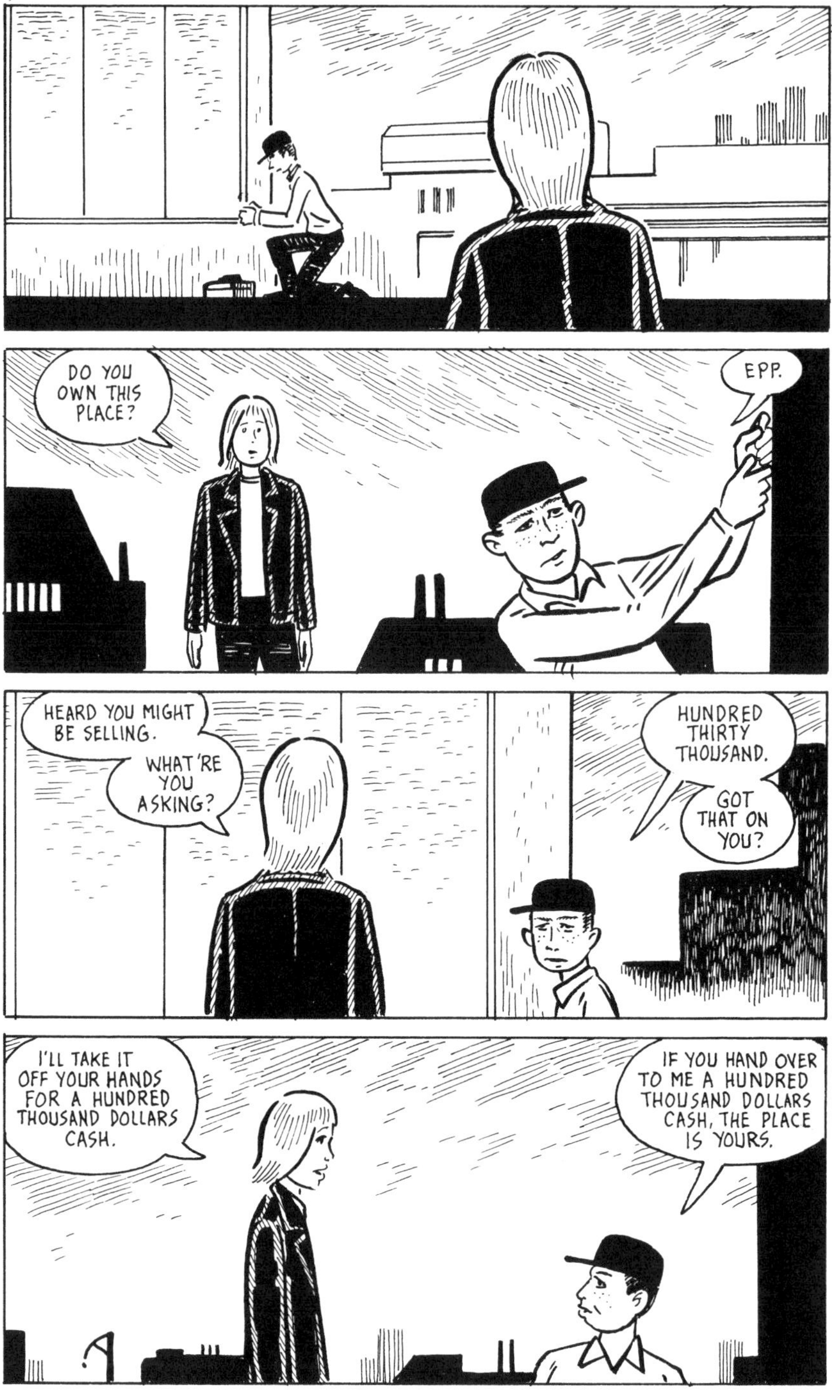
DO YOU OWN THIS PLACE?
EPP.
HEARD YOU MIGHT BE SELLING.
WHAT'RE YOU ASKING?
HUNDRED THIRTY THOUSAND.
GOT THAT ON YOU?
I'LL TAKE IT OFF YOUR HANDS FOR A HUNDRED THOUSAND DOLLARS CASH.
IF YOU HAND OVER TO ME A HUNDRED THOUSAND DOLLARS CASH, THE PLACE IS YOURS.

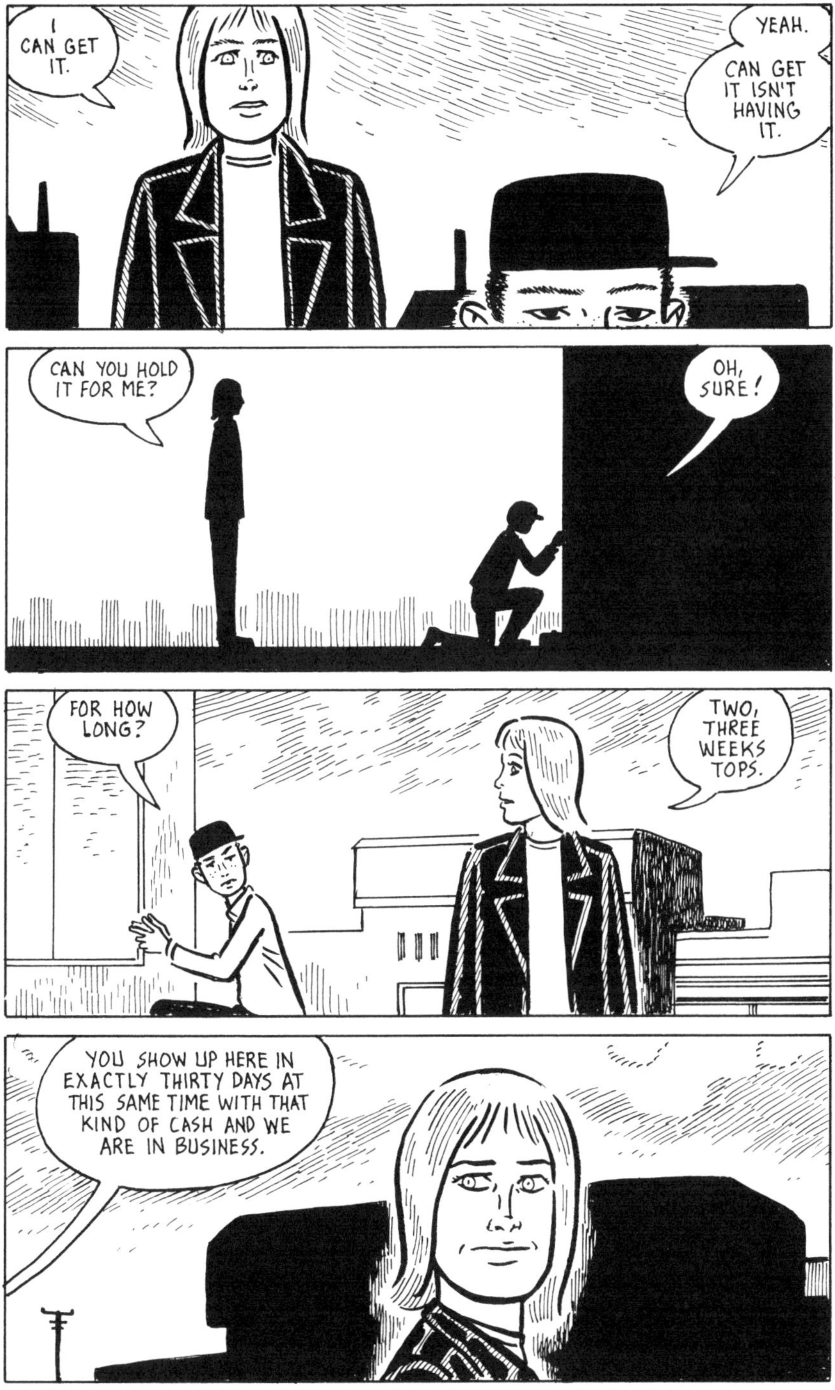
I CAN GET IT.
YEAH.
CAN GET IT ISN'T HAVING IT.
CAN YOU HOLD IT FOR ME?
OH, SURE!
FOR HOW LONG?
TWO, THREE WEEKS TOPS.
YOU SHOW UP HERE IN EXACTLY THIRTY DAYS AT THIS SAME TIME WITH THAT KIND OF CASH AND WE ARE IN BUSINESS.

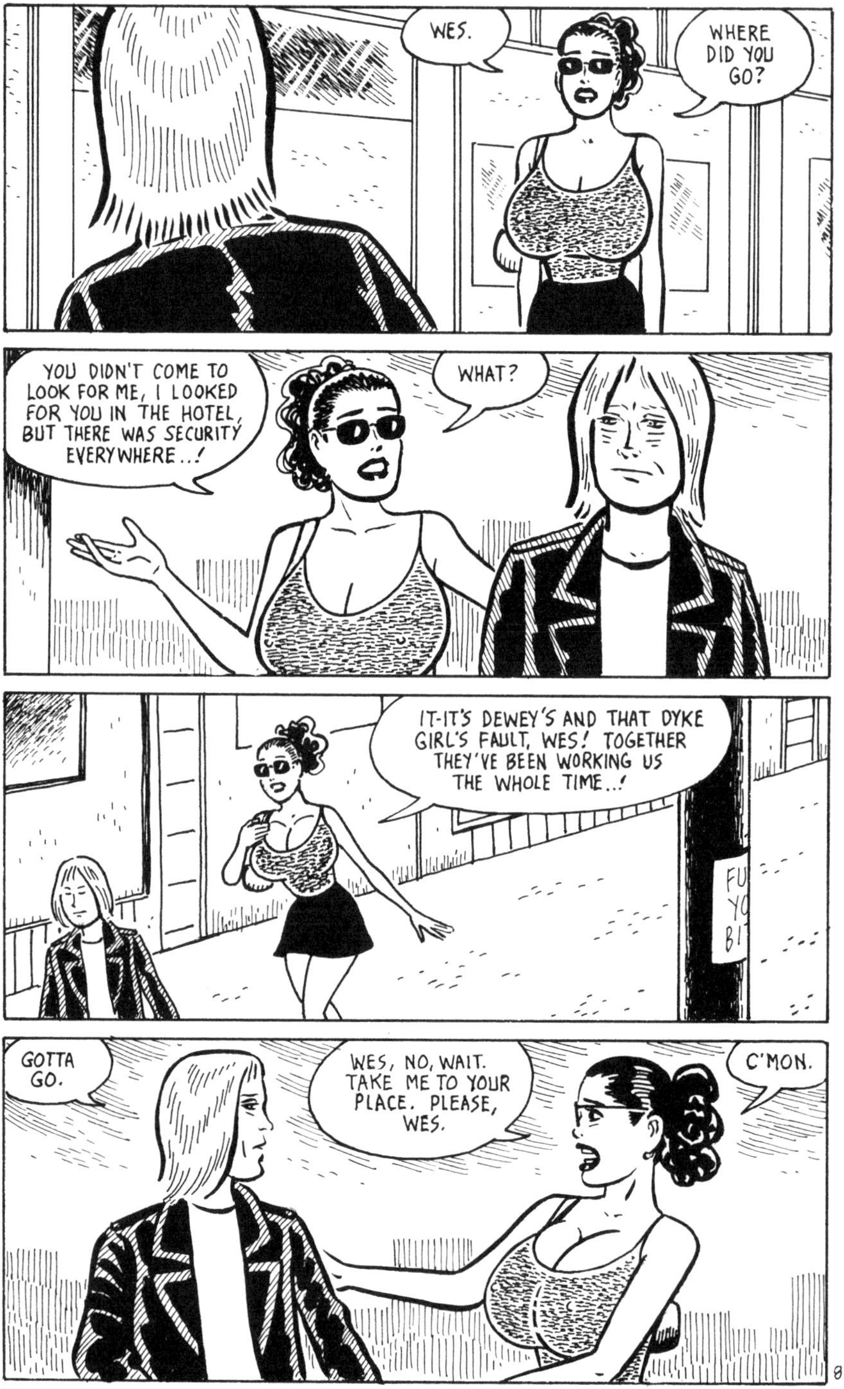
WES.
WHERE DID YOU GO?
YOU DIDN'T COME TO LOOK FOR ME, I LOOKED FOR YOU IN THE HOTEL, BUT THERE WAS SECURITY EVERYWHERE..!
WHAT?
IT-IT'S DEWEY'S AND THAT DYKE GIRL'S FAULT, WES! TOGETHER THEY'VE BEEN WORKING US THE WHOLE TIME..!
GOTTA GO.
WES, NO, WAIT. TAKE ME TO YOUR PLACE. PLEASE, WES.
C'MON.

WES, PLEASE.

I CAN'T LOSE YOU AGAIN.

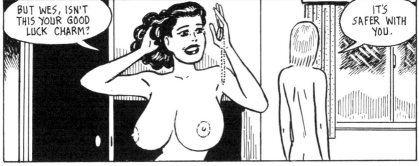

BUT WES, ISN'T THIS YOUR GOOD LUCK CHARM?

IT'S SAFER WITH YOU.

GUY...

I KNOW HOW MUCH IT MEANS TO YOU.

I HAVE TO LEARN HOW TO GET ALONG WITHOUT A SUPERSTITIOUS CRUTCH, NAL.

83

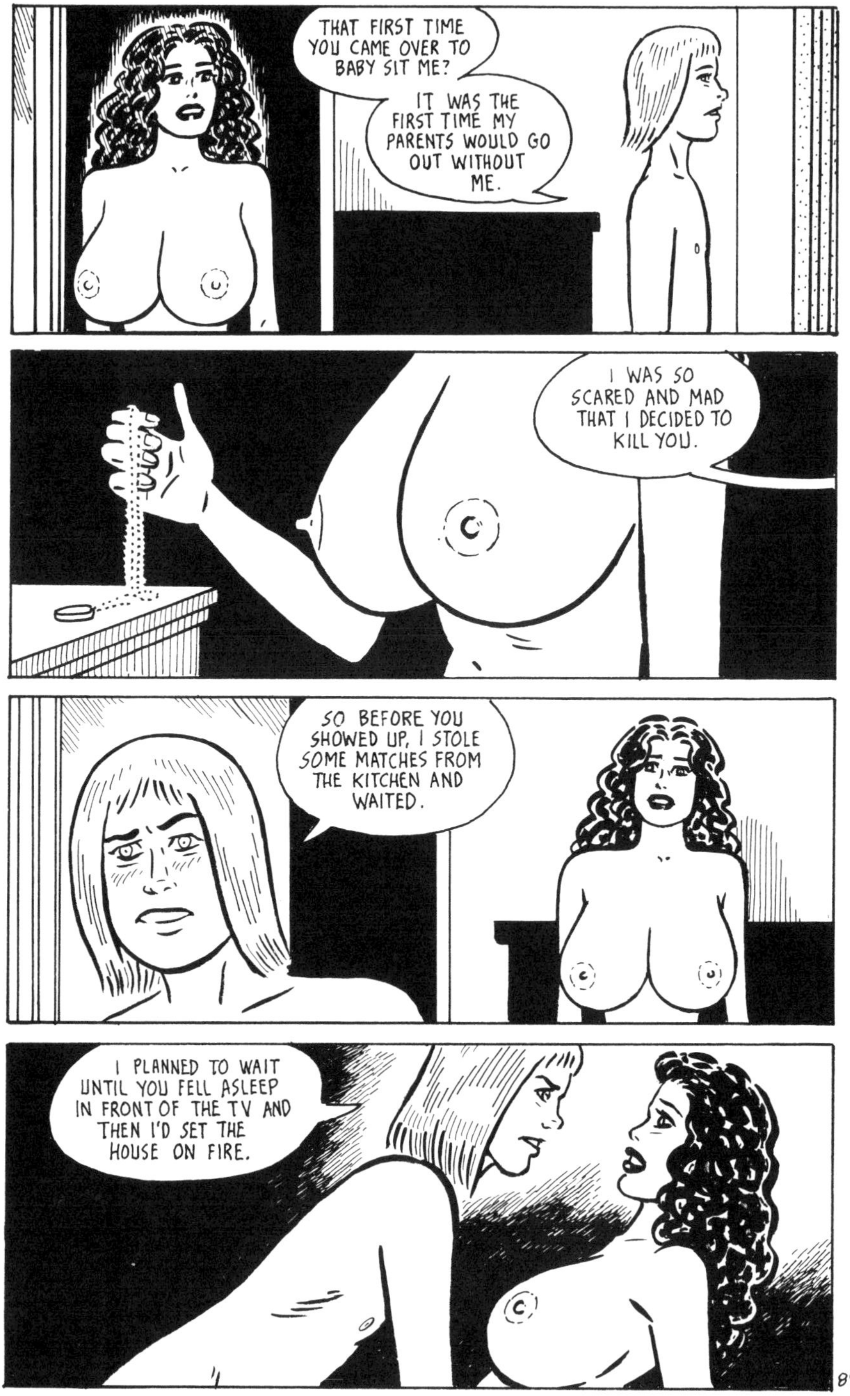
THAT FIRST TIME YOU CAME OVER TO BABY SIT ME?
IT WAS THE FIRST TIME MY PARENTS WOULD GO OUT WITHOUT ME.
I WAS SO SCARED AND MAD THAT I DECIDED TO KILL YOU.
SO BEFORE YOU SHOWED UP, I STOLE SOME MATCHES FROM THE KITCHEN AND WAITED.
I PLANNED TO WAIT UNTIL YOU FELL ASLEEP IN FRONT OF THE TV AND THEN I'D SET THE HOUSE ON FIRE.

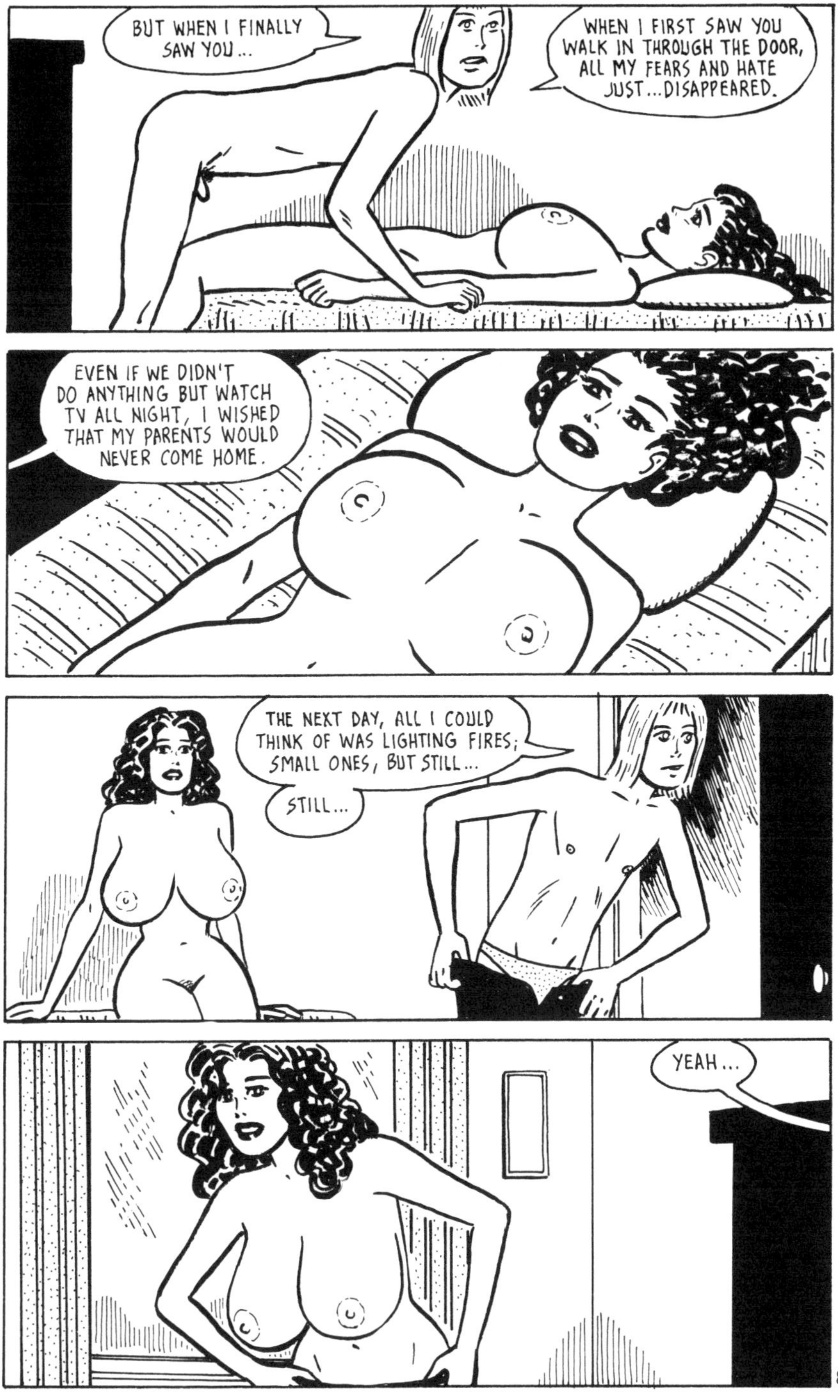
BUT WHEN I FINALLY SAW YOU...
WHEN I FIRST SAW YOU WALK IN THROUGH THE DOOR, ALL MY FEARS AND HATE JUST...DISAPPEARED.
EVEN IF WE DIDN'T DO ANYTHING BUT WATCH TV ALL NIGHT, I WISHED THAT MY PARENTS WOULD NEVER COME HOME.
THE NEXT DAY, ALL I COULD THINK OF WAS LIGHTING FIRES; SMALL ONES, BUT STILL...
STILL...
YEAH...

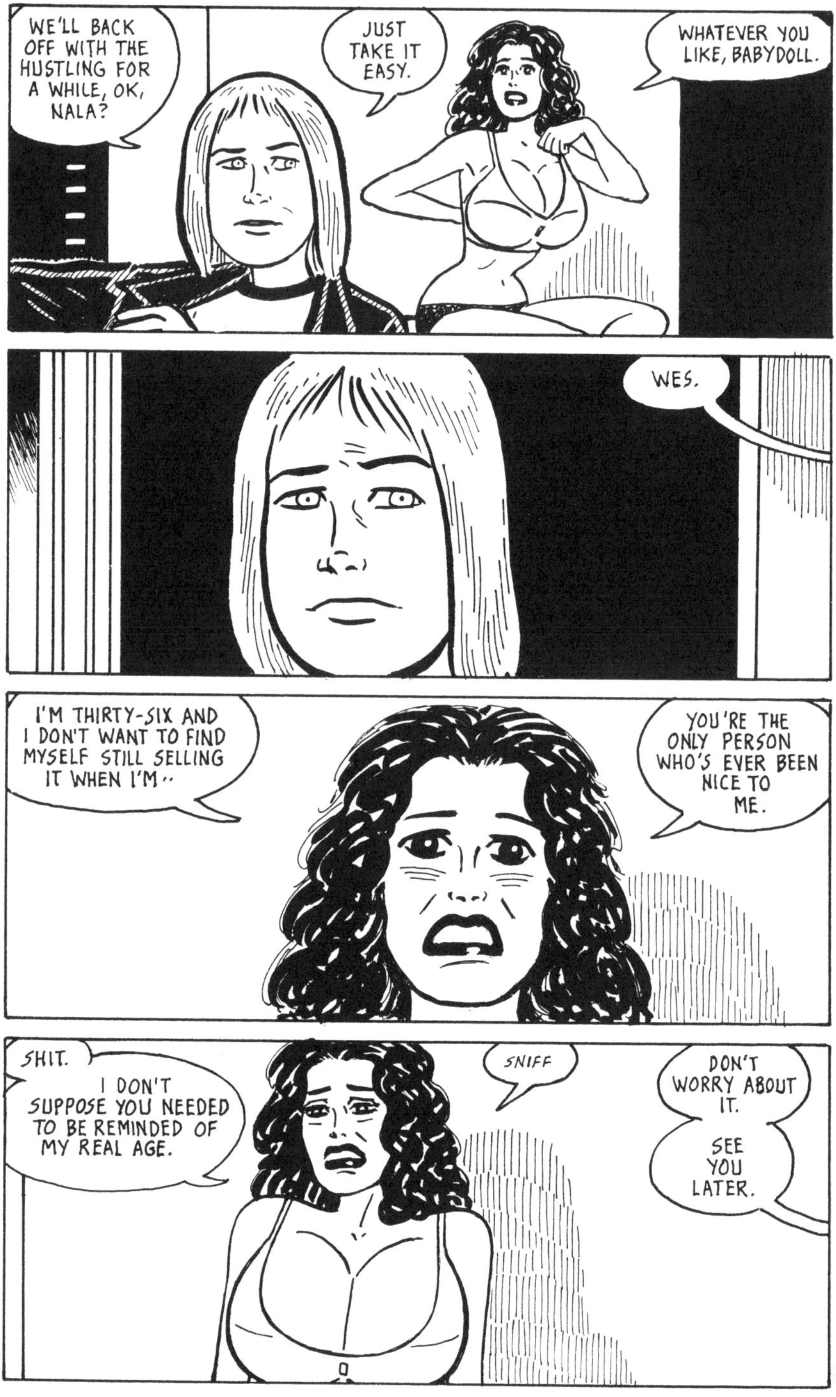
WE'LL BACK OFF WITH THE HUSTLING FOR A WHILE, OK, NALA?
JUST TAKE IT EASY.
WHATEVER YOU LIKE, BABYDOLL.
WES.
I'M THIRTY-SIX AND I DON'T WANT TO FIND MYSELF STILL SELLING IT WHEN I'M..
YOU'RE THE ONLY PERSON WHO'S EVER BEEN NICE TO ME.
SHIT.
I DON'T SUPPOSE YOU NEEDED TO BE REMINDED OF MY REAL AGE.
SNIFF
DON'T WORRY ABOUT IT.
SEE YOU LATER.

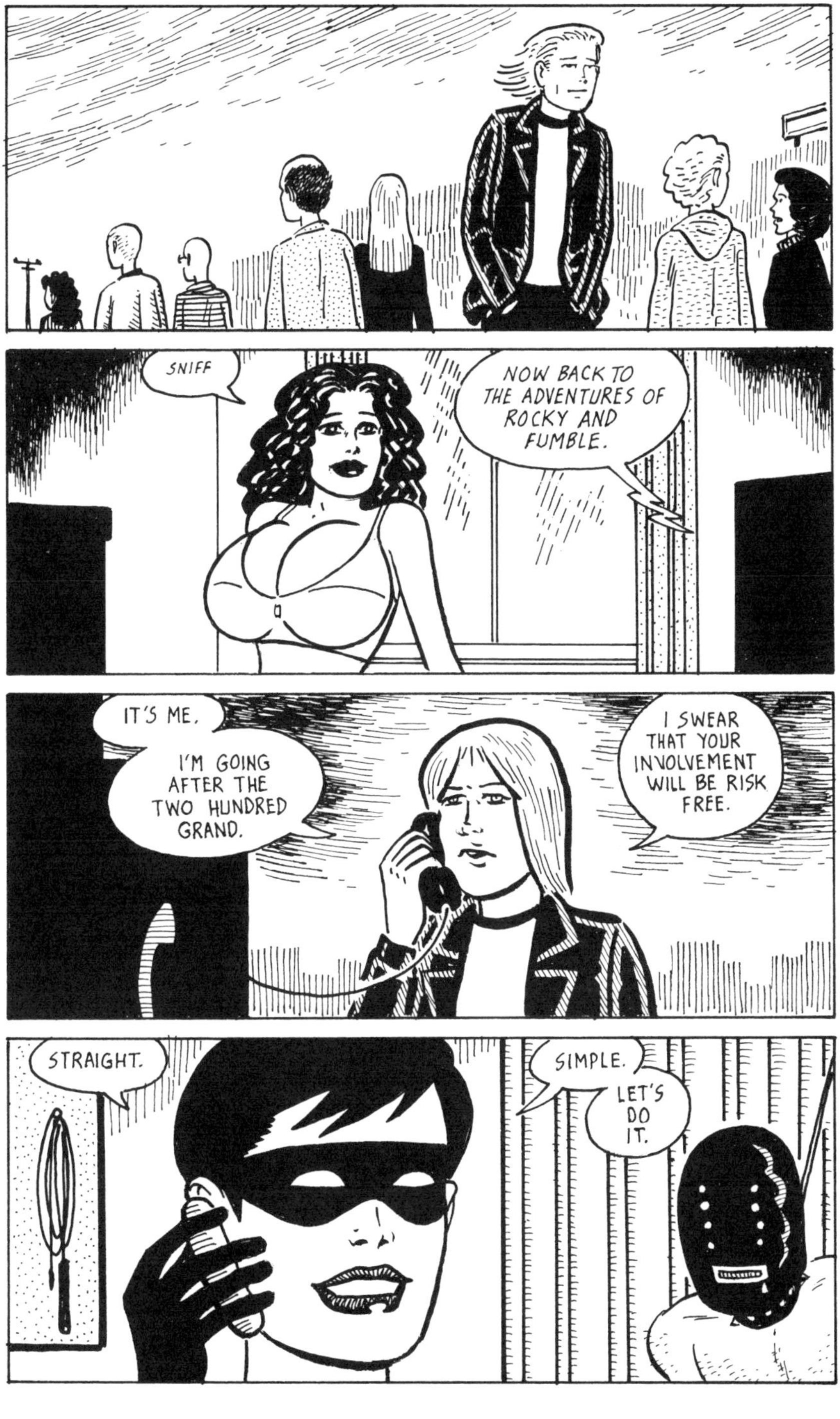
SNIFF
NOW BACK TO THE ADVENTURES OF ROCKY AND FUMBLE.
IT'S ME.
I'M GOING AFTER THE TWO HUNDRED GRAND.
I SWEAR THAT YOUR INVOLVEMENT WILL BE RISK FREE.
STRAIGHT.
SIMPLE.
LET'S DO IT.

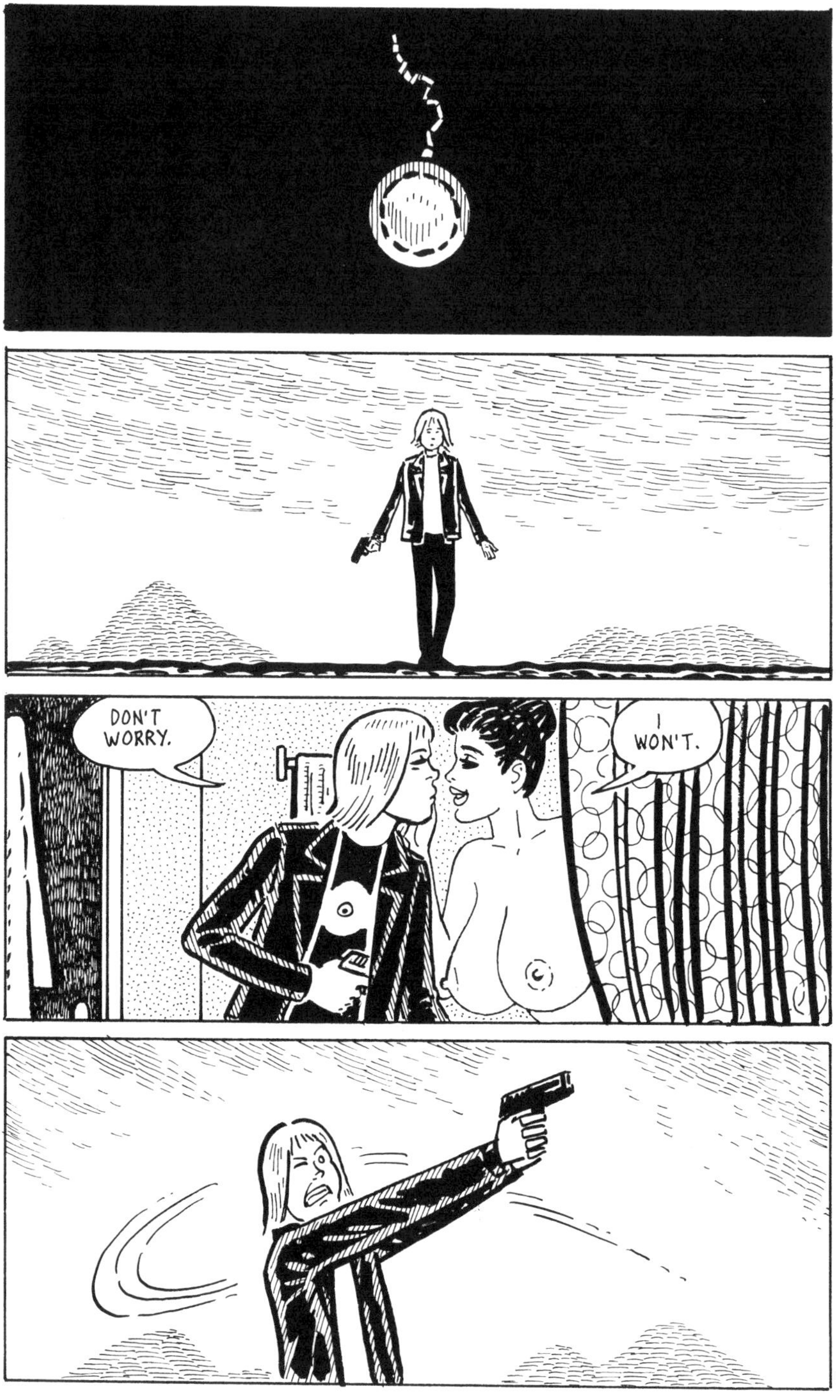
DON'T WORRY.
I WON'T.

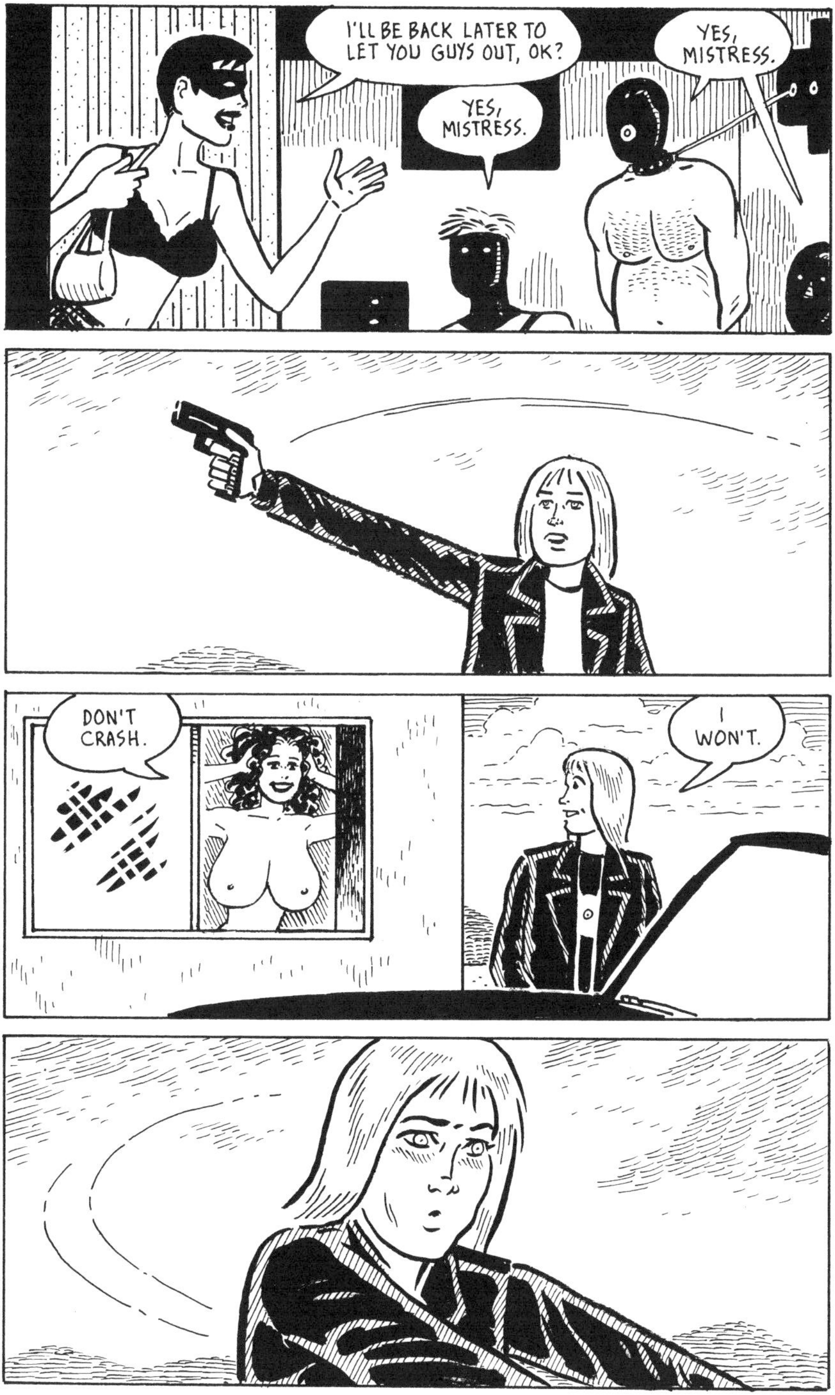
I'LL BE BACK LATER TO LET YOU GUYS OUT, OK?
YES, MISTRESS.
YES, MISTRESS.
DON'T CRASH.
I WON'T.

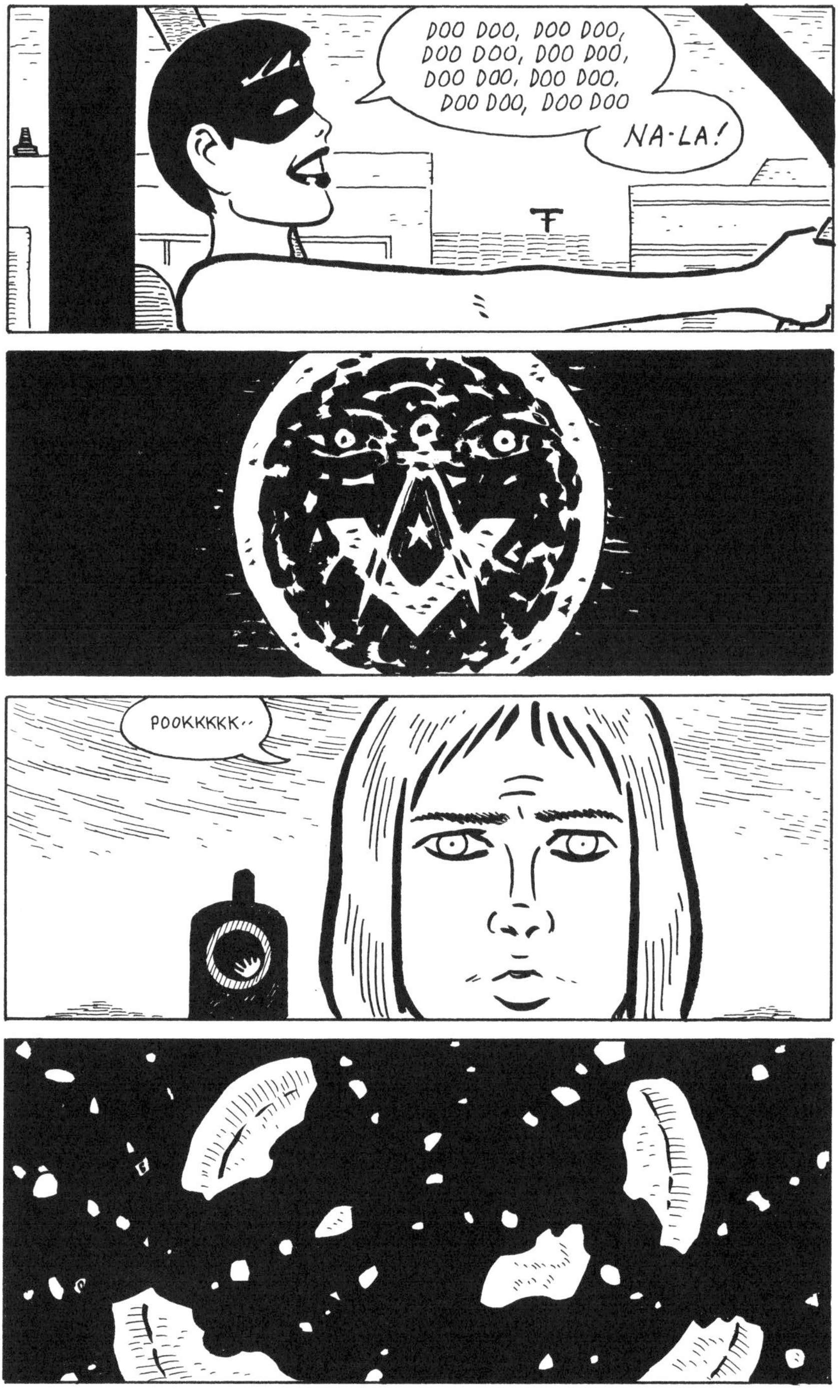
DOO DOO, DOO DOO, DOO DOO, DOO DOO, DOO DOO, DOO DOO, DOO DOO, DOO DOO
NA-LA!
POOKKKKK..

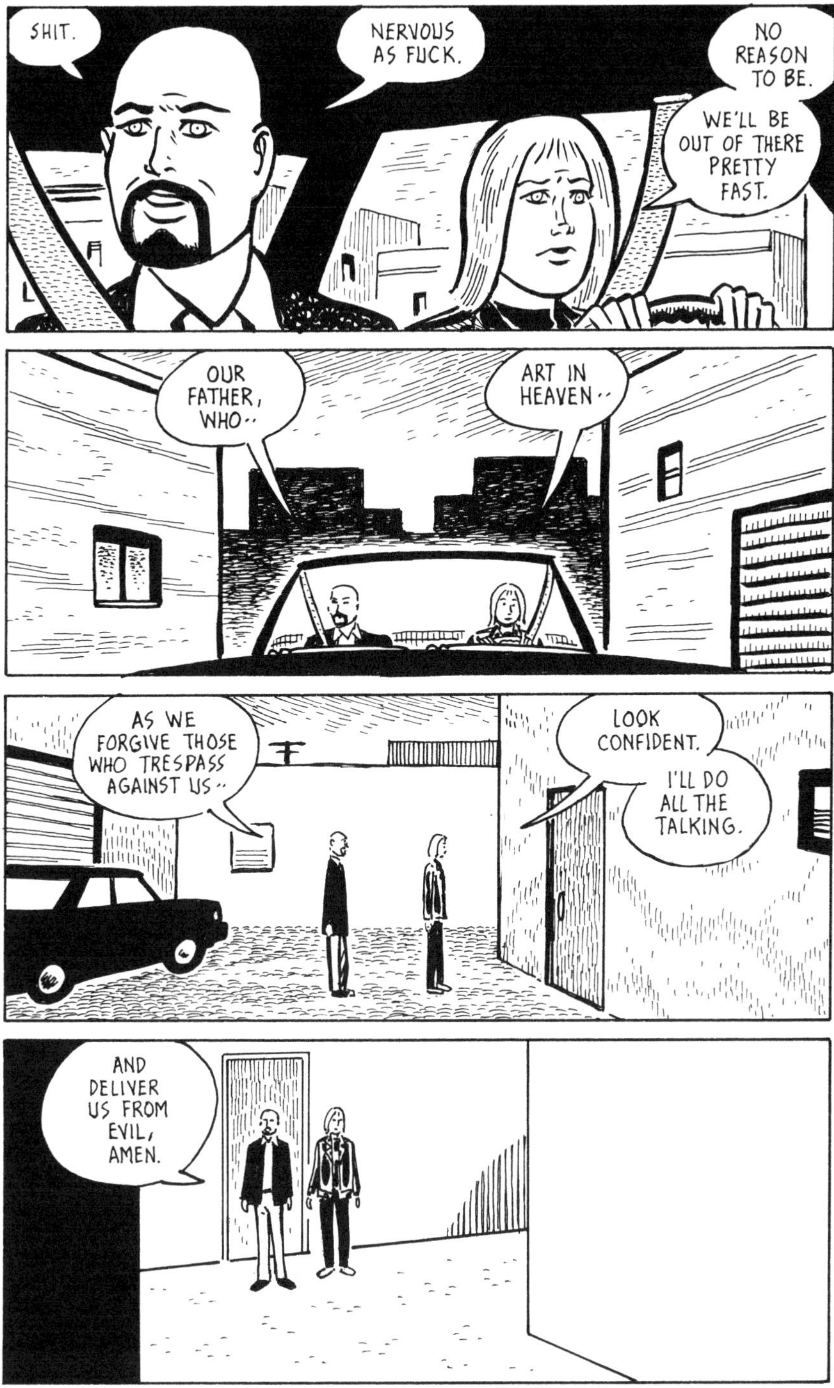
SHIT.
NERVOUS AS FUCK.
NO REASON TO BE.
WE'LL BE OUT OF THERE PRETTY FAST.
OUR FATHER, WHO..
ART IN HEAVEN..
AS WE FORGIVE THOSE WHO TRESPASS AGAINST US..
LOOK CONFIDENT.
I'LL DO ALL THE TALKING.
AND DELIVER US FROM EVIL, AMEN.

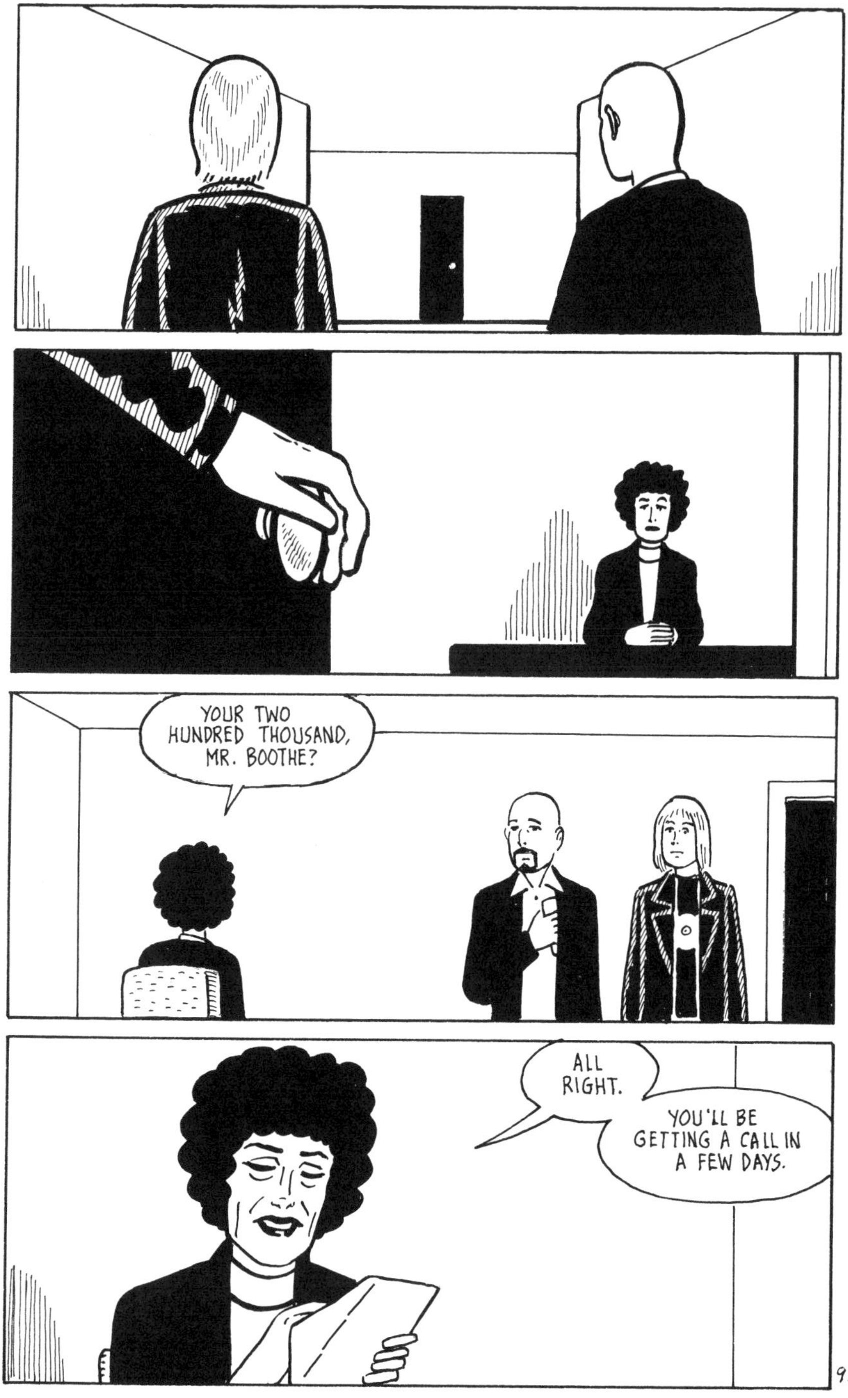
YOUR TWO HUNDRED THOUSAND, MR. BOOTHE?
ALL RIGHT.
YOU'LL BE GETTING A CALL IN A FEW DAYS.

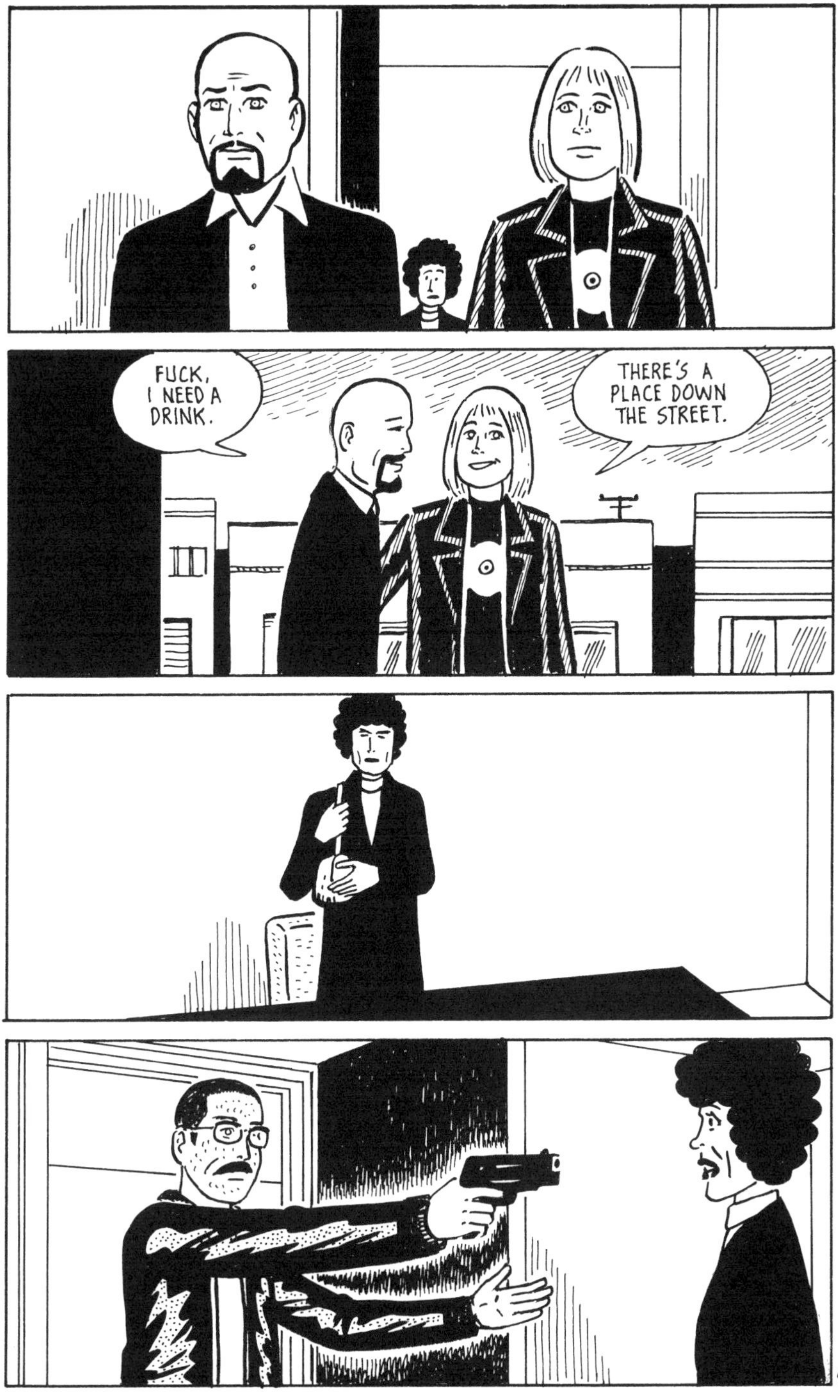
FUCK, I NEED A DRINK.
THERE'S A PLACE DOWN THE STREET.

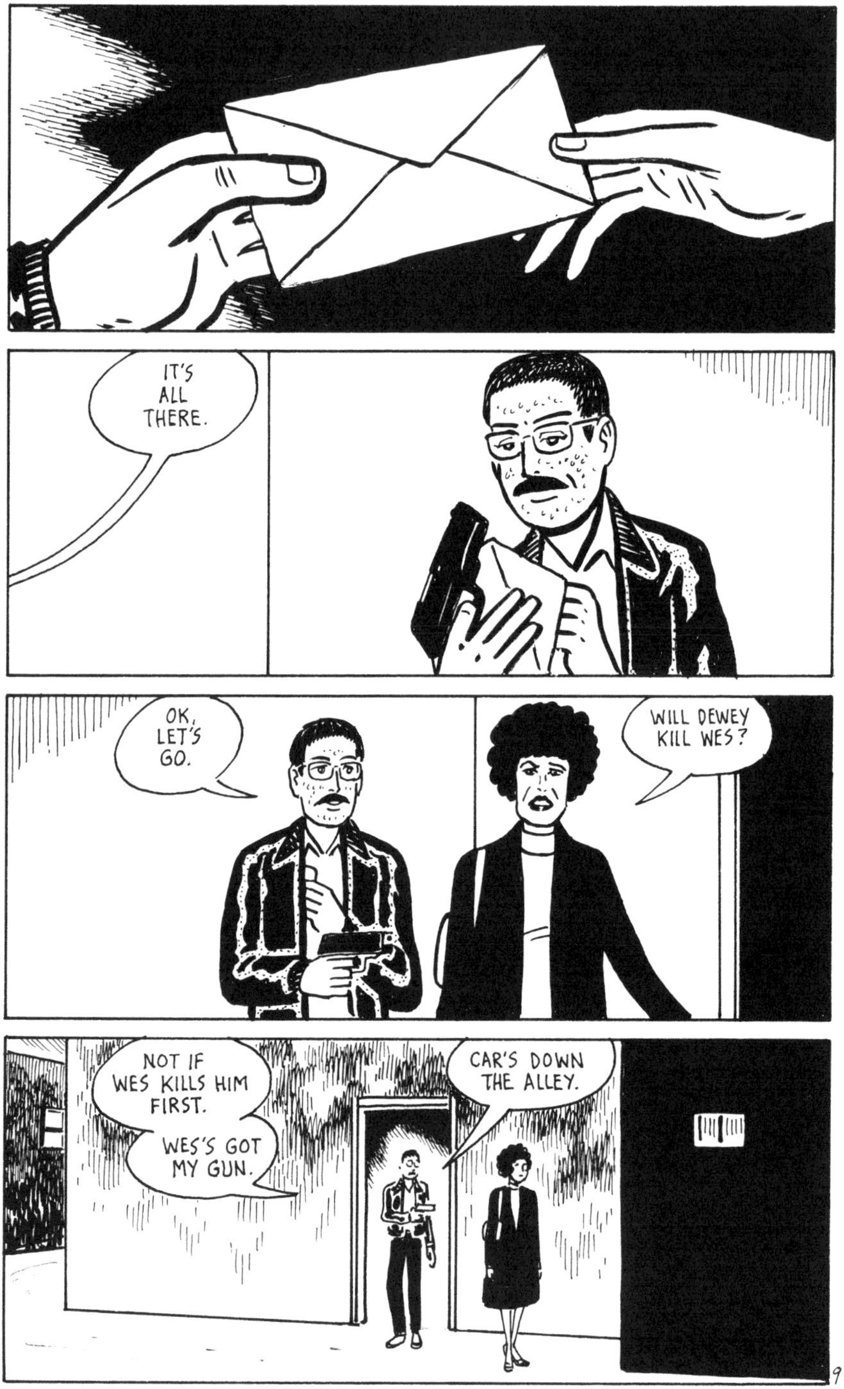
IT'S ALL THERE.
OK, LET'S GO.
WILL DEWEY KILL WES?
NOT IF WES KILLS HIM FIRST.
WES'S GOT MY GUN.
CAR'S DOWN THE ALLEY.

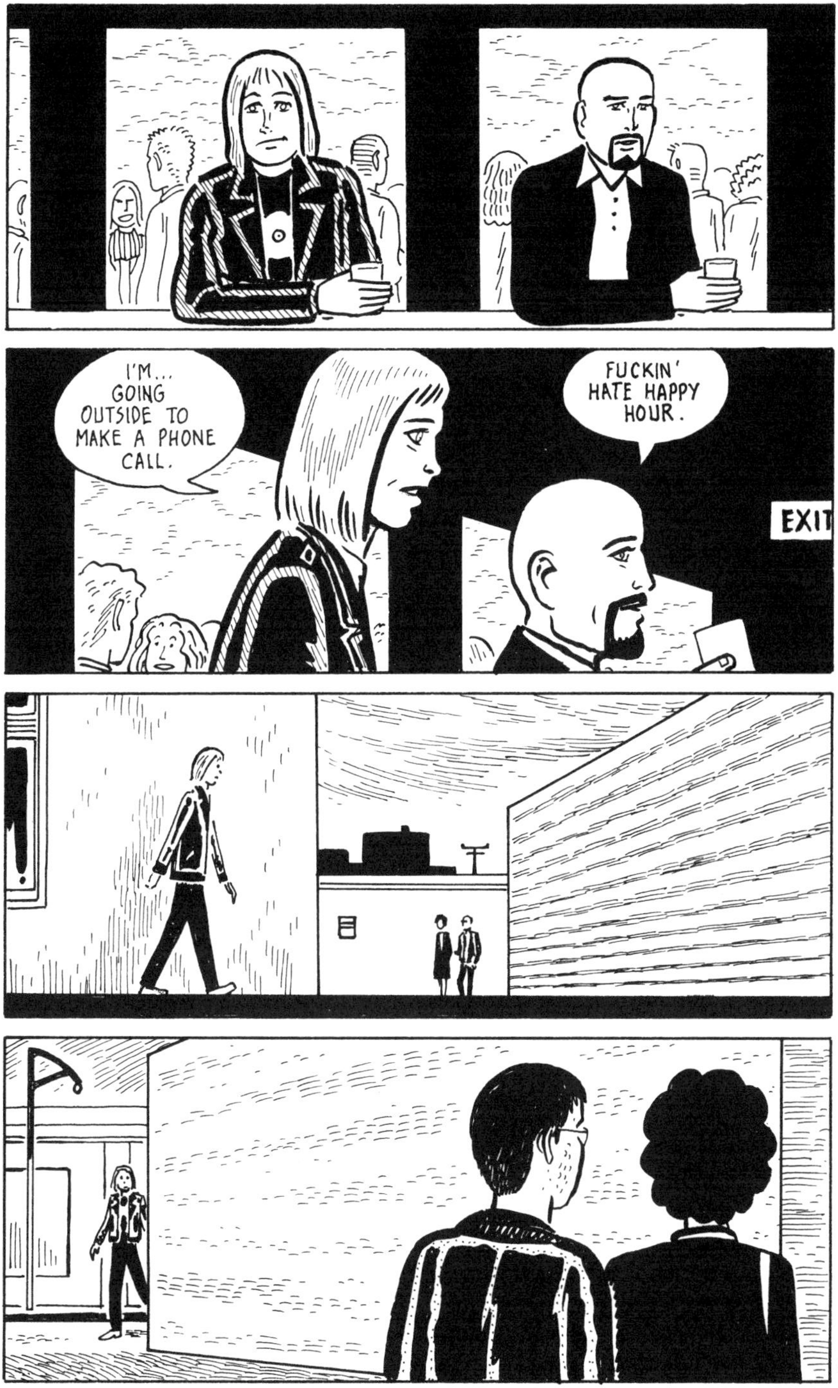
I'M... GOING OUTSIDE TO MAKE A PHONE CALL.
FUCKIN' HATE HAPPY HOUR.
EXIT

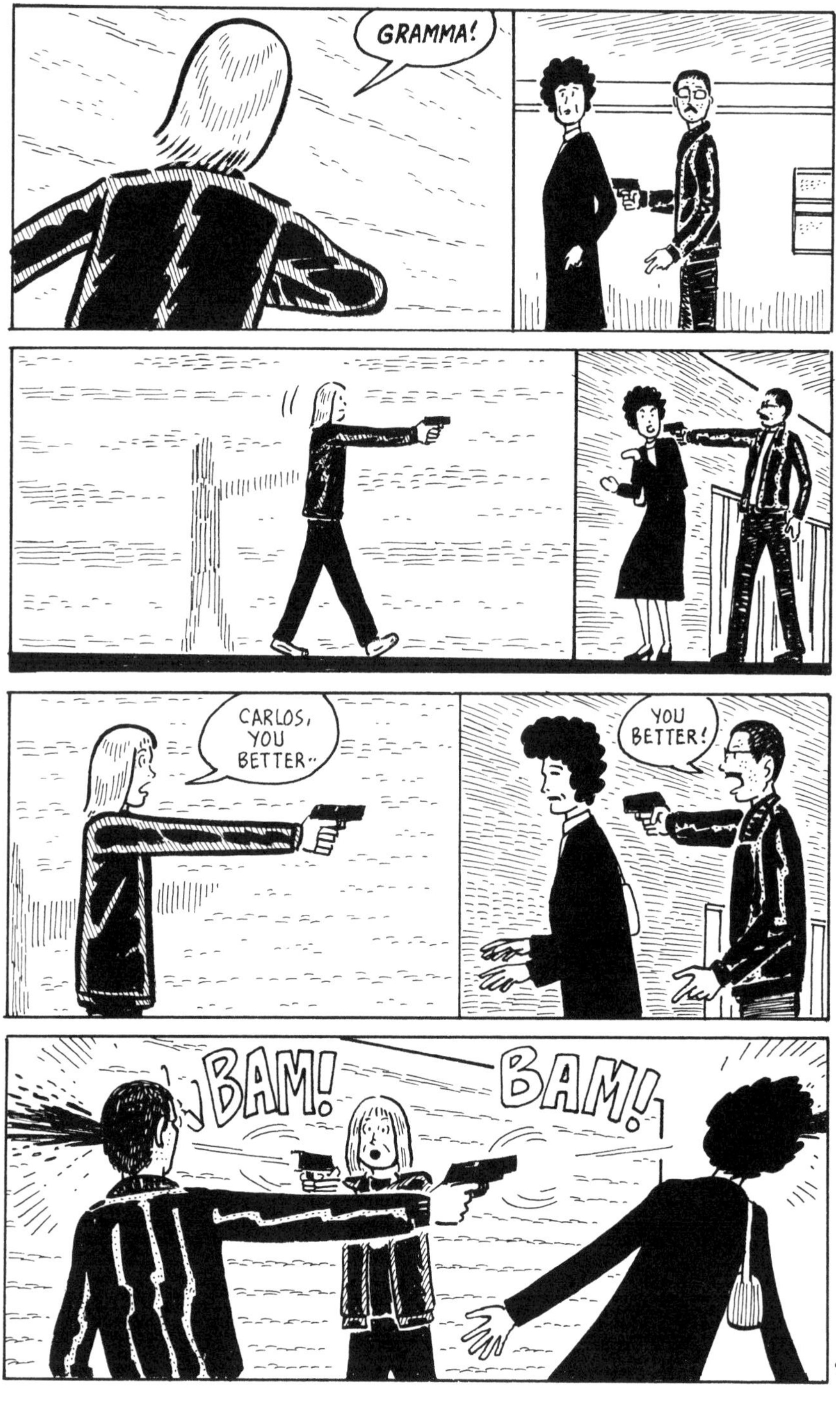
GRAMMA!
CARLOS, YOU BETTER..
YOU BETTER!
BAM!
BAM!

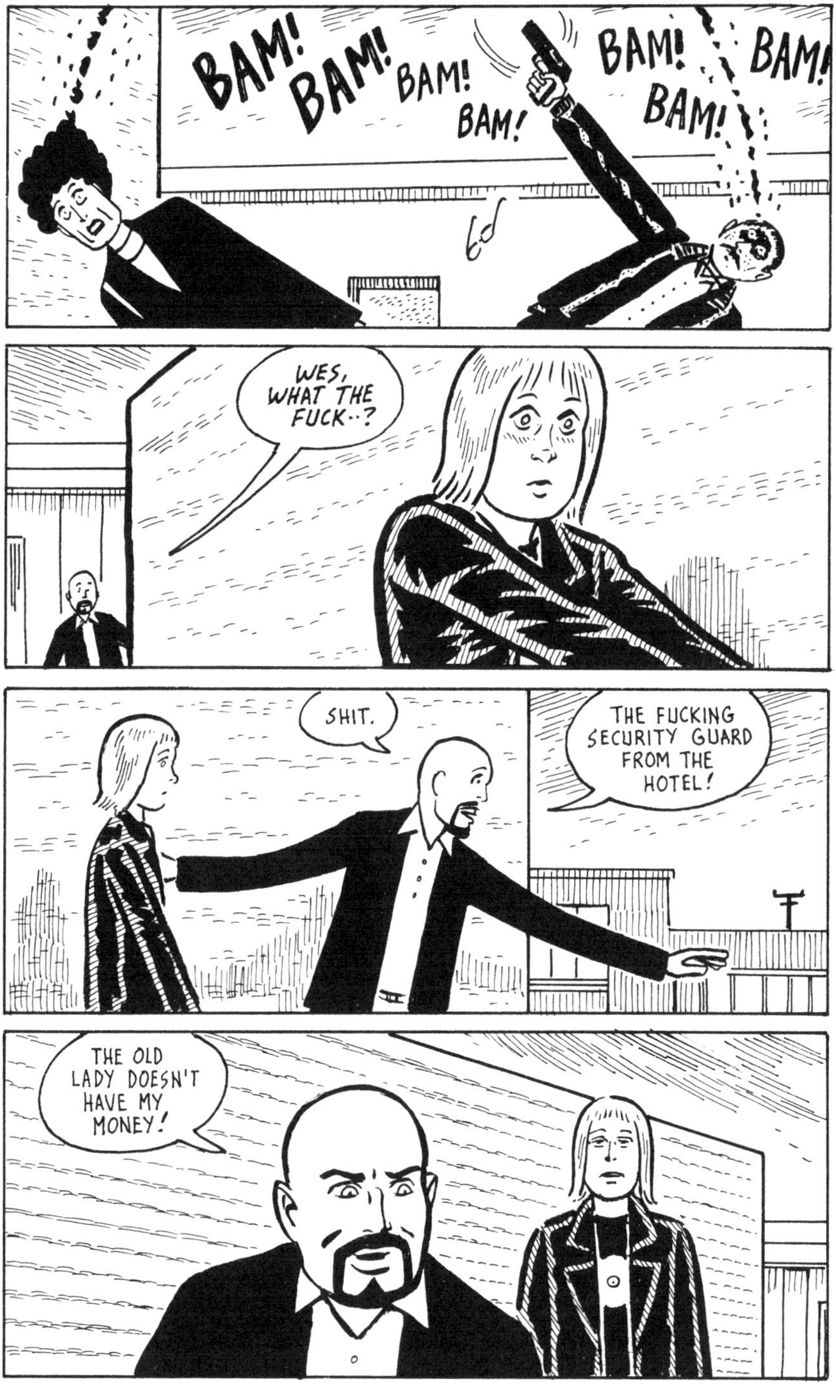

BAM!
BAM!
BAM!
BAM!
BAM!
BAM!
BAM!
WES, WHAT THE FUCK..?
SHIT.
THE FUCKING SECURITY GUARD FROM THE HOTEL!
THE OLD LADY DOESN'T HAVE MY MONEY!

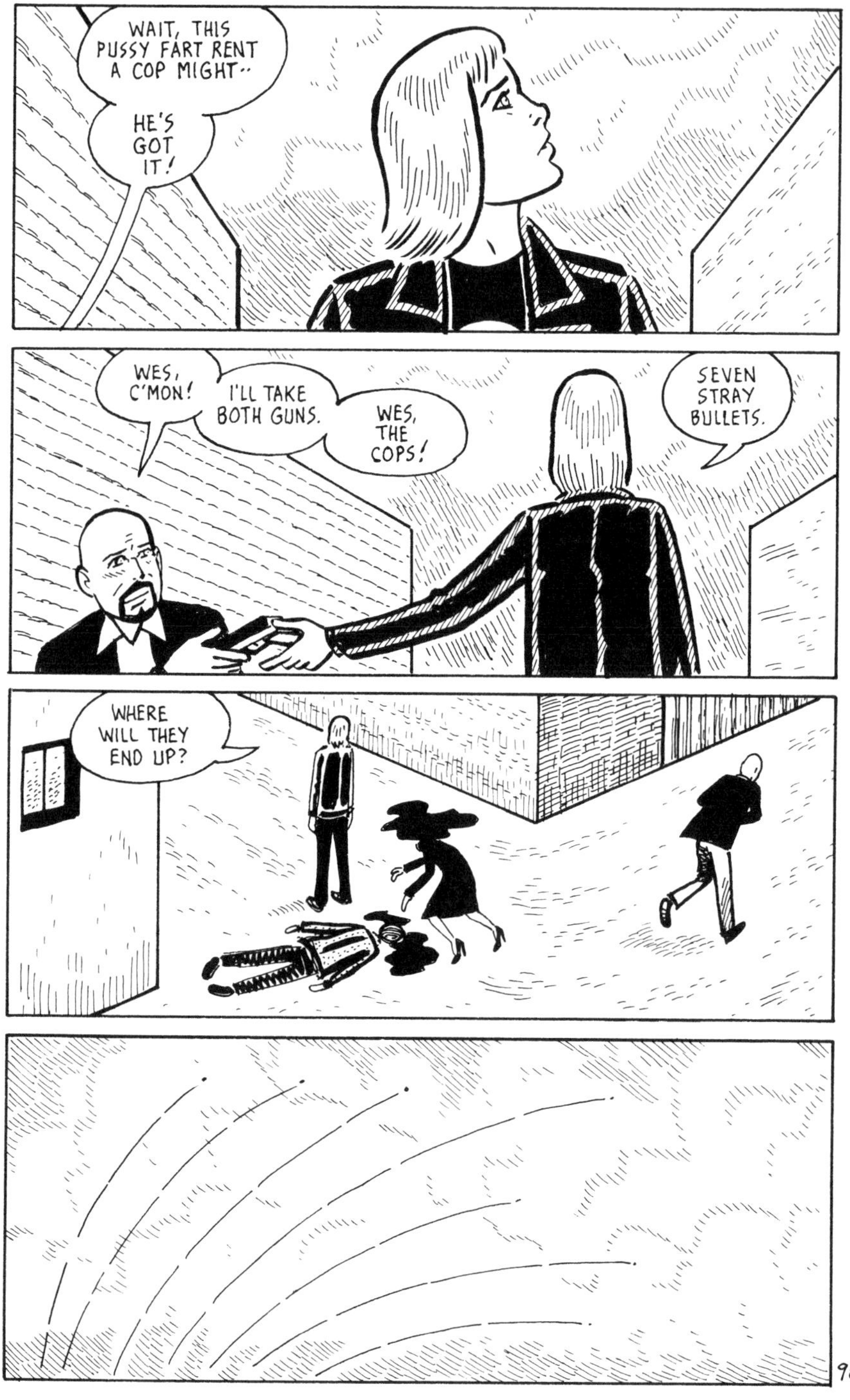
WAIT, THIS PUSSY FART RENT A COP MIGHT..
HE'S GOT IT!
WES, C'MON!
I'LL TAKE BOTH GUNS.
WES, THE COPS!
SEVEN STRAY BULLETS.
WHERE WILL THEY END UP?

ONE OF THOSE STRAY BULLETS COULD HIT NALA.
I GET OFF WORK AT NINE.
12 PAKS
20%

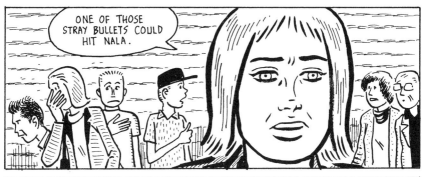

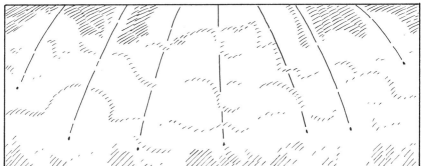

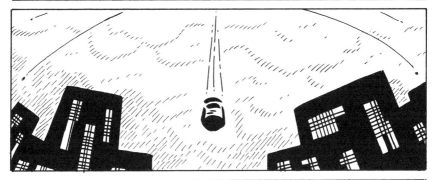

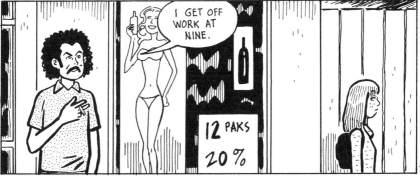

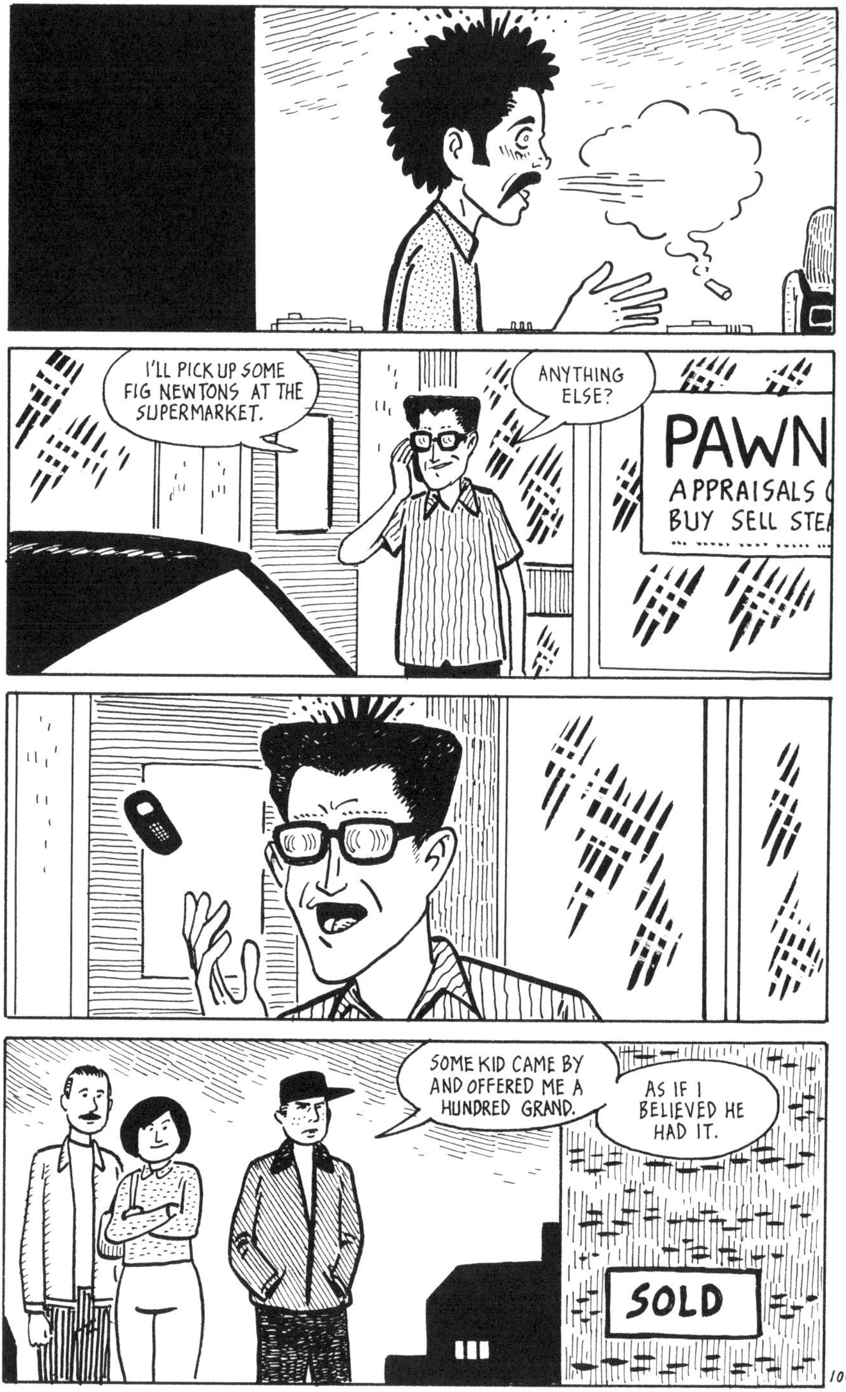
I'LL PICK UP SOME FIG NEWTONS AT THE SUPERMARKET.
ANYTHING ELSE?
PAWN
APPRAISALS
BUY SELL STE
SOME KID CAME BY AND OFFERED ME A HUNDRED GRAND.
AS IF I BELIEVED HE HAD IT.
SOLD

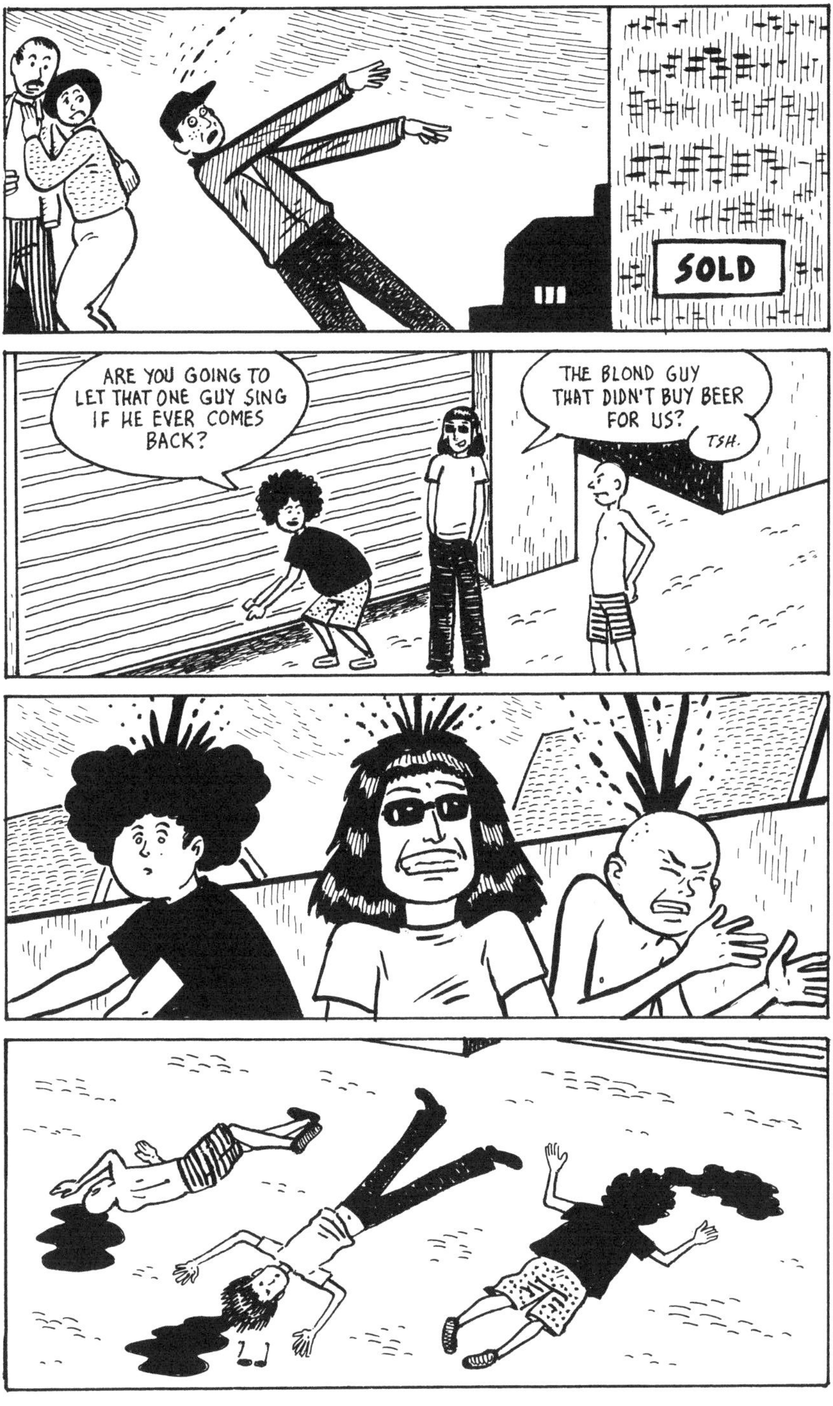
SOLD
ARE YOU GOING TO LET THAT ONE GUY SING IF HE EVER COMES BACK?
THE BLOND GUY THAT DIDN'T BUY BEER FOR US?
TSH.

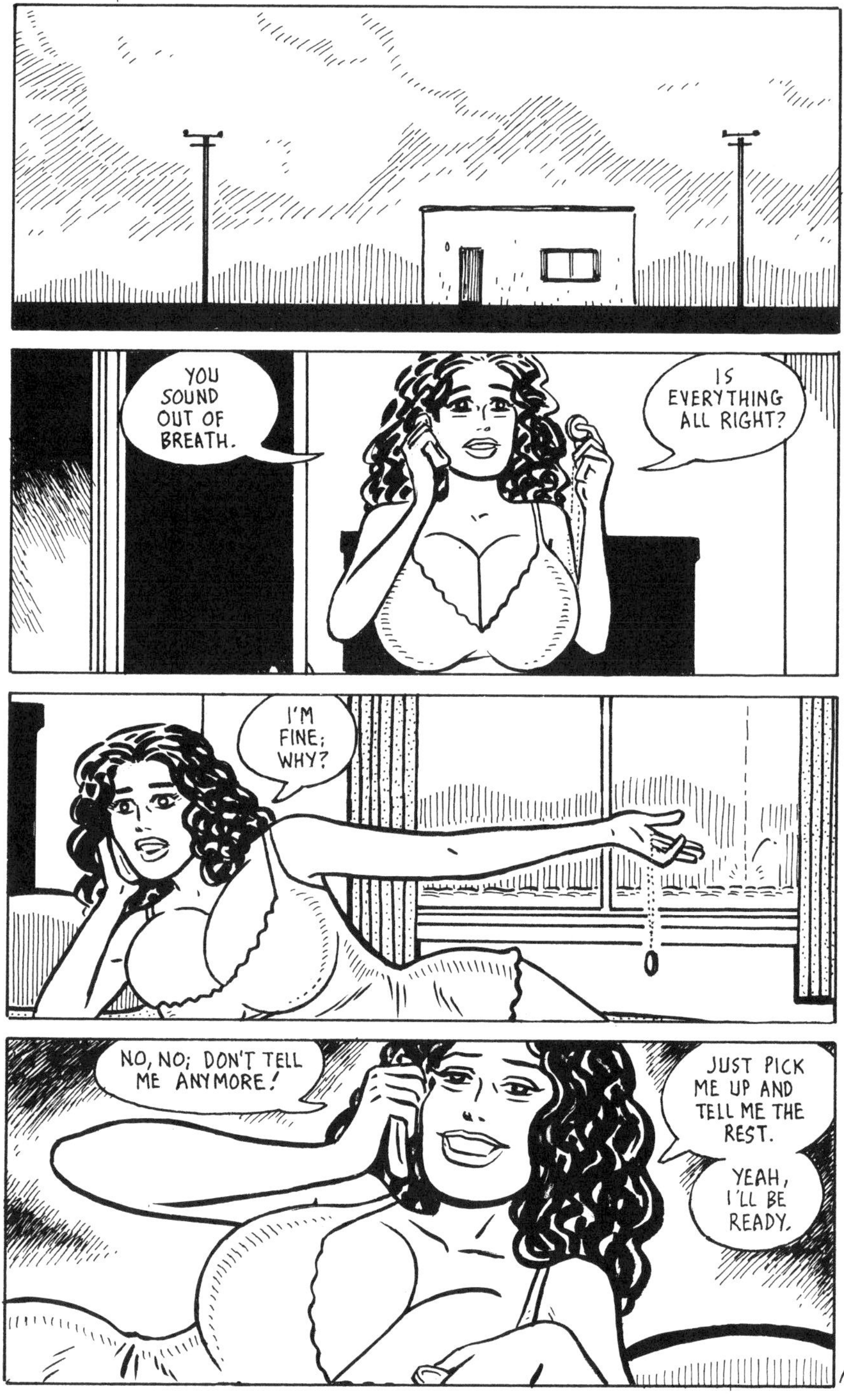
YOU SOUND OUT OF BREATH.
IS EVERYTHING ALL RIGHT?
I'M FINE; WHY?
NO, NO; DON'T TELL ME ANYMORE!
JUST PICK ME UP AND TELL ME THE REST.
YEAH, I'LL BE READY.

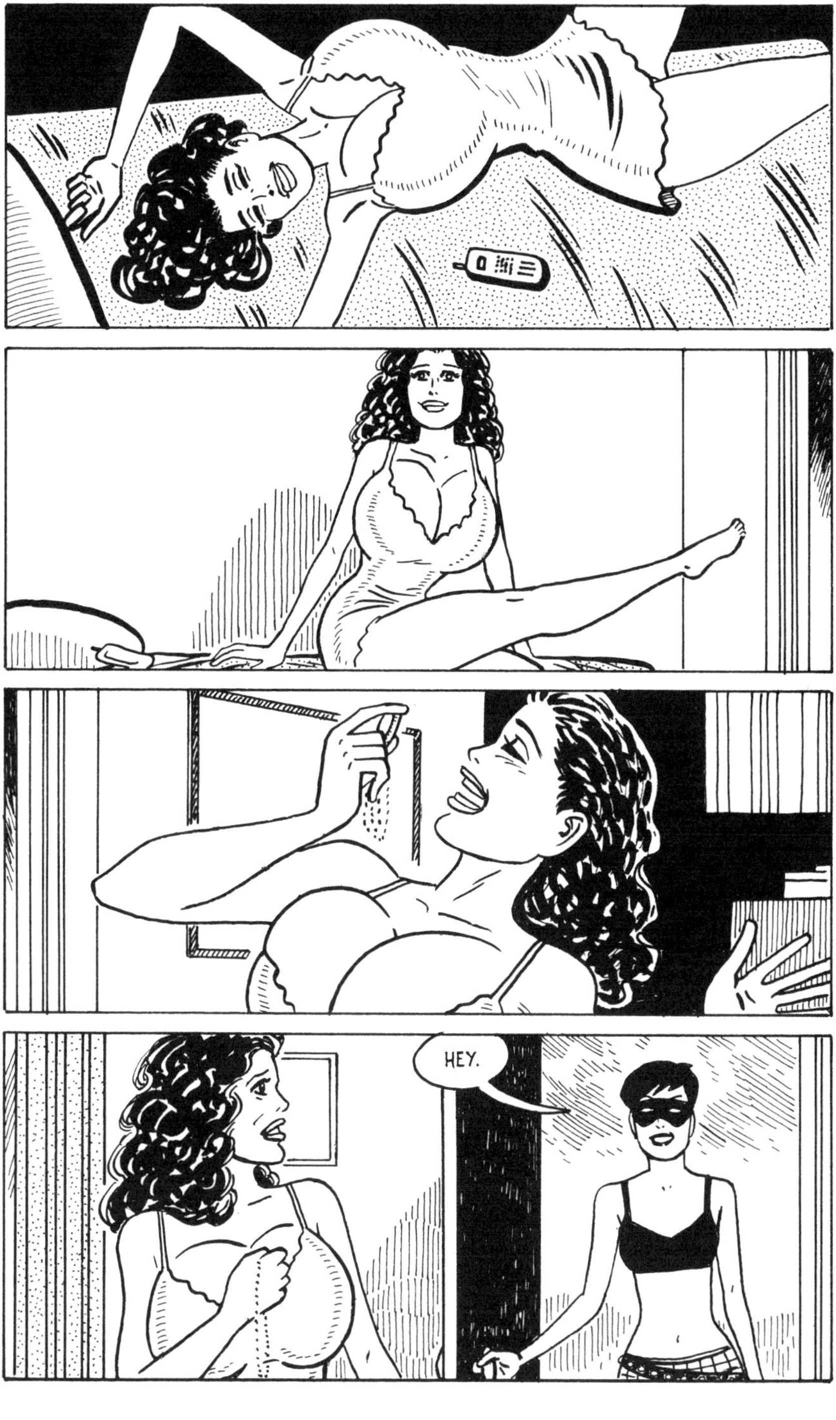
HEY.

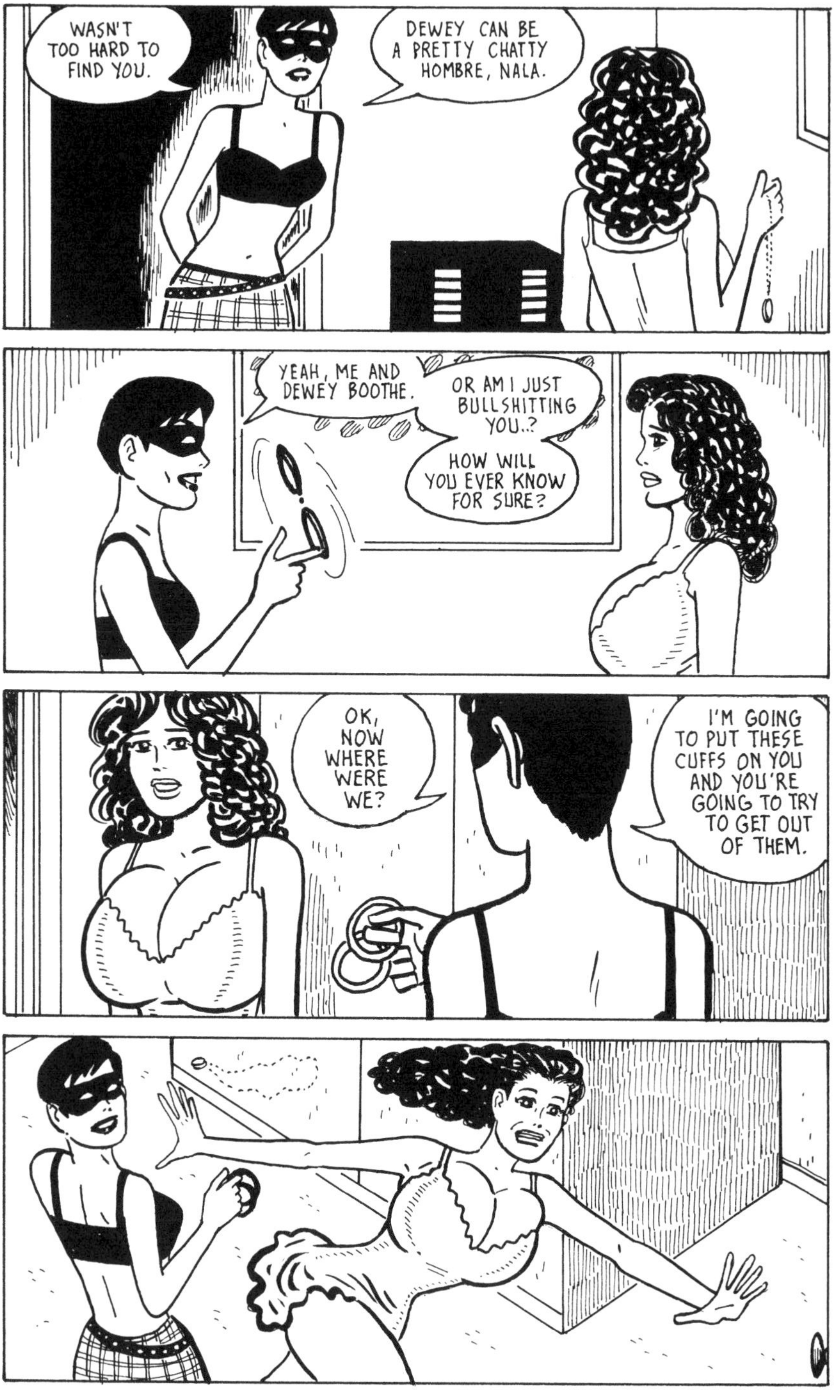
WASN'T TOO HARD TO FIND YOU.
DEWEY CAN BE A PRETTY CHATTY HOMBRE, NALA.
YEAH, ME AND DEWEY BOOTHE.
OR AM I JUST BULLSHITTING YOU..?
HOW WILL YOU EVER KNOW FOR SURE?
OK, NOW WHERE WERE WE?
I'M GOING TO PUT THESE CUFFS ON YOU AND YOU'RE GOING TO TRY TO GET OUT OF THEM.

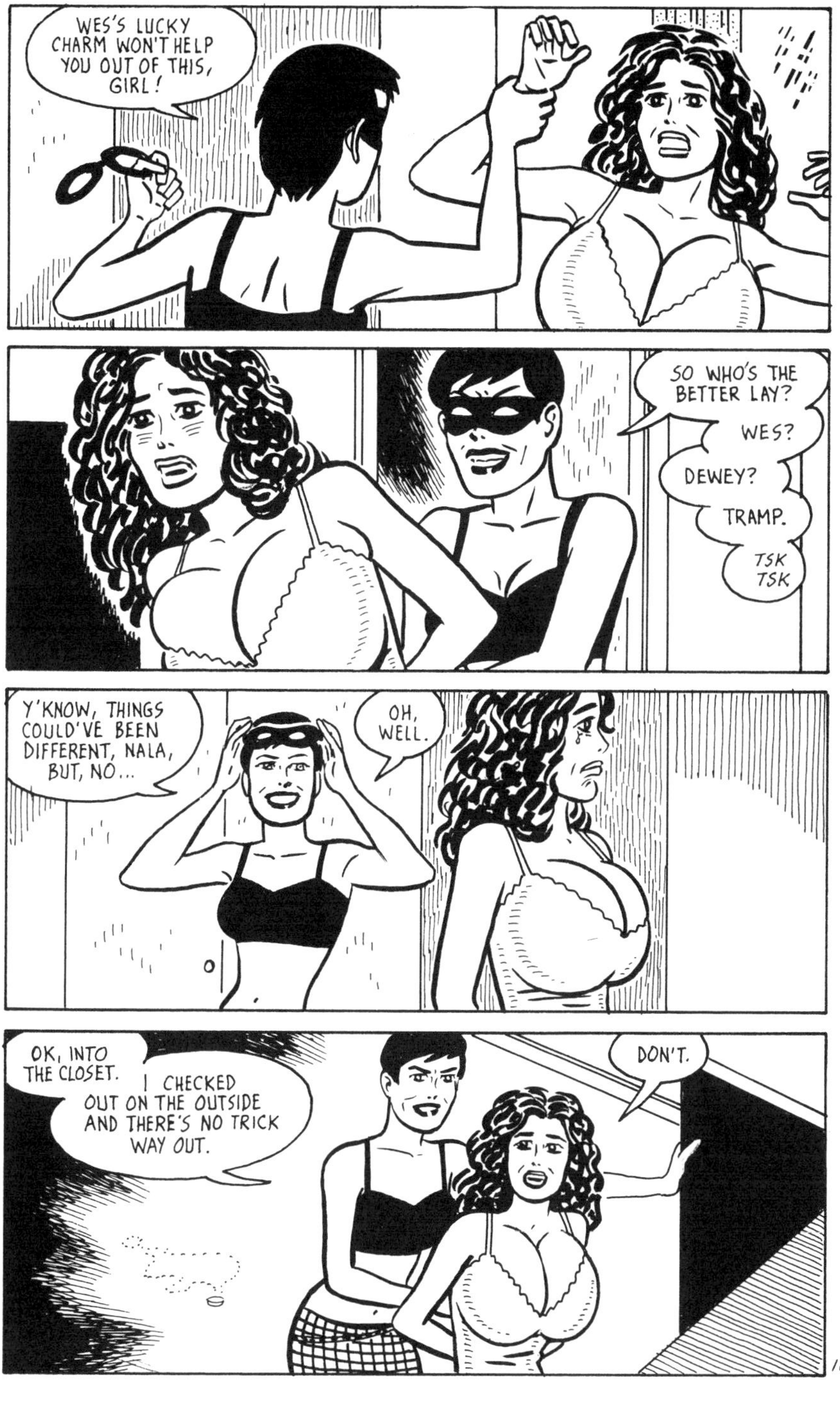
WES'S LUCKY CHARM WON'T HELP YOU OUT OF THIS, GIRL!
SO WHO'S THE BETTER LAY?
WES?
DEWEY?
TRAMP.
TSK TSK
Y'KNOW, THINGS COULD'VE BEEN DIFFERENT, NALA, BUT, NO...
OH, WELL.
OK, INTO THE CLOSET.
I CHECKED OUT ON THE OUTSIDE AND THERE'S NO TRICK WAY OUT.
DON'T.

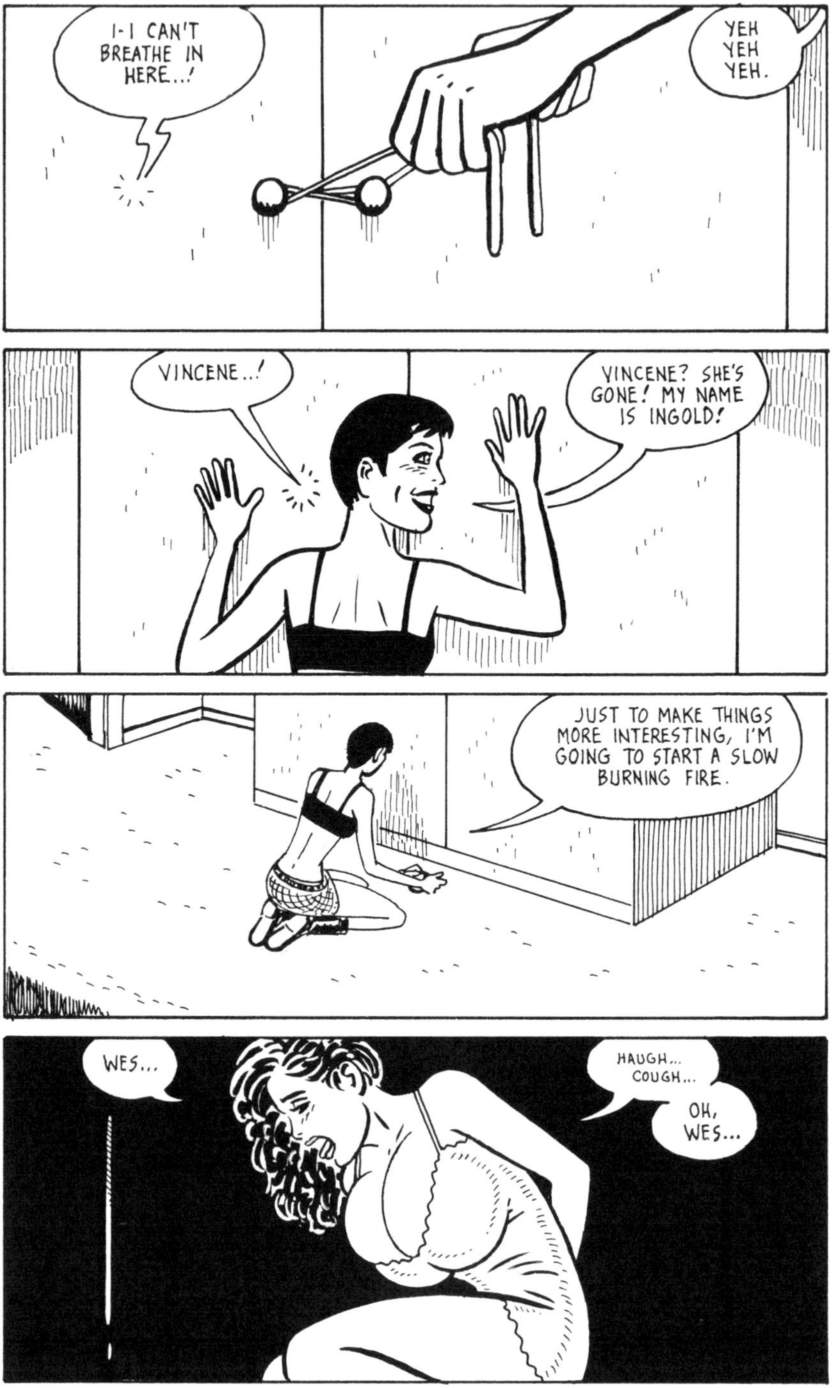
I-I CAN'T BREATHE IN HERE...!
YEH YEH YEH.
VINCENE...!
VINCENE? SHE'S GONE! MY NAME IS INGOLD!
JUST TO MAKE THINGS MORE INTERESTING, I'M GOING TO START A SLOW BURNING FIRE.
WES...
HAUGH... COUGH...
OH, WES...

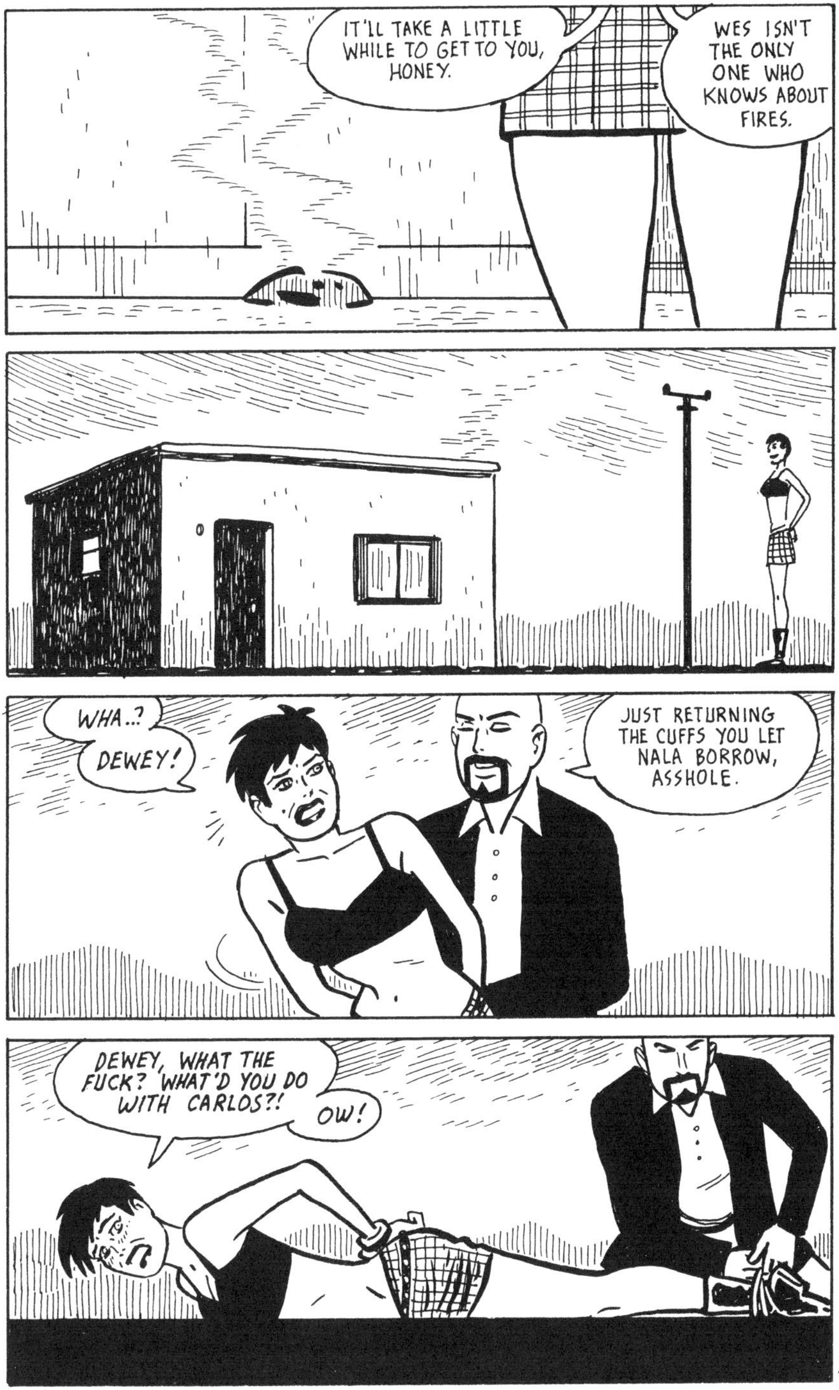
IT'LL TAKE A LITTLE WHILE TO GET TO YOU, HONEY.
WES ISN'T THE ONLY ONE WHO KNOWS ABOUT FIRES.
WHA..?
DEWEY!
JUST RETURNING THE CUFFS YOU LET NALA BORROW, ASSHOLE.
DEWEY, WHAT THE FUCK? WHAT'D YOU DO WITH CARLOS?!
OW!

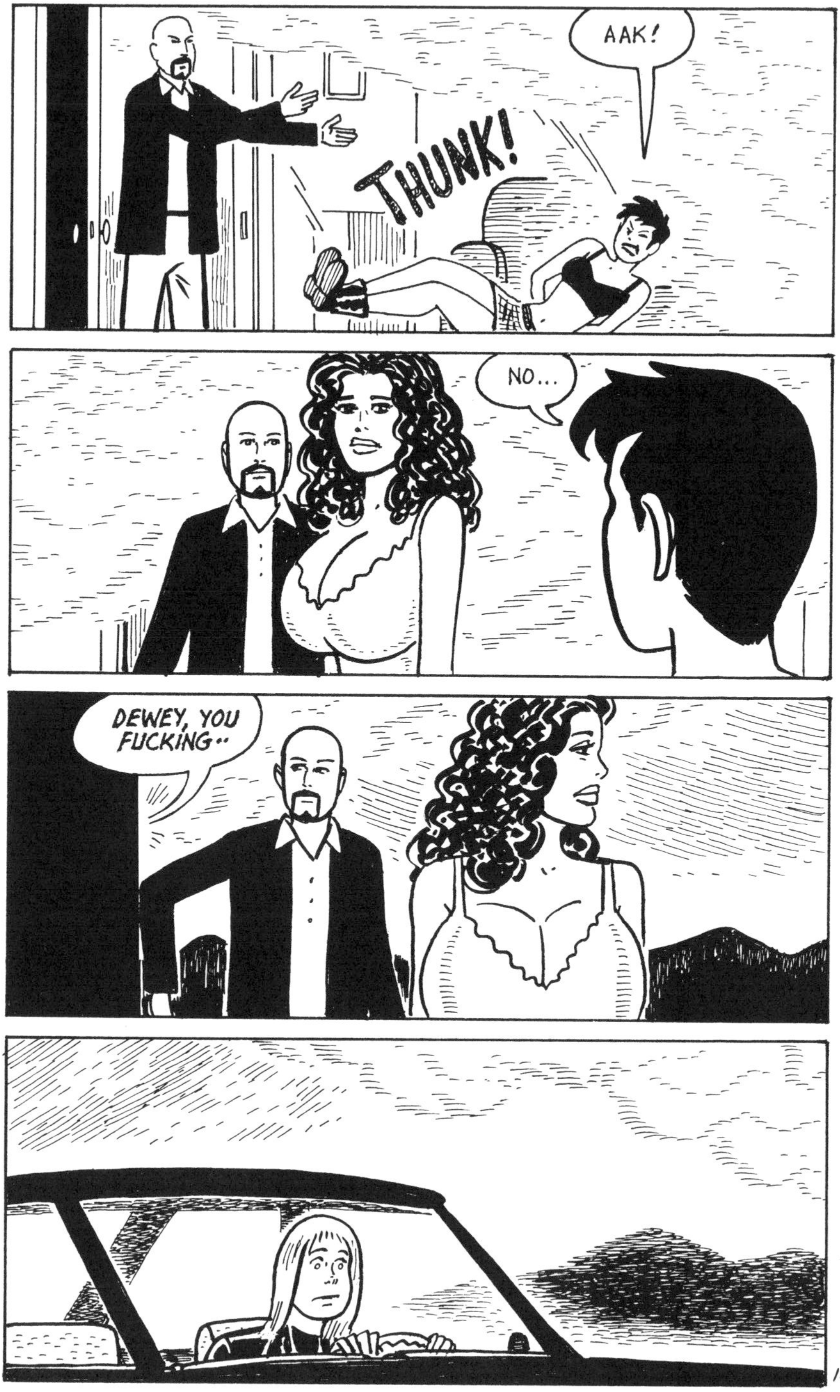
THUNK!
AAK!
NO...
DEWEY, YOU FUCKING..

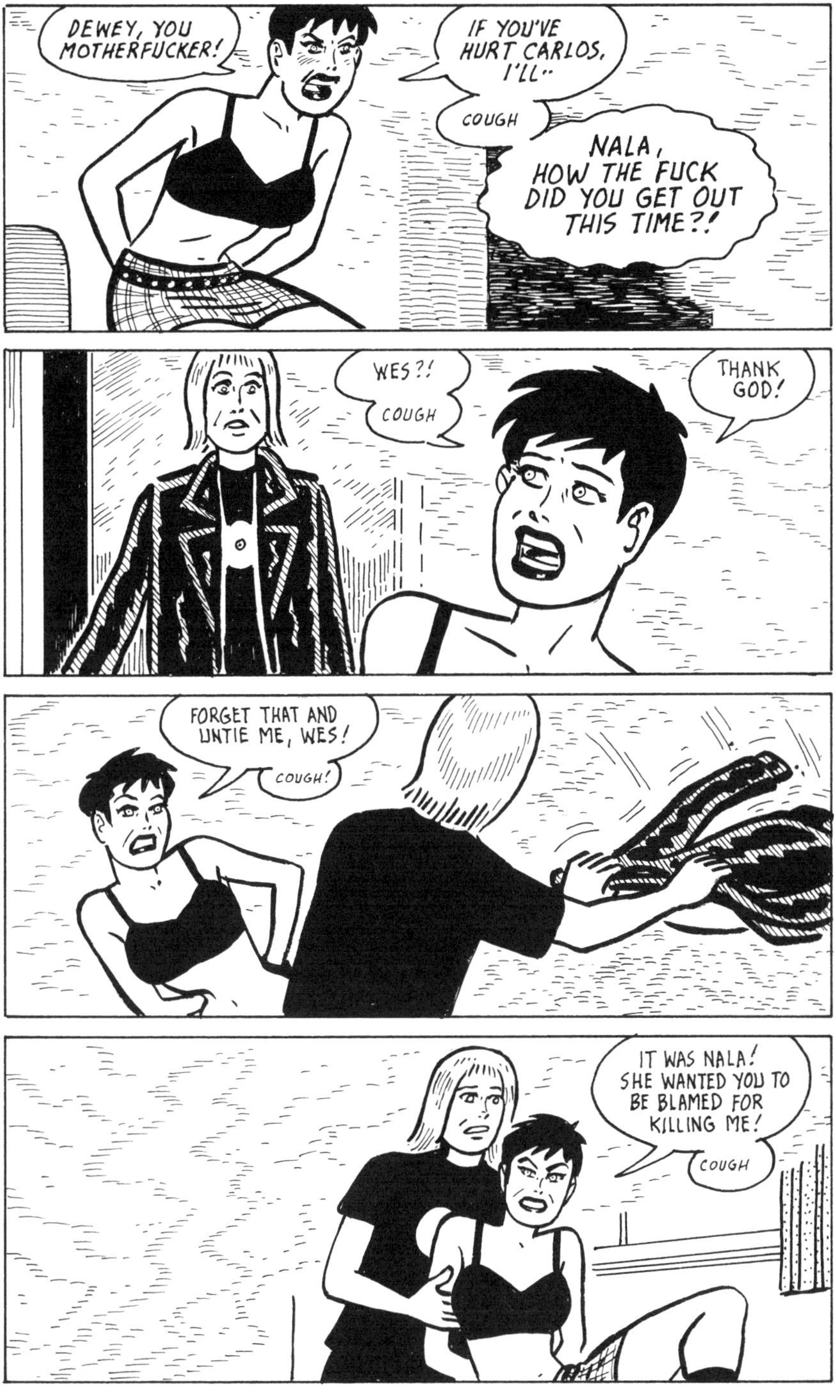
DEWEY, YOU MOTHERFUCKER!
IF YOU'VE HURT CARLOS, I'LL..
COUGH
NALA, HOW THE FUCK DID YOU GET OUT THIS TIME?!
WES?!
COUGH
THANK GOD!
FORGET THAT AND UNTIE ME, WES!
COUGH!
IT WAS NALA! SHE WANTED YOU TO BE BLAMED FOR KILLING ME!
COUGH

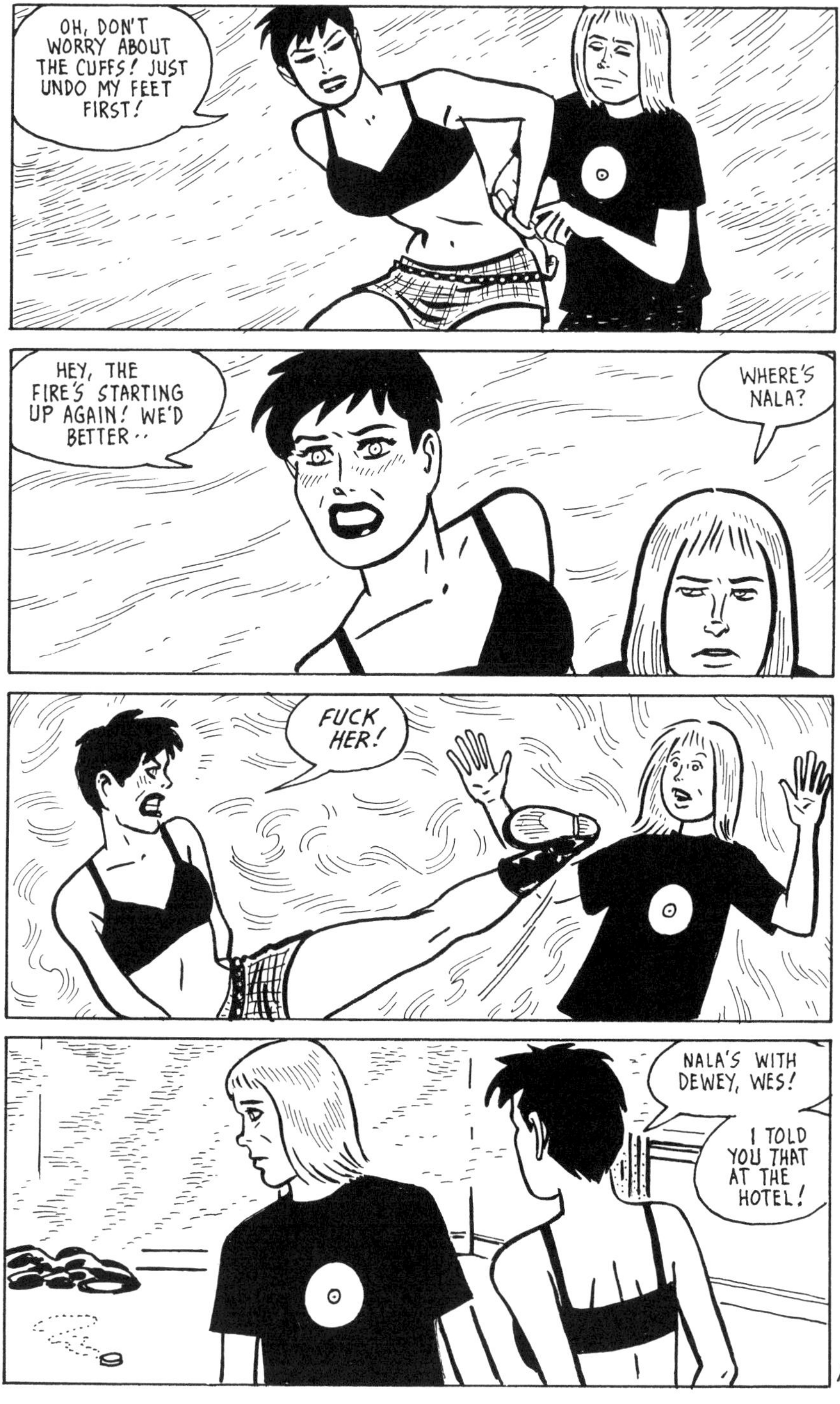
OH, DON'T WORRY ABOUT THE CUFFS! JUST UNDO MY FEET FIRST!
HEY, THE FIRE'S STARTING UP AGAIN! WE'D BETTER··
WHERE'S NALA?
FUCK HER!
NALA'S WITH DEWEY, WES!
I TOLD YOU THAT AT THE HOTEL!

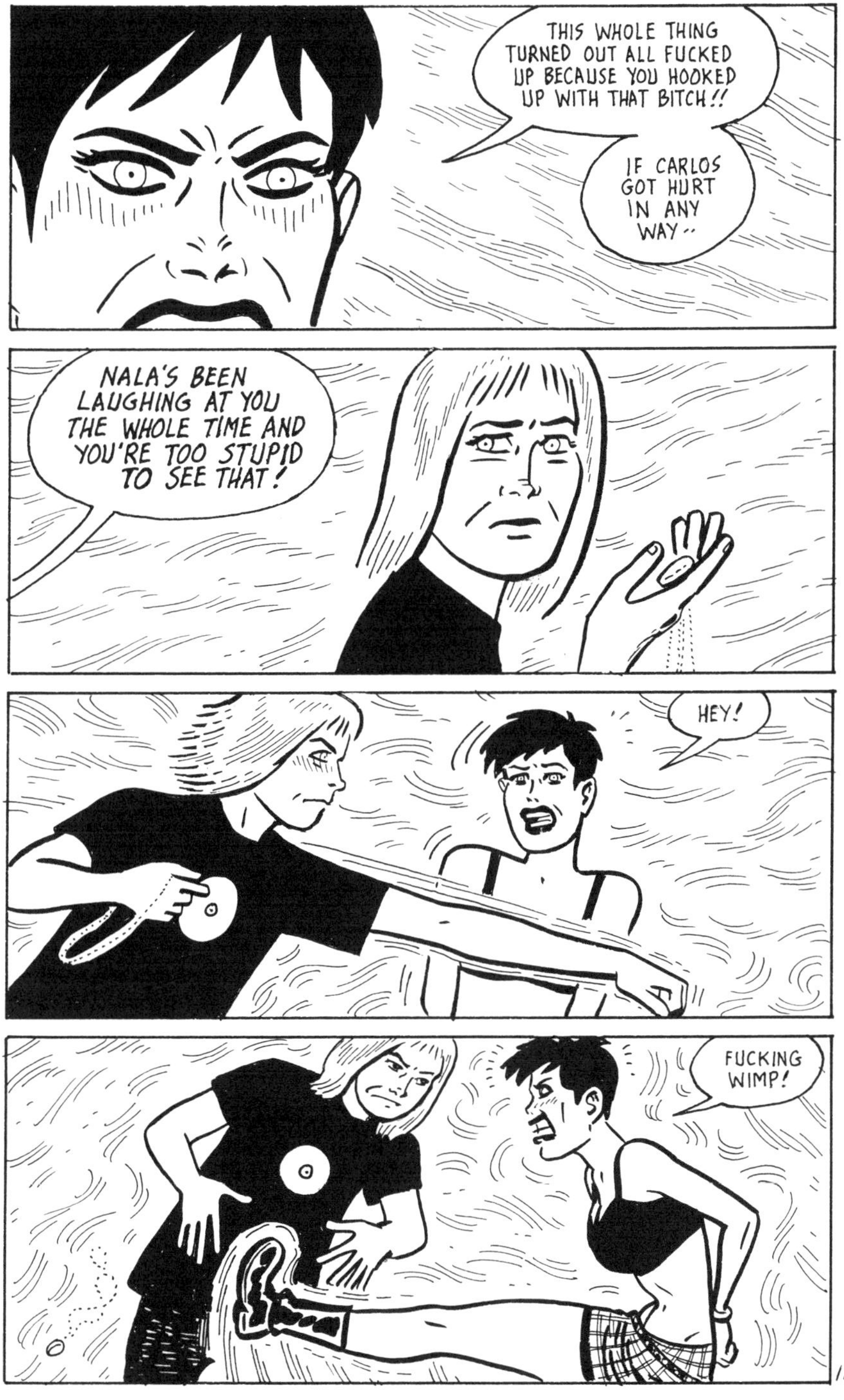
THIS WHOLE THING TURNED OUT ALL FUCKED UP BECAUSE YOU HOOKED UP WITH THAT BITCH!!
IF CARLOS GOT HURT IN ANY WAY..
NALA'S BEEN LAUGHING AT YOU THE WHOLE TIME AND YOU'RE TOO STUPID TO SEE THAT!
HEY!
FUCKING WIMP!

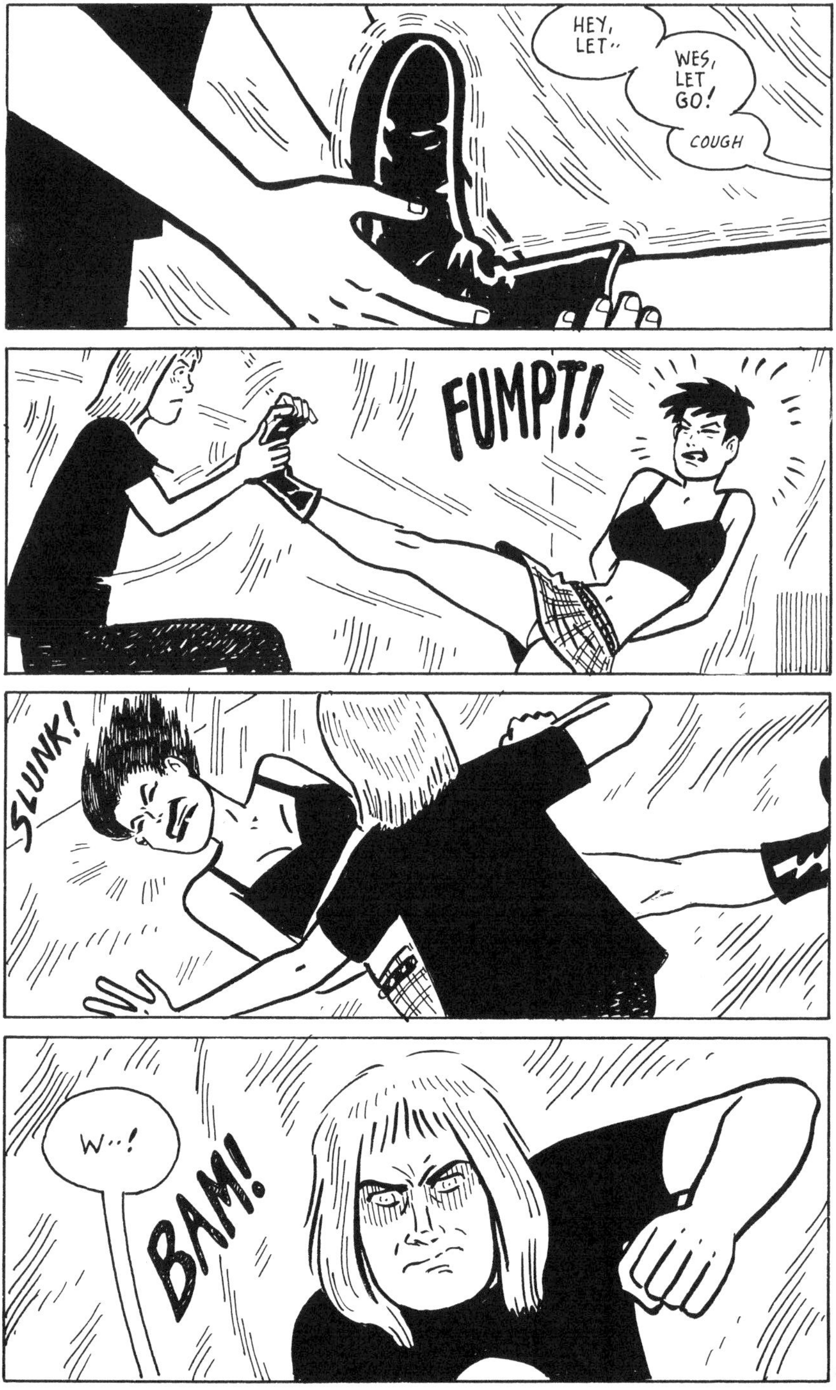
HEY, LET··
WES, LET GO!
COUGH
FUMPT!
SLUNK!
W··!
BAM!

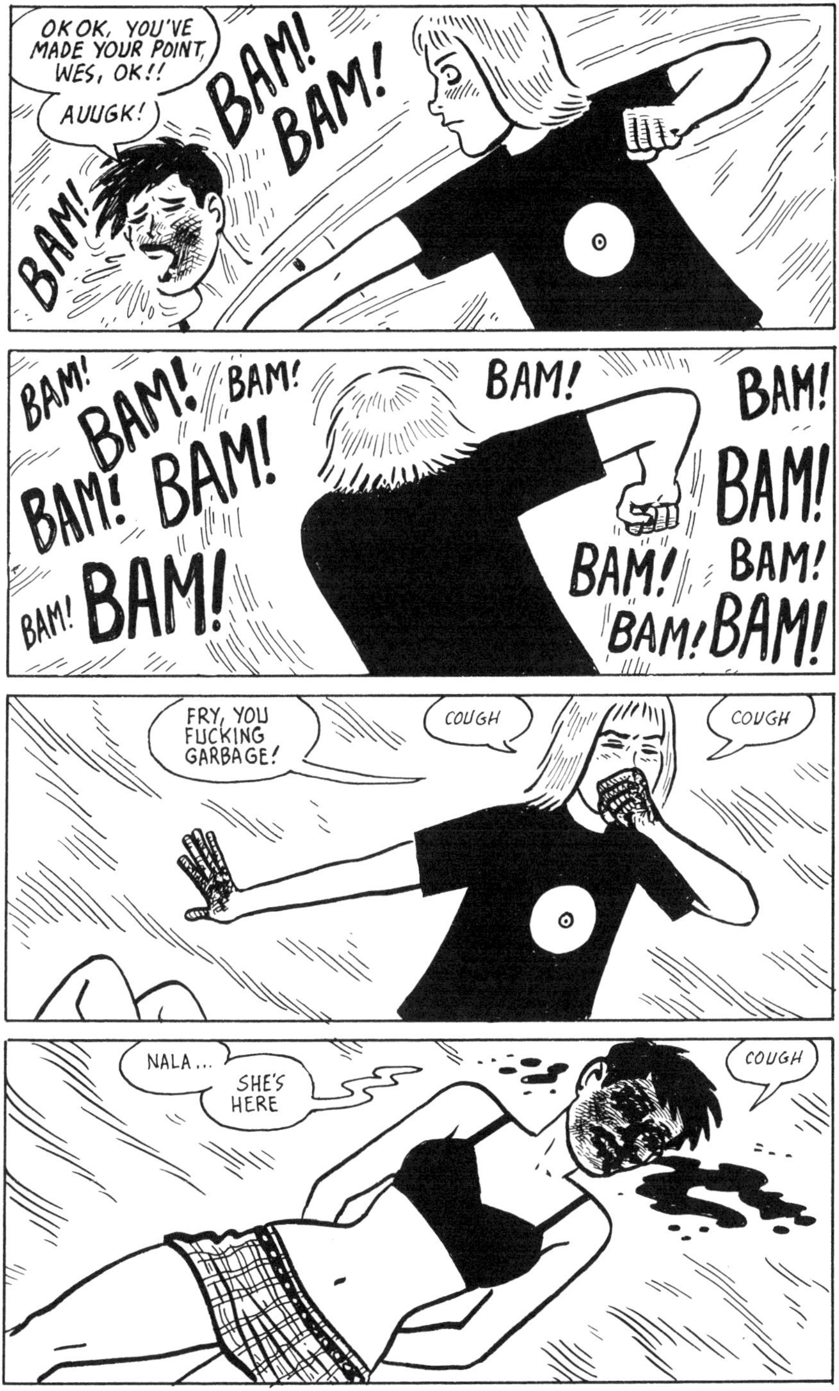
OK OK, YOU'VE MADE YOUR POINT, WES, OK!!
AUUGK!
BAM!
BAM!
BAM!
BAM!
BAM!
BAM!
BAM!
BAM!
BAM!
BAM!
BAM!
BAM!
BAM!
BAM!
BAM!
BAM!
BAM!
BAM!
FRY, YOU FUCKING GARBAGE!
COUGH
COUGH
NALA...
SHE'S HERE
COUGH

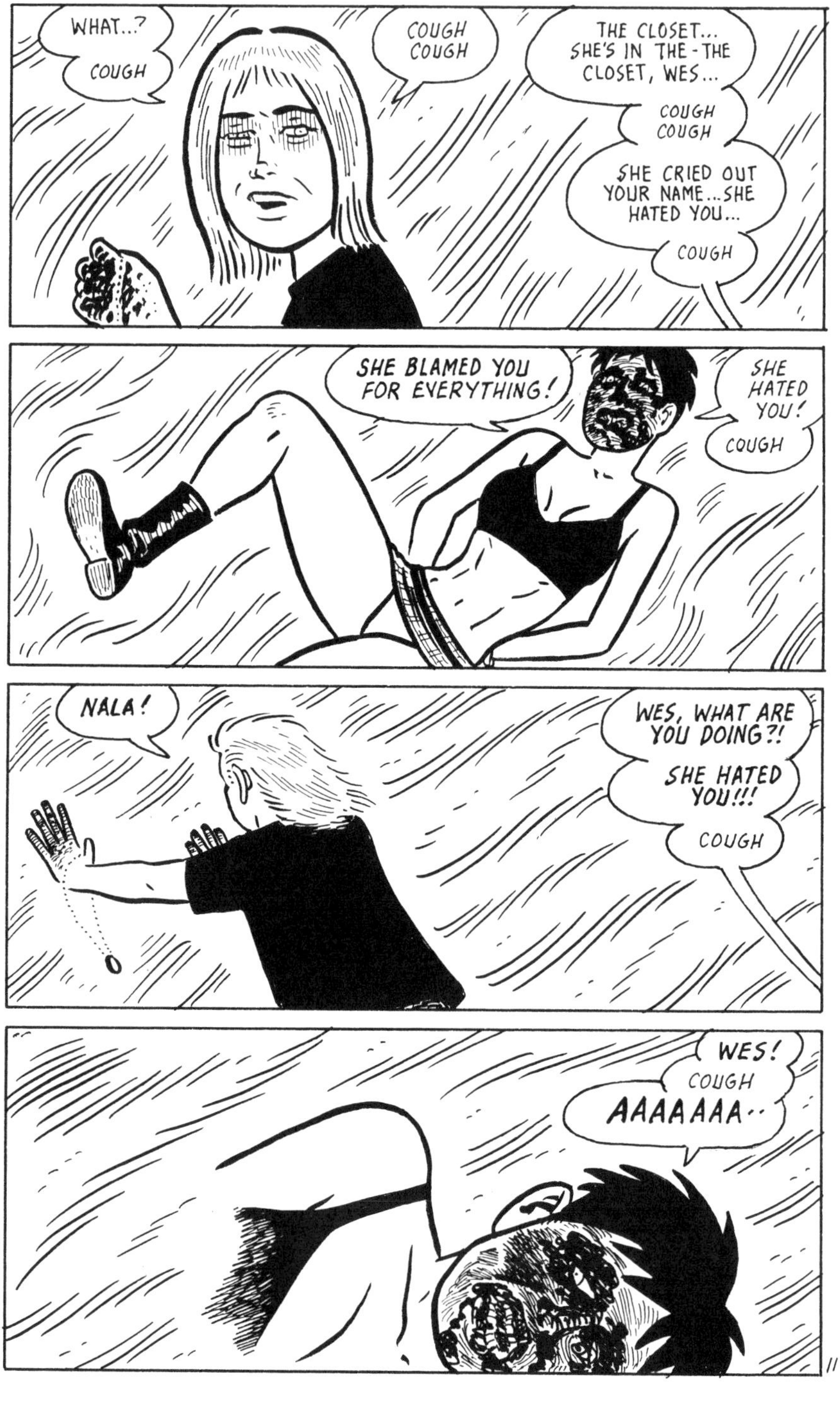
WHAT..?
COUGH
COUGH COUGH
THE CLOSET... SHE'S IN THE-THE CLOSET, WES...
COUGH COUGH
SHE CRIED OUT YOUR NAME...SHE HATED YOU...
COUGH
SHE BLAMED YOU FOR EVERYTHING!
SHE HATED YOU!
COUGH
NALA!
WES, WHAT ARE YOU DOING?!
SHE HATED YOU!!!
COUGH
WES!
COUGH
AAAAAAA..

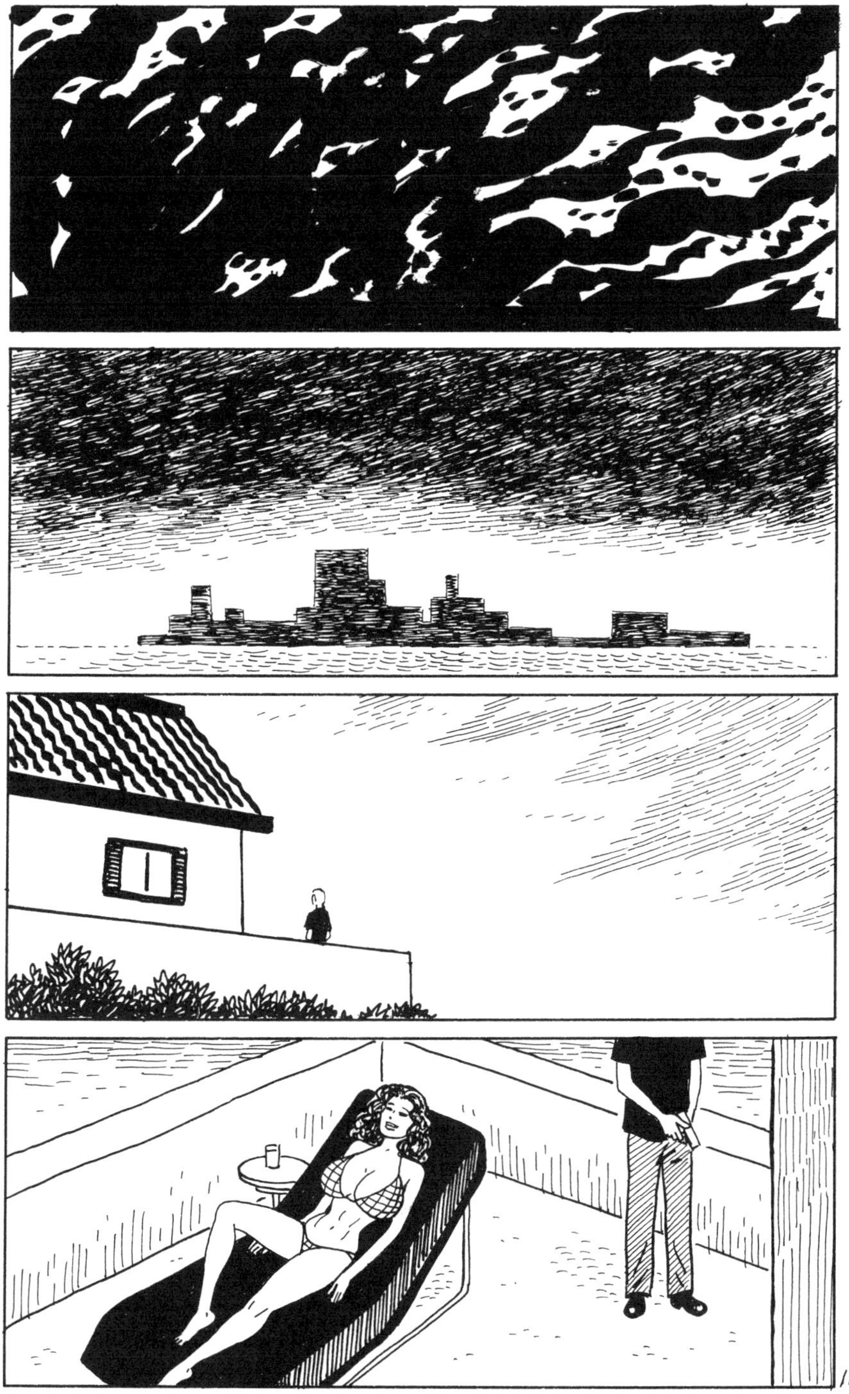

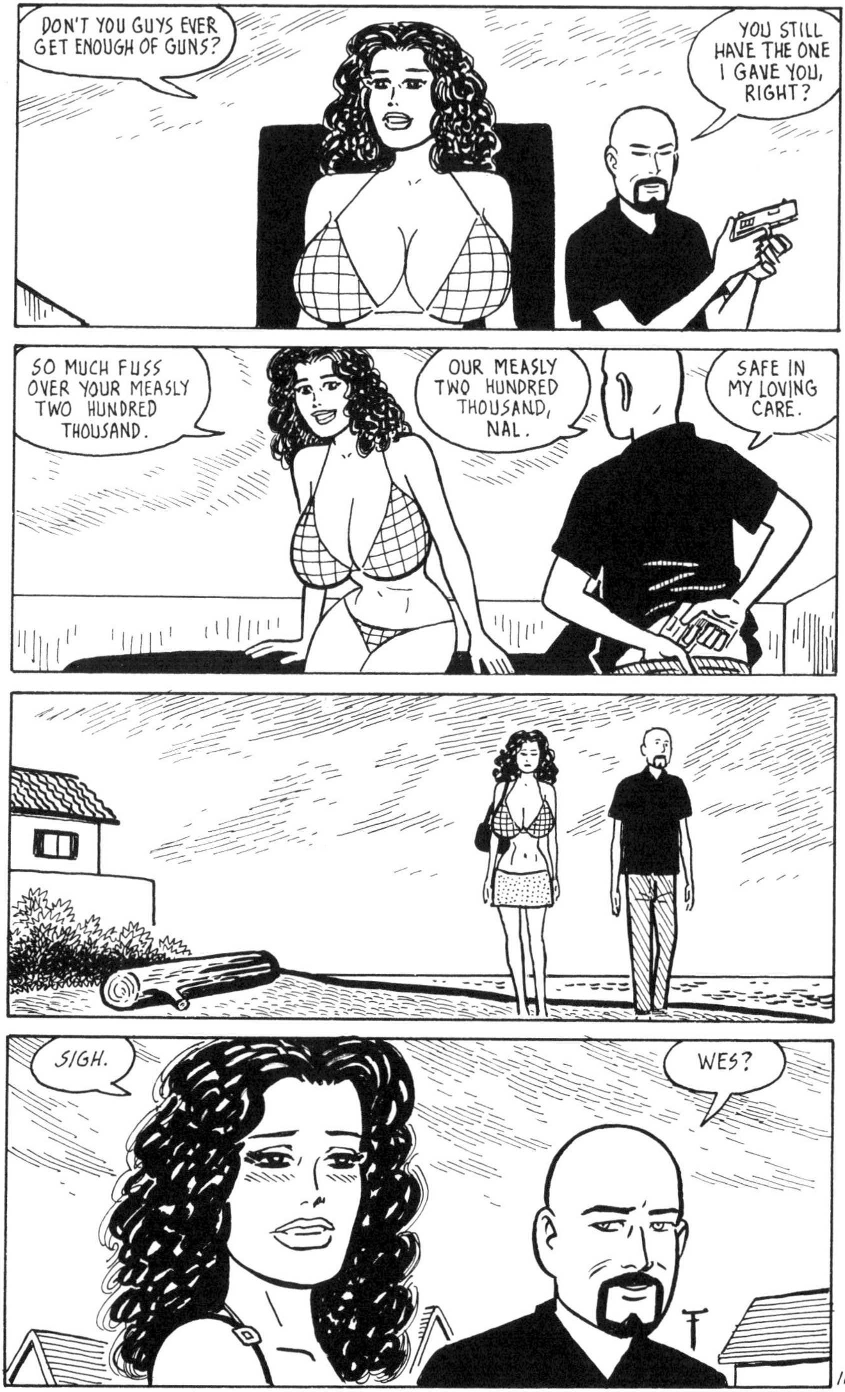
DON'T YOU GUYS EVER GET ENOUGH OF GUNS?
YOU STILL HAVE THE ONE I GAVE YOU, RIGHT?
SO MUCH FUSS OVER YOUR MEASLY TWO HUNDRED THOUSAND.
OUR MEASLY TWO HUNDRED THOUSAND, NAL.
SAFE IN MY LOVING CARE.
SIGH.
WES?

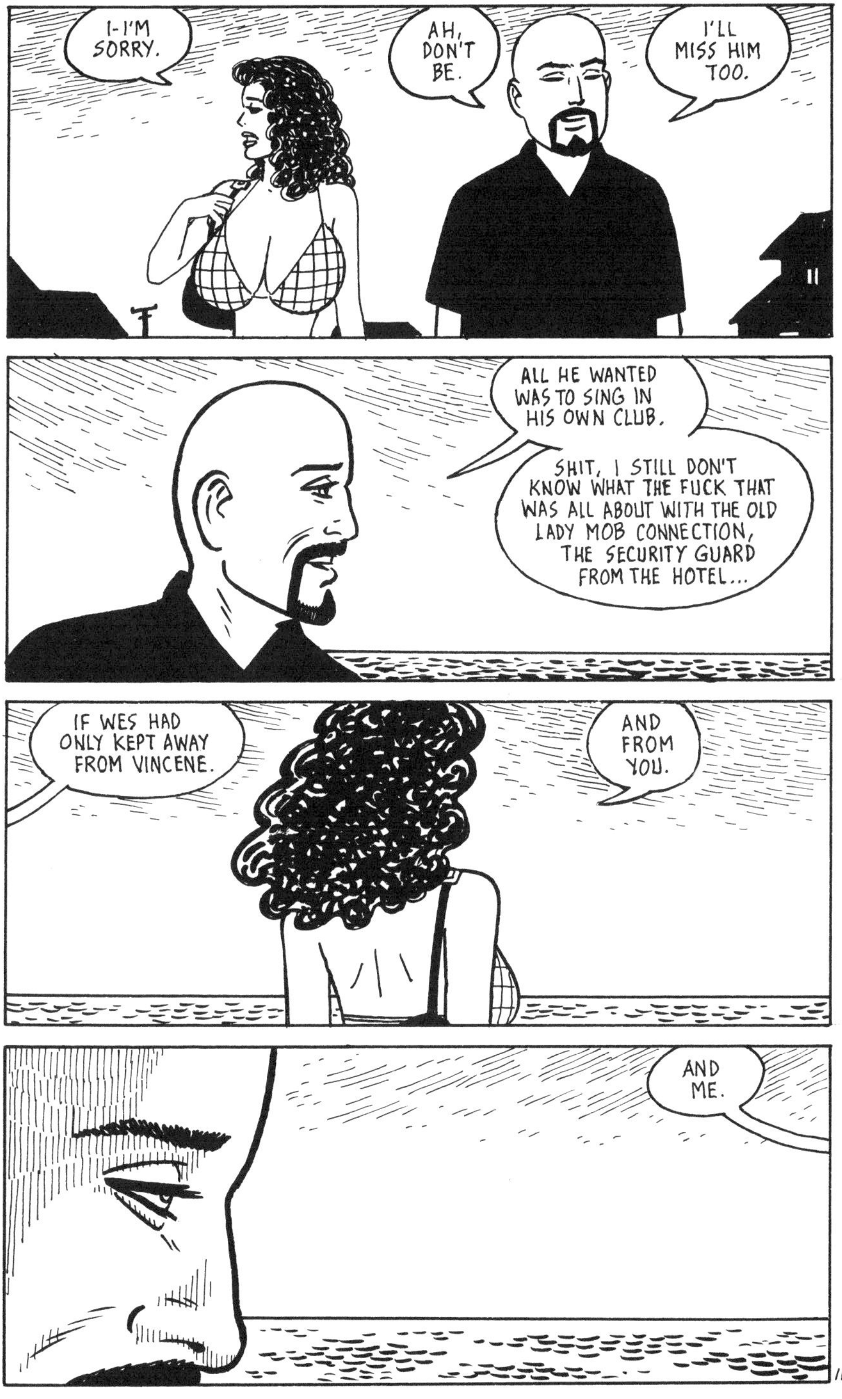
I-I'M SORRY.
AH, DON'T BE.
I'LL MISS HIM TOO.
ALL HE WANTED WAS TO SING IN HIS OWN CLUB.
SHIT, I STILL DON'T KNOW WHAT THE FUCK THAT WAS ALL ABOUT WITH THE OLD LADY MOB CONNECTION, THE SECURITY GUARD FROM THE HOTEL...
IF WES HAD ONLY KEPT AWAY FROM VINCENE.
AND FROM YOU.
AND ME.

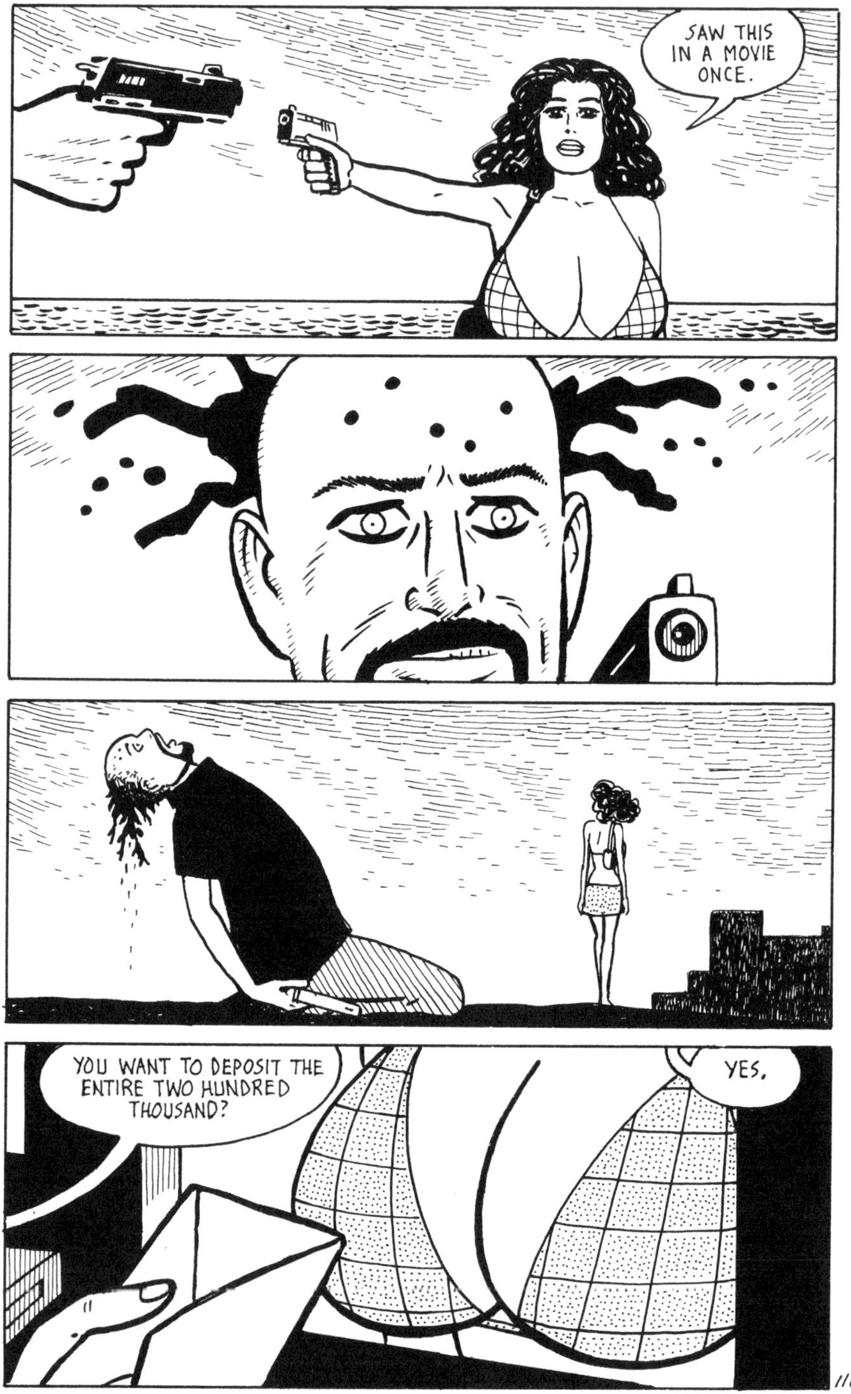
SAW THIS IN A MOVIE ONCE.
YOU WANT TO DEPOSIT THE ENTIRE TWO HUNDRED THOUSAND?
YES.

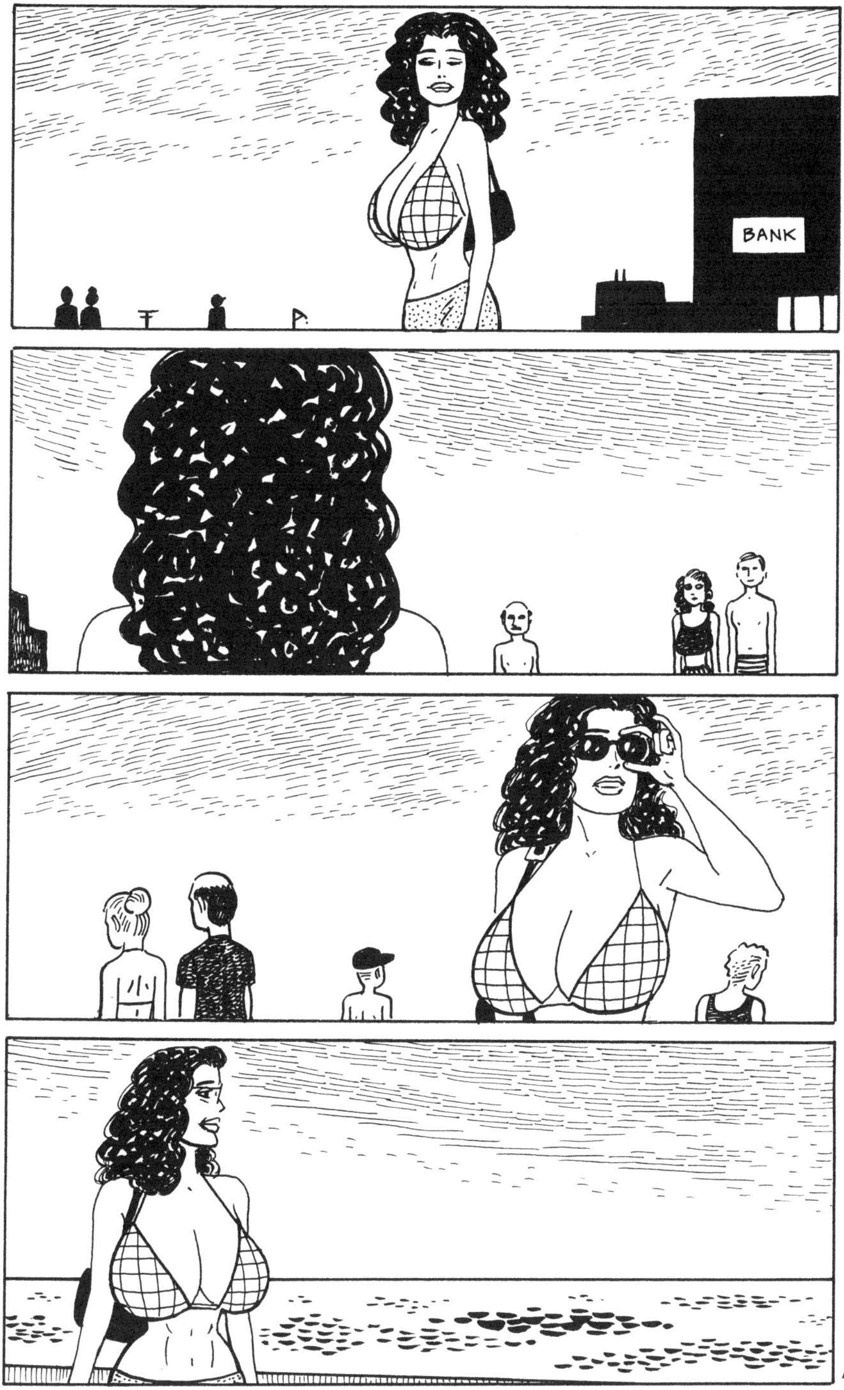
BANK

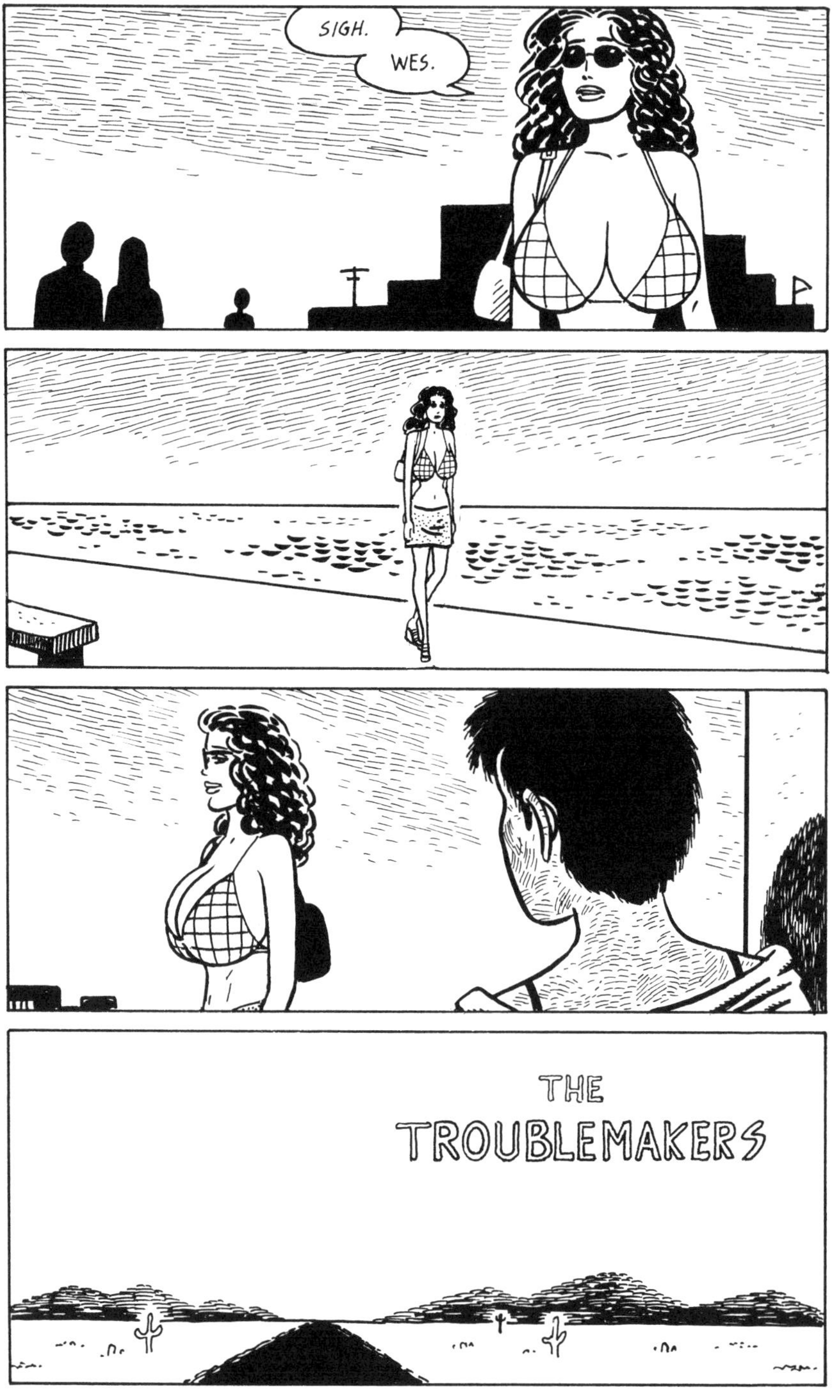
SIGH.
WES.
THE TROUBLEMAKERS

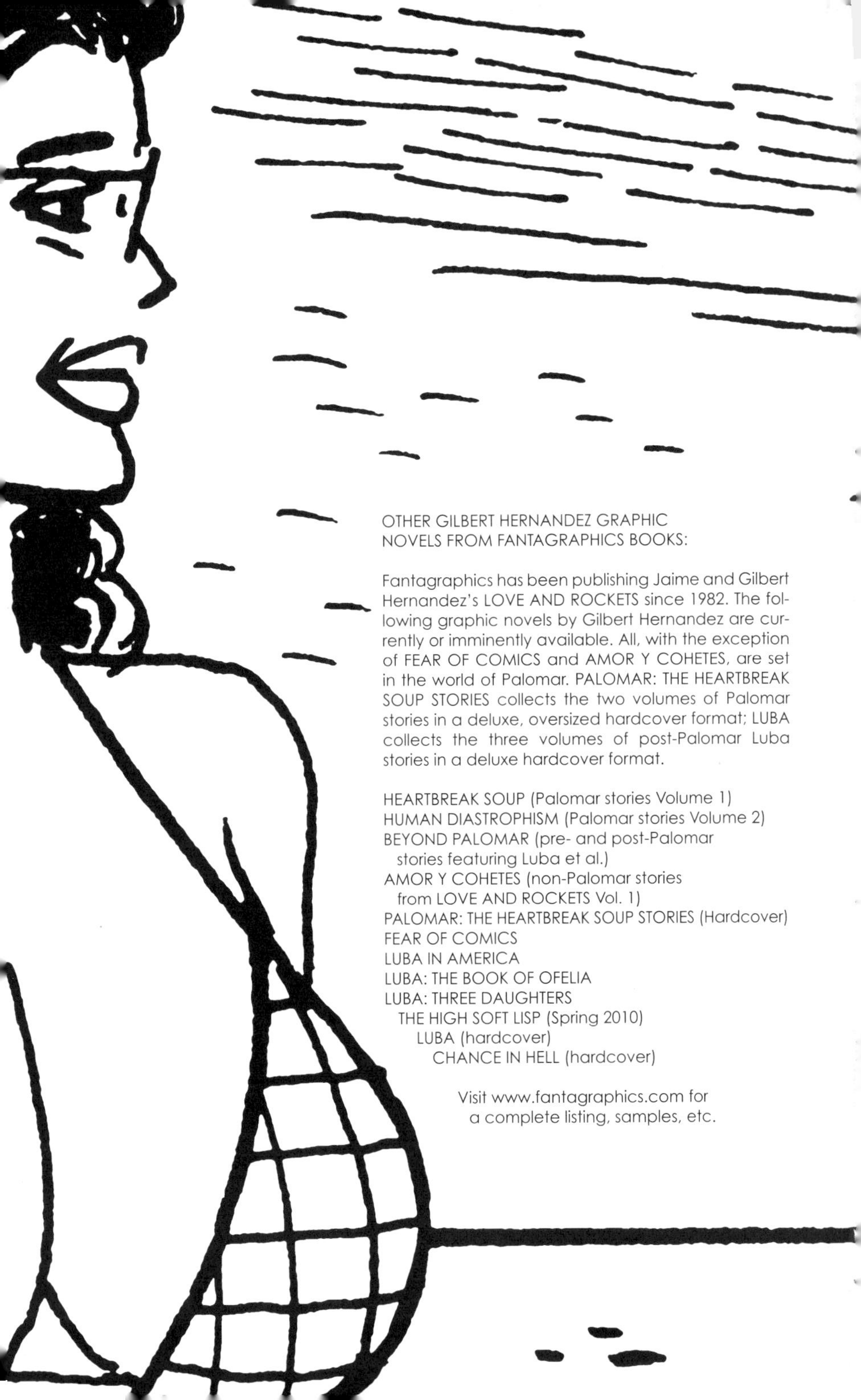

OTHER GILBERT HERNANDEZ GRAPHIC NOVELS FROM FANTAGRAPHICS BOOKS:

Fantagraphics has been publishing Jaime and Gilbert Hernandez's LOVE AND ROCKETS since 1982. The following graphic novels by Gilbert Hernandez are currently or imminently available. All, with the exception of FEAR OF COMICS and AMOR Y COHETES, are set in the world of Palomar. PALOMAR: THE HEARTBREAK SOUP STORIES collects the two volumes of Palomar stories in a deluxe, oversized hardcover format; LUBA collects the three volumes of post-Palomar Luba stories in a deluxe hardcover format.

HEARTBREAK SOUP (Palomar stories Volume 1)
HUMAN DIASTROPHISM (Palomar stories Volume 2)
BEYOND PALOMAR (pre- and post-Palomar stories featuring Luba et al.)
AMOR Y COHETES (non-Palomar stories from LOVE AND ROCKETS Vol. 1)
PALOMAR: THE HEARTBREAK SOUP STORIES (Hardcover)
FEAR OF COMICS
LUBA IN AMERICA
LUBA: THE BOOK OF OFELIA
LUBA: THREE DAUGHTERS
THE HIGH SOFT LISP (Spring 2010)
LUBA (hardcover)
CHANCE IN HELL (hardcover)

Visit www.fantagraphics.com for a complete listing, samples, etc.

SCARLETT by STARLIGHT

KING VAMPIRE

LIE DOWN IN THE DARK

The MIDNIGHT PEOPLE

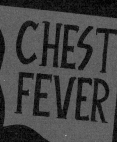

CHEST FEVER

HYPNOTWIST

SEVEN BULLETS TO HELL

AMERICAN CULT ACTRESS

The EARTHIANS

FANCY

E DEVIL